Novell®
GroupWise 7
User's Handbook

ERIC RAFF

Novell
PRESS™

Novell.

Published by Pearson Education, Inc.
800 East 96th Street, Indianapolis, Indiana 46240 USA

Novell® GroupWise 7 User's Handbook

Copyright © 2006 by Novell, Inc.

International Standard Book Number: 0-672-32789-9

Library of Congress Catalog Card Number: 2004195540

Printed in the United States of America

First Printing: August 2005

08   07   06   05   4   3   2   1

Trademarks

Warning and Disclaimer

Bulk Sales

Pearson offers excellent discounts on this book when ordered in quantity for bulk purchases or special sales. For more information, please contact

U.S. Corporate and Government Sales
1-800-382-3419
corpsales@pearsontechgroup.com

For sales outside of the U.S., please contact

International Sales
international@pearsoned.com

Novell Press is the exclusive publisher of trade computer technology books that have been authorized by Novell, Inc. Novell Press books are written and reviewed by the world's leading authorities on Novell and related technologies, and are edited, produced, and distributed by the Que/Sams Publishing group of Pearson Education, the worldwide leader in integrated education and computer technology publishing. For more information on Novell Press and Novell Press books, please go to www.novellpress.com.

Associate Publisher	Program Manager, Novell, Inc.	Marketing Manager
Mark Taber	Darrin Vandenbos	Doug Ingersoll

Acquisitions Editor
Jenny Watson

Development Editor
Emmett Dulaney

Managing Editor
Charlotte Clapp

Project Editor
Seth Kerney

Copy Editor
Chuck Hutchinson

Indexer
Chris Barrick

Proofreader
Melinda Gutowski

Technical Editor
Dave Muldoon

Publishing Coordinator
Vanessa Evans

Designer
Gary Adair

Page Layout
Toi Davis

Contents at a Glance

Table of Contents

About the Author

Eric Raff has been working in the computer industry throughout his career. He formerly held the position of GroupWise Support Engineer at Novell for six years and is known worldwide as a leading authority in the GroupWise community. He has been a featured speaker and presenter for Novell Brainshare, as well as at each of the GroupWise Advisor conferences and GWAVACon 2004. He is also a coauthor of the Caledonia GroupWise 6.5 upgrade guide, is a technical editor for the Novell Press GroupWise 6 and 6.5 Admin guides, and is currently acting as a contributing editor for the *GroupWise Advisor Magazine*. He is the recipient of the Super Star award from the Software Support Professional Association (SSPA) and has consistently been an avid advocate in the GroupWise community. Eric is currently working as a Senior Messaging Engineer for one of Novell's largest customers.

Dedication

I dedicate this book to Jalene, Bryanna, Dayton, and Jacob. You are all the light of my life.

—Eric Raff

We Want to Hear from You!

As the reader of this book, *you* are our most important critic and commentator. We value your opinion and want to know what we're doing right, what we could do better, what areas you'd like to see us publish in, and any other words of wisdom you're willing to pass our way.

You can email or write me directly to let me know what you did or didn't like about this book—as well as what we can do to make our books better.

Please note that I cannot help you with technical problems related to the topic of this book, and that due to the high volume of mail I receive, I may not be able to reply to every message.

When you write, please be sure to include this book's title and author as well as your name, email address, and phone number. I will carefully review your comments and share them with the author and editors who worked on the book.

Email: feedback@novellpress.com

Mail: Mark Taber
             Associate Publisher
             Novell Press/Pearson Education
             800 East 96th Street
             Indianapolis, IN 46240 USA

Reader Services

For more information about this book or others from Novell Press, visit our website at www.novellpress.com. Type the ISBN or the title of a book in the Search field to find the page you're looking for.

Introduction to GroupWise 7

Welcome to GroupWise 7! You have in front of you a tool to open the vast world of collaboration with your peers—within your company and with your partners, vendors, suppliers, and customers—regardless of your location.

Of course, email itself has been and continues to be a popular method of communication. GroupWise goes way beyond simple email (which it does very well) to act as a very effective collaboration tool, contact manager, daily planner, and document interface.

GroupWise is flexible enough to work for you at whatever level you feel comfortable with. If you just need email, fine! If you want to share a folder and build rules to automatically place all project emails in that shared folder, great! If you are a member of an Internet newsgroup and want access to those messages, excellent!

GroupWise fits the bill perfectly.

Chapter 1: Introduction to GroupWise 7

In this chapter, we introduce you to the overall functionality of GroupWise and discuss its interface—the main screen—and how to navigate through it. We focus on the Windows GroupWise program using the "New Look" of the GroupWise client (the web browser version, called GroupWise WebAccess, is covered in Chapter 13, "GroupWise WebAccess"). Additional items covered in this chapter include starting GroupWise, using the "New Look" versus the "Classic Look," looking at how to use folders, and navigating through GroupWise. If you are a long-time user of GroupWise, this chapter is key to understanding the new user interface. When you finish this chapter, you will understand how the interface works and how you can use it to access the information sources covered in subsequent chapters.

Chapter 2: What's New in GroupWise 7

In this chapter, we look at all the new features for GroupWise 7. For this version, Novell put most of the development into the client software that you run to access the information in GroupWise. The goal was to make the client interface more intuitive with a clean, uncluttered look and feel. As a result of this development effort, you can now choose between the "New Look" or the "Classic Look" when working in the GroupWise client. Many new client features and enhancements make using the GroupWise client very exciting.

In addition, GroupWise 7 adds significant new features, such as Multiple Calendars, Instant Messaging presence awareness, HTML/multiple signatures, and spell check as you type. Also added to GroupWise 7 is the ability to edit system distribution lists from the client, making distribution list administration a task that can now be delegated to select users. There are also many enhancements that allow you to more fully customize the client in a simple, intuitive manor. This allows you to interact with the GroupWise content using your own style and preferences.

Chapter 3: Messaging Fundamentals

This chapter explains how to use the core features of GroupWise—sending and receiving email messages. We cover the different GroupWise modes that are available; the different message types; and how to read, respond to, forward, and delete messages. Whether you have used email for years or are just beginning with GroupWise, you'll find that this chapter makes you much more productive with the most popular message type—email. Included in this chapter are many tips and notes that provide extra content and information that you should find very useful when using GroupWise.

Chapter 4: The GroupWise Address Book

In this chapter, we explore each aspect of the GroupWise Address Book and how to effectively use the Address Book and its features. We cover the Frequent Contacts address book and how it is different from other address books, how to manage the Name Completion Search capabilities, how to utilize multiple address books, and how to share personal address books. You will also find many other useful and time-saving tips and tricks for working with the GroupWise Address Book.

In addition, we cover a new and very useful feature of the GroupWise System Address Book that allows you to manage and update system distribution lists from within your GroupWise Address Book.

Chapter 5: Message Management

The amount of information that people receive and send on a daily basis in the form of email is staggering, and it never seems to lessen. You get more and more email every day, and this chapter focuses on how to manage that influx of information. Organizing messages using the Cabinet, managing outgoing messages, and deleting messages are all covered in this chapter. This chapter also deals with how to locate information; using filters, printing, and archiving messages are also covered.

Chapter 6: Personal Calendaring and Task Management

In this chapter, we discuss how to leverage the Calendar system within GroupWise 7 to effectively manage your personal time using appointments, tasks, and reminder notes. We introduce you to the Calendar interface and walk you through creating posted appointments, tasks, and reminder notes. You will also learn all the ins and outs of setting up and working with multiple calendars, making it a snap to keep business versus personal appointments, tasks, notes, and so on, separated and easily distinguishable.

In addition, we show you several easy and convenient methods to manage your calendar, including rescheduling and changing Calendar entries from one type to another.

Chapter 7: Group Calendaring and Task Management

Taking personal calendaring to the next level, this chapter deals with collaborating with others using meetings, delegating tasks, and sending reminder notes to others. We show you how to monitor those invitations, how to retract or reschedule them, and how to set up recurring events. Finally, we cover additional Calendar topics, such as how to view multiple calendars at the same time and how to print a calendar using the many different printing formats built in to GroupWise 7.

Chapter 8: Advanced Features

This is the chapter that really sets you apart as a true GroupWise 7 power user. It covers the advanced features of GroupWise that allow you to use the program to its fullest potential. We cover such topics as GroupWise rules, Proxy, discussions, Junk Mail Handling, and advanced security options. You will also find configuration options for customizing the appearance of GroupWise, using message notification, managing your mailbox size, repairing your mailbox, and using other new advanced features. Finally, we cover accessing other email accounts with GroupWise, including how to import settings, email, and addresses into GroupWise from other mail accounts.

Chapter 9: Document Management

The built-in document management system (DMS) in GroupWise 7 allows you to tightly integrate your information management of everyday documents, spreadsheets, and presentations into your GroupWise program. Using GroupWise DMS, you can create, open, and share your documents with other users, as well as leverage powerful features such as version control, historical access, and document security. We also show you how to import your existing documents into document libraries with GroupWise.

Chapter 10: Remote Access

In today's mobile society, accessing information regardless of your location is a key requirement for many users. GroupWise offers several different options on remote access. This chapter covers using the primary Windows-based GroupWise client in remote and cache modes, allowing you to work on your messages, appointments, and documents while disconnected from the network. When you once again have a network connection, the GroupWise client will synchronize with the master mailbox, keeping everything in sync. GroupWise cache and remote modes are extremely valuable to users who are mobile and use a laptop as their primary computer.

This chapter covers how to prepare GroupWise for remote access and how to use GroupWise in remote and cache modes.

Chapter 11: Customizing GroupWise

Out of all the chapters in this book, you're sure to find this chapter to be the most fun because it deals with customizing GroupWise to suit your tastes. For example, if you would like the three functions you use most often as the only buttons on the Toolbar, we show you how to accomplish this. We also show you how to customize your Home view, allowing you to place only the content you deem most important on this view. In addition, we discuss how to customize your folders; set default fonts and views for reading and sending messages; and display messages in different formats, such as discussion threads.

Chapter 12: GroupWise on a PDA

This chapter discusses how you can use the new GroupWise PDA Connect program to synchronize your Palm or PocketPC device to your GroupWise mailbox.

In addition, we discuss how to access your GroupWise mailbox over the Internet from a number of wireless devices, including personal digital assistants (PDAs), cell phones, and other devices dedicated to messaging (such as BlackBerry's RIM devices). We show you how GroupWise automatically senses the device you are connecting with and formats the information appropriately.

Chapter 13: GroupWise WebAccess

One of the strongest and most versatile features of GroupWise 7 is the ability to access all your information using a web browser without having to sacrifice the most powerful features of the full Windows-based client. GroupWise 7 WebAccess allows you to open a web browser from anywhere in the world and operate almost exactly as though you were in front of your computer in the office. New features such as right-click functions, autoname completion, and drag-and-drop capabilities are now integrated into GroupWise WebAccess. We show you this easy-to-use interface and describe how to access your messages, folders, Calendar information, address books, and documents. We also discuss accessing rules, proxy, signature lines, and send options from the WebAccess interface.

Appendix A: GroupWise Cross-Platform Client

Appendix A discusses the GroupWise Cross-Platform client that runs on either the Macintosh or Linux platform. The Cross-Platform client allows users on either of these platforms to enjoy the benefit of a full feature-rich client to interact with their mail. Because of the differences between the Mac/Linux and Windows environments, there are a few differences between the Windows GroupWise client and the Cross-Platform client. These differences are discussed and identified.

Appendix B: GroupWise Startup Options

This appendix covers the options that allow the GroupWise client to operate in online, cache, or remote mode. Also, other relevant startup switches that affect the client load behavior are explained.

Appendix C: Additional GroupWise Resources

This appendix provides numerous additional resources for finding more GroupWise information—sources on the Internet, within the GroupWise Help facility, and in the "Cool Solutions" community.

Appendix D: POP Versus IMAP Accounts

This appendix provides a quick and easy reference on what POP and IMAP accounts are. It explains what these protocols are, how they are used by the GroupWise client, and how you can identify which protocol may work the best for accessing your Internet mail accounts.

CHAPTER 1

Introduction to GroupWise 7

In this chapter, you learn about the GroupWise 7 client interface. The GroupWise client is the software you use to interact with a GroupWise system or another type of email system. This interface is the user's view of a program (it's what you, the user, interact with to control the program). This chapter briefly introduces you to the main parts of the GroupWise client interface.

Different Versions of GroupWise

The GroupWise 7 client is supported on Microsoft Windows 2000, Windows XP, and Windows 2003. GroupWise also has a special WebAccess client that can be used through any of the popular Internet-browsing programs, such as Microsoft Internet Explorer and Mozilla Firefox. Using the WebAccess client, you access your GroupWise account from other operating systems that support web browsing, such as Macintosh, UNIX, and Linux. You can also use a personal digital assistant (PDA) or a wireless telephone to access information in a GroupWise system. No matter which one you use to access GroupWise, each client or device has basically the same features, but the way you use those features can vary depending on the capabilities of the environment.

In this book, we emphasize the GroupWise client for the Microsoft Windows platform. We also devote several pages to the GroupWise WebAccess client. These are the two most commonly used means of accessing your GroupWise account. Appendix A, "GroupWise Cross-Platform Client," discusses the GroupWise Cross-Platform client that you can run on a Macintosh or Linux workstation.

No matter which method you use to interact with GroupWise, all GroupWise users deal with common message formats. It doesn't matter which version of the client you use to create a message, and it doesn't matter which version of the client the recipient uses to read the message. (In fact, if you are communicating through the Internet with users outside your company's GroupWise installation, those users are very likely using completely different email systems.) The point is that you can send messages to people using different email systems, different computing platforms, and different email interfaces without knowing anything about those other systems, platforms, or interfaces.

Starting GroupWise

You can launch the GroupWise program in different ways. The most common is to simply double-click the GroupWise icon located on your Windows desktop. If the icon is not available on your desktop, you can navigate to the Start menu and then choose Programs, Novell GroupWise, GroupWise. Normally, when you perform one of these actions, GroupWise simply opens your mailbox.

NOTE

This book was written based on a GroupWise 7 default client installation running on Windows XP Professional. If you are running a different version of Windows, or if you or your administrator has customized the installation, you might use a slightly different procedure to launch GroupWise.

The first time you run GroupWise, however, you might see the GroupWise Startup screen. You use this screen to provide GroupWise with your user ID, post office information, and TCP/IP settings. Don't panic if you encounter this screen. Your system administrator can give you all the necessary information. For the rest of the chapter, we assume that you don't need to deal with the Startup screen.

NOTE

Appendix B, "GroupWise Startup Options," provides more information about the Startup screen.

The Main GroupWise Screen

When you open the GroupWise 7 client for the first time, the screen shown in Figure 1.1 appears automatically. You access all the GroupWise features from this screen. We call this part of the interface the *main GroupWise screen*. From the main GroupWise screen, you access your incoming messages, outgoing messages, deleted messages, documents stored in a GroupWise library, and any items on your calendar. You can also access other email accounts you might happen to use. (We explain how to set up these features in Chapter 8, "Advanced Features.") The GroupWise interface looks similar to other Windows applications. In particular, it bears close resemblance to Windows Explorer, and it functions in much the same way.

FIGURE 1.1

The GroupWise interface provides access to all GroupWise features.

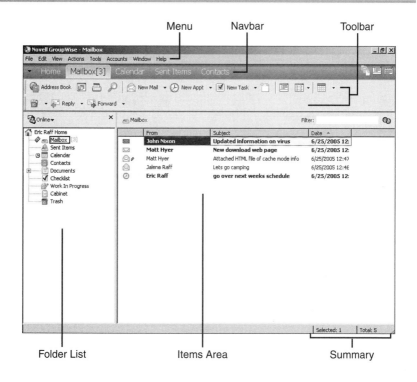

NOTE

You can open multiple GroupWise windows and customize each one with a different view of your GroupWise information.

As you can see in Figure 1.1, the main screen has six principal areas:

- **Main menu**—The GroupWise Options menu, under the title bar. This can be hidden, so you may not see it by default. If it is hidden, you can access the main menu options by clicking on the black down arrow on the far left of the Nav bar.

- **Navigation bar**—The GroupWise Navigation or Nav bar is located under the main menu. It consists of tabs that take you to various folders in GroupWise.

- **Toolbar**—Buttons that provide shortcuts to commonly used menu options.

- **Folder list**—The list of folder icons where your messages are organized. The folder list may be hidden also. Clicking the folders icon on the right side of the Nav bar will show or hide the folder list.

- **Items area**—The area where messages are stored.

- **Summary**—An indicator that shows the number of selected and total messages in the highlighted folder.

These interface elements comprise the basic control elements of the main GroupWise screen and allow you to interact with the program efficiently.

NOTE

Your system administrator may have changed the default settings for your organization. As a result, you may see a slightly different interface when you first launch the GroupWise 7 client.

The right side of the Nav bar contains three icons. They allow you to show or hide the folder list, QuickViewer, or main menu.

The Home View

New to GroupWise 7 is the Home view. It is extremely powerful in that it allows you to see any information contained within GroupWise through one window. The first time you access the Home view, a help screen providing basic information about the Home view and how you can begin customizing it will appear. By default, when you click on the Home tab in the Nav bar or select your Home view from the Folder list, you see your calendar for the day, your checklist items, and any unread information in your mailbox. The Home view uses *panels* to display various content inside the Home view. The true power of the Home view is in the panels. Panels can be added, rearranged, and customized to display anything in any format you desire. Customizing the Home view is covered in Chapter 11, "Customizing GroupWise."

The Folder List and Items Area

The Folder list contains a hierarchical structure of the folders that are used to organize and hold messages and documents. The items area displays the individual messages located in the selected folder. The Folder list and items area are linked to each other. To view the items in a folder, simply select the folder in the Folder list on the left; the items in that folder then appear in the items area on the right.

Nine folders appear automatically in the main GroupWise screen. In Chapter 5, "Message Management," you learn how to adjust the settings for these folders and how to create new folders for storing your messages. Table 1.1 lists the nine system-generated default folders and describes their functions.

TABLE 1.1
Default GroupWise Folders

FOLDER NAME	DESCRIPTION
Mailbox	Displays the messages you have received. (Mailbox management is explained in Chapter 5.
Sent Items	Displays the messages you have sent to other email recipients and allows you to obtain the status of the messages and perform other actions on those messages.
Calendar	Displays your calendar, which stores information about your appointments, notes, and tasks. (Calendar management is explained in Chapter 6, "Personal Calendaring and Task Management.")
Contacts	Displays your personal contacts. These contacts are in your Frequent Contacts address book. (The Address Book is explained in Chapter 4, "The Address Book and the Address Selector.")

TABLE 1.1
Default GroupWise Folders (continued)

FOLDER NAME	DESCRIPTION
Documents	Contains subfolders that display the documents you have authored and the documents in your default library. (Document management is explained in Chapter 9, "Document Management.")
Checklist	Displays a list of items that require an action of some type. This folder can be used for task management. (Task management is discussed in Chapter 7, "Group Calendaring and Task Management.")
Work In Progress	Keeps drafts of unsent messages until you're ready to send them.
Cabinet	Displays the messages you have filed for storage. (Message management is explained in Chapter 5.)
Trash	Displays the items you have deleted along with the date the item was deleted.

TIP

You can use the Nav bar to navigate to different folders. You can also add any folder to the Nav bar by right-clicking it and selecting Customize Nav Bar. Having more tabbed areas allows you to hide the Folder list, giving you more screen space to view your items.

The following sections describe each of the default system folders in more detail.

Mailbox

When you want to see your new messages, you must open the Mailbox folder. When you receive a new message, an unopened envelope icon appears next to the Mailbox folder. The number of unopened messages in your mailbox is also displayed to the right of the Mailbox folder. This number is also displayed to the right of the Mailbox tab on the Nav bar. When you're in the Home view, new items are displayed in the Unread Items panel.

You open the Mailbox folder simply by clicking it. You see a list of your opened and unopened messages in the items area, as shown earlier in Figure 1.1. To read a message, double-click the message line. The message opens in a new window. To open an item through the Unread Items panel, simply double-click the item.

NOTE

After an item has been opened, it will stay visible in the Unread Items panel until you navigate off and then back to the Home view. This allows you to delete or reply to the message you have just read from within the Home view.

Sent Items

The Sent Items folder is your outbox. You use this folder to manage the messages you have sent, and you can perform these three useful tasks:

- View the status of the messages you have sent
- Resend messages
- Retract messages you have sent (provided that the recipient has not yet opened the message)

Figure 1.2 shows the Sent Items folder. The first time you double-click an item in the Sent Items folder, a dialog box appears asking what you want the double-click action to perform in the future. You have the choice of either having the message open or having the status information appear. This dialog box appears only the first time you double-click a sent item. Your choice in this dialog box becomes your default action. (You can change this option later by clicking Tools, Options, Environment and clicking the Default Actions tab.)

TIP

All sent items have a red arrow next to them indicating that the item was sent from your GroupWise account.

When you view the status information of a message, you can see detailed information about what has happened to the message since you sent it. GroupWise 7 provides two views into the properties of a message: Basic and Advanced. Basic shows you information such as when the message was delivered, opened, deleted, completed (if the message was a task), forwarded, accepted, or declined (if the message was an appointment or a task). Advanced displays additional information that is useful if you're troubleshooting message delivery issues.

From the Sent Items folder, you can resend messages that need to be updated, modified, or sent to additional recipients. To resend a message, select the Resend option after right-clicking on the message. You can also resend from the Actions menu. When you edit and resend a message, you can retract the original message as long as the recipient has not opened it yet.

FIGURE 1.2
The Sent Items folder allows you to access and manage messages you have sent.

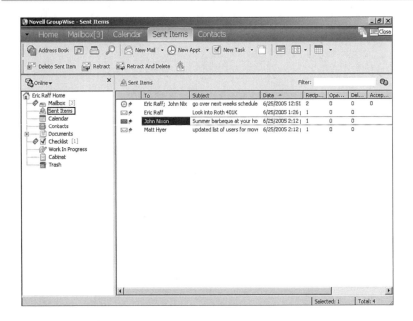

To retract a message, highlight the message in the Sent Items screen and press the Delete key. Next, select either Recipient's Mailbox or All Mailboxes. (Selecting the My Mailbox feature does not retract the message but instead deletes it from your Sent Items folder.) Deleting from the recipient's mailbox retracts the message and leaves a copy of the message in your Sent Items folder. Deleting from all mailboxes retracts the message and also deletes the message from your Sent Items folder.

TIP

You can retract only messages that have not been opened by the recipient. Also, the recipient is not warned that a message is being retracted. GroupWise simply removes the message from the recipient's mailbox unless it has already been read. You can see if the recipient has already opened the message by viewing the properties of the sent item. If a message is sent to multiple recipients and some but not all have opened it, when you retract the message, it will be retracted from only those recipients who have not opened it.

Calendar

The calendar feature enables you to create, view, and manage your appointments, tasks, and notes. These calendar items can be personal items (for example, a personal note to yourself), or they can be group items (for example, a meeting request). Figure 1.3 shows the calendar.

FIGURE 1.3
The calendar provides access to your appointments, tasks, and notes.

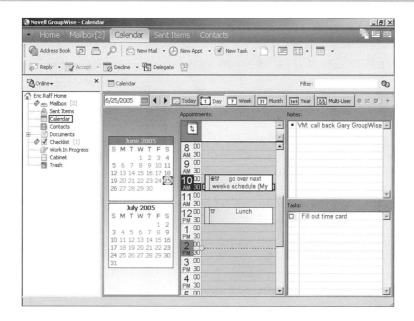

NOTE

Chapters 6 and 7 explain personal and group calendaring in more detail.

You can view your calendar items in the items area by clicking the Calendar folder. To view the calendar as its own window, click Window and choose Calendar. Then select the Calendar view you want to see, such as Day, Week, or Month. You can also click the Calendar tab on the Nav bar.

Contacts

The Contacts folder stores your mail contacts. For each contact, you can enter several different types of information such as name, birthday, email address(es),

Instant Messaging IDs, comments, and so on. By default, the Contacts folder is linked to the GroupWise Frequent Contacts address book. You can manage the contacts from this Contacts folder or from within the address book. There is also a History tab available when you look at the details of a contact that will display all the mail sent to or from this contact in one window. To learn more about working with and managing your contacts, see Chapter 4.

Documents

GroupWise can be used as a full-featured document management system (DMS). The Documents folder displays references to documents that have been stored in a GroupWise library. They might be documents you have created or documents created by other individuals. GroupWise document management is explained in Chapter 9.

Checklist

The Checklist folder enables you to keep track of items requiring an action. It displays items in your personal Task List. (The first time you open the Checklist folder, you see an information screen that gives you an overview of this folder; this screen goes away after you place an item into the folder.) This folder includes both items that you have created yourself and tasks others have assigned to you. (Tasks are explained in more detail in Chapters 6 and 7.)

A task is something that requires an action on your part, such as following up on an email message or returning a telephone call. Each task has a start date and a due date. Overdue tasks are carried forward in the Calendar views and are then displayed in red, indicating past-due status.

If you send a task item to someone else and that person accepts the task, you can track its status by opening the task from the Sent Items folder and viewing its properties.

Work In Progress

You can use the Work In Progress folder to store drafts of messages that have not been sent, as shown in Figure 1.4. For example, if you begin writing a message and run out of time to complete it or need to obtain additional infor-mation, you can save a draft of the message in the Work In Progress folder. Later, you can retrieve the message from this folder, complete it, and send the message along to the recipients. The Work In Progress folder is accessible from the GroupWise WebAccess client as well. This feature allows you to work on items in the office, save them, and then finish them from wherever you have access to a web browser.

FIGURE 1.4
Work In Progress allows you to save drafts of messages for later completion.

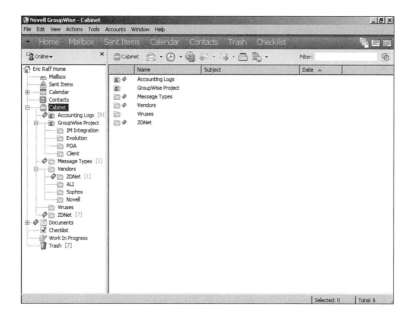

NOTE

Saving reoccurring appointments to the Work In Progress folder creates multiple occurrences of the items and unlinks the items so that you cannot send them without reconfiguring the reoccurring date.

The Work In Progress folder is also useful for storing drafts of documents if you are using the document management features of GroupWise.

Cabinet

The Cabinet folder is the place where you can create additional folders that you use to organize your messages. Figure 1.5 shows an example of the Cabinet. You use this folder to organize messages in the same way you use the directory and subdirectory structure on your computer to organize files. You can place messages that pertain to the same project in a folder, nest folders inside other folders, and link messages to multiple folders. (Chapter 5 explains more about folders and how to manage your messages.)

FIGURE 1.5
The GroupWise Cabinet allows you to organize and manage your messages by creating additional folders under it.

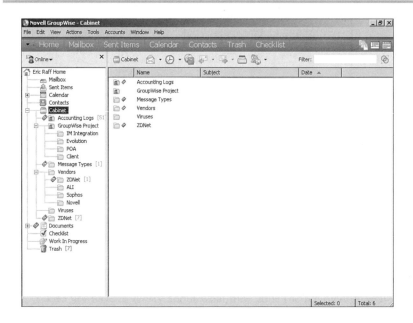

Trash

When you delete a message from anywhere in GroupWise, the message goes into the Trash. Later, if you need to undelete the message, you can retrieve it from the Trash, provided that the Trash has not been emptied. (Chapter 5 discusses managing messages in the Trash folder.)

To view the messages in the Trash, simply click the Trash folder. Figure 1.6 shows how the Trash folder looks when it is open. Messages do not remain in the Trash forever. They stay there for a specified period of time and then are emptied from the Trash by the GroupWise server. When a message is emptied from the Trash, it is completely deleted from your GroupWise mailbox, and you cannot retrieve it again. (Your GroupWise system administrator might be able to recover items that have been deleted from the Trash. Contact your system administrator if a situation arises in which you absolutely must retrieve items that have been deleted from the Trash.)

By default, messages are automatically emptied from the Trash after seven days unless your administrator has made changes to this setting. You may also be able to adjust this number. To choose the number of days you want deleted messages to stay in the Trash before they are automatically emptied, edit the value by choosing Tools, Options, Environment and then selecting the Cleanup tab associated with Trash. (Chapter 11 explains how to set this option.)

In some GroupWise configurations, you might be prompted to confirm a final deletion of an item that the GroupWise system has not yet backed up. If the GroupWise system has not backed up a document, it cannot be restored at a later date. This is a special protection mechanism known as a *smart purge*, which your GroupWise system administrator may or may not have enabled. If you receive this prompt, make sure the message is not needed again for any reason.

FIGURE 1.6
The Trash stores your deleted messages.

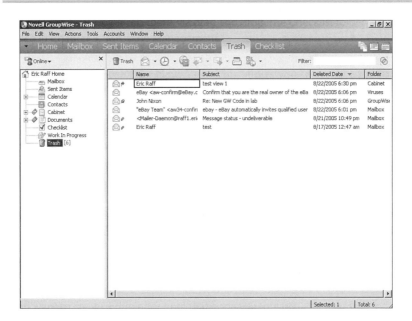

Navigating Within GroupWise

As you work with GroupWise, you will discover that you can accomplish individual tasks in many different ways. In this book, we try to consistently explain the easiest steps to follow. Like other Windows-based applications, the GroupWise client contains pull-down menus; scrollbars; and minimize, maximize, and close buttons consistent with accepted Windows conventions.

You can click any corner of the GroupWise interface and drag it to a new position on the screen to resize the main GroupWise screen. You can also click and drag the dividing bar between different panes of the main screen to resize the panes. Likewise, you can click and drag messages from the items area to the folders in the Cabinet or other system folders.

In many situations, you can use alternative methods to execute the menu commands. For example, to compose a mail message, you can choose File, New, Mail. Alternatively, you can simply click the New Mail button on the Toolbar, or you can press Ctrl+M.

Several GroupWise features can help you navigate within GroupWise more quickly and efficiently. These features include the Toolbar, keystroke shortcuts, QuickMenus, and QuickViewer.

NOTE

Throughout this book, you will find instructions explaining how to accomplish various tasks. Many of these tasks work off the main menu. If the main menu is hidden, the instructions may be confusing. Showing the main menu is as simple as clicking the far right icon in the Nav bar to toggle it on.

The Toolbar

The Toolbar, shown in Figure 1.7, is the row of buttons under the menu bar in the main GroupWise screen. You can use the buttons on the Toolbar as shortcuts to activate options that otherwise appear under the pull-down menus. Using the Toolbar, you can quickly access the GroupWise features you use most often. Editing functions (such as Cut, Copy, and Paste), Spell Check, and Online Help are examples of buttons you can add to the Toolbar, saving you the trouble of selecting these options from the menus. You can use the Toolbar in message views as well as in the main GroupWise screen. (In Chapter 11, we explain how to customize the Toolbar.)

Keystroke Shortcuts

Many of the options in the pull-down menus can also be accessed by keystroke sequences, allowing you to efficiently perform GroupWise tasks without reaching for the mouse. For example, you can compose a new message by choosing the New, Mail option from the File pull-down menu, or you can simply press Ctrl+M to achieve the same result. Not all functions have keystroke shortcuts, however. If a pull-down menu command has a keystroke shortcut, it is listed next to the function in the pull-down menu. A comprehensive list is available in Online Help. Look under the Index for "Keys."

FIGURE 1.7
The Toolbar provides quick access to the most commonly used GroupWise functions.

QuickMenus

QuickMenus, shown in Figure 1.8, is a GroupWise feature that adds function-ality to the right mouse button. When you are accessing different areas of the interface, right-clicking the mouse button displays a short menu of actions that is relevant to the item or area you are clicking.

FIGURE 1.8
QuickMenus provides context-sensitive shortcut menus for common GroupWise functions.

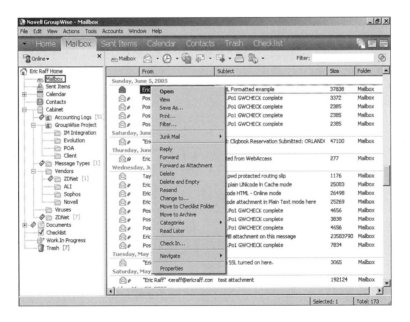

Remember if you ever are unsure how or what you can do to a particular item, just start right-clicking to open a list of available options. This is a great way to become familiar with what actions you can take in GroupWise as well.

NOTE

GroupWise WebAccess supports context-sensitive QuickMenus through the right-click functionality as well.

QuickViewer

By enabling the GroupWise QuickViewer, you can read messages and view their attachments without double-clicking these items. You can place the GroupWise QuickViewer across the bottom or on the right side of the screen. Placing the QuickViewer on the right side of the screen allows for more content to be displayed in it. Figure 1.9 shows the QuickViewer being displayed on the right side of the screen. When you select a message in the items area, the main GroupWise screen's QuickViewer pane displays the message contents automatically.

FIGURE 1.9

The QuickViewer provides an instant view of message contents.

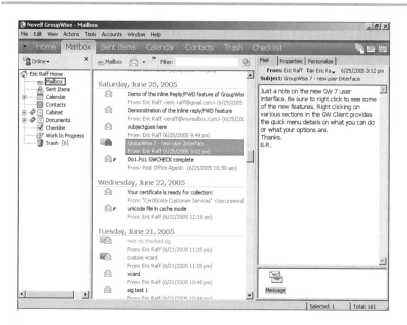

Summary

In this chapter, you learned about the GroupWise interface, which gives you access to many different messaging and calendaring functions, and you also learned some tricks that will help you navigate the interface. The next chapter explains the important new functions that appear in GroupWise 7.

CHAPTER 2

What's New in GroupWise 7

The GroupWise User program has several new features and enhancements. This chapter describes each one of them and shows how they can make your collaboration activities more productive.

The intent here is to provide a concise overview of these features, not to delve into the details of each. We briefly describe each feature and provide a graphic of most of them. If you are familiar with GroupWise, this chapter should help you quickly get up to speed on the new additions to the end-user interface.

This chapter is divided into four groupings of new features: look and feel, functionality, management, and new WebAccess client features. Look-and-feel features are those that add to or change how you access or utilize functions within GroupWise. Functionality features are those that provide totally new user capabilities. Management features enhance your ability to organize and keep track of the messages and information stored in GroupWise. Finally, we describe the new GroupWise WebAccess client features.

Look and Feel

GroupWise 7 takes a major step forward in regards to its look and feel. The features in the following sections provide new ways for you to access information and functions with the GroupWise 7 application. We encourage you to try out these features on your own; for more detailed, step-by-step instruction, we refer you to the chapter where each feature is covered in detail.

NOTE

Chapter 11, "Customizing GroupWise," discusses customizing the look and feel of GroupWise.

Appearance Schemes

GroupWise 7 supports a new look and feel. It also supports the capability to switch back to a GroupWise 6.5 scheme or create your own custom scheme. The scheme entails items such as the main menu, Nav bar, Main Toolbar, folder list, and QuickViewer settings. The client schemes are defined under Tools, Options, Environment, Appearance. Figure 2.1 shows a customized scheme for the client.

FIGURE 2.1
A customized appearance scheme.

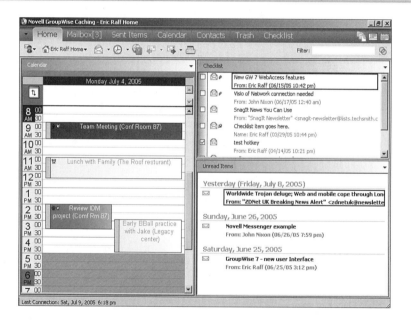

Color Schemes

Along with the appearance schemes you can customize, you can also choose from several color schemes. When you apply a color scheme to GroupWise, it affects the entire color layout of the GroupWise client. Possible color schemes are Blue, Sky Blue (default), Olive Green, Spring Green, Silver, and Sterling

Silver. You can modify the color scheme by right-clicking on the Nav bar and selecting Customize Nav Bar. At the bottom are the available color schemes. Alternatively, you can make these and other modifications by choosing Tools, Options, Environment and selecting the Appearance tab.

Customizable Navigation Bar

GroupWise 7 supports a new Navigation bar, known as the *Nav bar* for short. This horizontal bar contains tabs that represent any folder in your GroupWise mailbox. You can add any folder to the Nav bar to increase its functionality. This task is as simple as right-clicking the Nav bar and selecting Customize Nav Bar. Check the desired folder in GroupWise to have it appear on the Nav bar.

Updated Icons

As you know, GroupWise 7 sports an entirely new look and feel. This includes more than 140 updated icons for every component of the client.

Header Controls

Header controls allow you to adjust the text color and font size of your GroupWise headers. These changes affect the Nav bar in particular. You might want to increase the font size if you find the text to be too small. To adjust the header text color and font size, right-click on the Nav bar and select from either the Header Text Color or Font Size options.

Customized Calendar Background Color

You can change the background colors in the calendar's appointments, tasks, notes, and all-day-events sections. To accomplish this, right-click in any of the mentioned sections of the calendar and select Background Color. You can also remove the separating lines between tasks and notes from this interface.

Summary View and Group Labels of Items

GroupWise's new Summary view is designed to give you a summary of each item. It shows the From, Subject, and Date information, using two lines for each message. You might use the Summary view when you have the QuickViewer displayed on the right. You may also choose to enable the group labels feature. Group labels organize all mail for each day under a date group heading. Figure 2.2 displays the mailbox in the Summary view, group labels are enabled, and the QuickViewer is located to the right.

FIGURE 2.2
The Summary view with the QuickViewer displayed on the right.

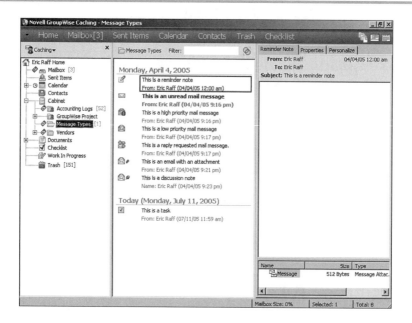

QuickViewer Placement Options

You can now place the QuickViewer on the right side of the screen. Traditionally, the QuickViewer was displayed horizontally across the bottom section of the client. See Figure 2.2 for an example of this view. To adjust the location of the QuickViewer, choose View, QuickView and then select Display at Bottom or Display at Right.

NOTE

Chapter 8, "Advanced Features," explains how to work with the QuickViewer.

Customized Inline Reply/Forward Layout

When replying to or forwarding a message that is inline (the original message is contained in the reply or forward message body), you can customize how the original text is defined and where your reply text is located. You can have your reply text placed at the top or bottom of the original text. You can also define separate settings for plain-text email and HTML messages. Figure 2.3 displays an HTML reply with the reply text at the top of the message and the message headers included.

FIGURE 2.3
Using customized inline reply/forward settings.

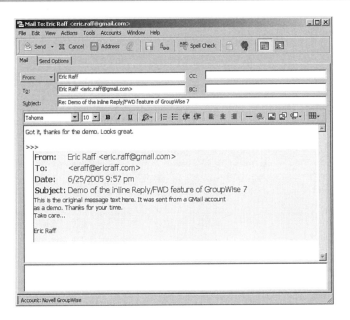

Functionality

The new functionality features in GroupWise 7 add capabilities not available in earlier versions of the program. The features described in the following sections provide more collaboration and information-management capabilities.

Multiple Calendars

With GroupWise 7, you can now create multiple calendars. This way, you can easily keep your work and family schedules separated. You can also keep work, project-oriented, personal, and other tasks and notes separated. For each calendar you create, you can define a color scheme. You can then view all calendars in one window and see all the appointments from the various calendars, each color-coded appropriately. You can drag and drop appointments, tasks, or notes between calendars as well. Figure 2.4 shows a second calendar called

Family. The main calendar is selected, and the check boxes next to each subcalendar cause the appointments to be visible from the main calendar.

FIGURE 2.4
Viewing multiple calendars superimposed over each other.

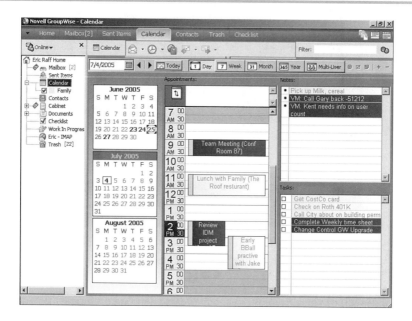

NOTE

Chapter 6, "Personal Calendaring and Task Management," explains how to set up and work with multiple calendars.

Print a Calendar in Full Color

When you print the calendar, it now retains any colors you have set on appointments. This feature allows you to retain the colors for additional calendars or categorized items when printing.

All-Day Events

When creating an appointment, you can easily flag it as an all-day event through the Actions menu or by checking the All Day Event option. All-day events are shown across the top of the appointment view window. Figure 2.5 shows an appointment being created with the all day event option checked.

FIGURE 2.5
Creating an all-day appointment.

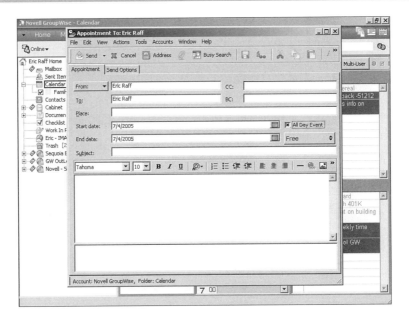

Chapters 5, "Message Management," and 6, "Personal Calendaring and Task Management," discuss working with calendar items.

Quick Filter

The quick filter is a great addition to GroupWise 7. It allows you to simply begin typing in a filter window to dynamically apply a filter to the selected folder. This makes locating messages fast and simple. The quick filter searches the From, To, and Subject fields. Figure 2.6 displays the quick filter box.

Search Attachments

When performing searches (searches and filters are different), GroupWise automatically searches the contents of attachments immediately. This provides a more comprehensive search and makes finding attachments that reference specific words or phrases much easier.

FIGURE 2.6
The quick filter interface in the GroupWise client.

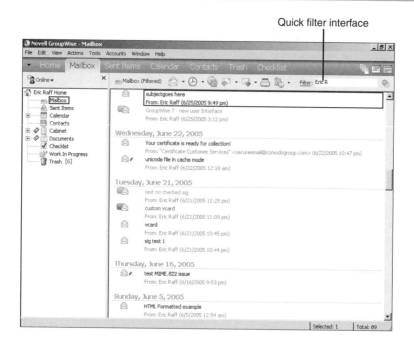

NOTE

Chapter 5 discusses using the Find feature.

Spell Check As You Type

GroupWise 7 now supports dynamic spell checking. This means that as you type in the message body or subject areas, any misspelled words are underlined in red. You can then right-click the misspelled word to see a list of possible correct spellings.

Messenger Presence

If your organization has implemented the Novell Instant Messenger product, the GroupWise 7 client now integrates with it for presence awareness. When you read a message from a fellow GroupWise user, you can see the status of the user who sent you the message from the Read view of the message. From this view, you can initiate a chat with the sender. This makes it simpler to communicate with users using a chat session rather than going back and forth with email messages. Figure 2.7 depicts this feature. Notice the Presence icon next to the From field. You can also right-click the Presence icon to add the sender to your IM Contact list.

FIGURE 2.7
Integration between the Novell Instant Messenger and GroupWise client.

Multiple HTML Signatures

GroupWise now supports the use of multiple signatures. This allows you to create a signature for personal use and a different one for business use, and so on. When you send a message, GroupWise prompts as to what signature you want to attach to the message. In addition to multiple signatures, you can format your signatures using HTML. This allows you to create a much more customized and creative signature.

NOTE

Chapter 11 explains how to use multiple signatures.

Block Images in HTML Messages

A common technique that spammers are using today is sending an HTML email that simply contains a link to an image hosted on an Internet server.

When you open the message, the link automatically retrieves the graphic or image and displays it inside the message. GroupWise 7 now blocks external images from being downloaded and displayed in the message when you read it. Instead, you are notified that the message contains a reference to an external image. If you want to see the images, you have to click on the notification message that is displayed across the top of the email. Figure 2.8 shows a message that contains links to external images and the GroupWise client blocking the download and display of these images.

FIGURE 2.8
GroupWise can block the automatic display of external images imbedded in an HTML message.

Notification of blocked images

Blocked images
display as a red X

NOTE

Chapter 11 explains how to configure the blocking of external images.

Additional Save As Formats

GroupWise 7 now supports four different Save As formats. You can save messages using the plain-text (.txt), rich text (.rtf), Internet mail (MIME) (.eml), or
GroupWise Classic (.doc) formats. When you save a message using the File,
Save As option, you see a new Saved Message Format drop-down list with
these available formats. When you select the desired format, the extension of
the Save File As field changes appropriately.

Work Offline When in Remote or Cache Mode

When working in remote or cache modes, you can now tell the GroupWise
client that you are offline. This capability is helpful if do not have a network
connection and are hence disconnected. While the offline setting is applied,
your GroupWise client will not try to send or synchronize with your master
mailbox. The Proxy and Busy Search features are also removed from the client
interface while you are set to work offline. Figure 2.9 displays where you apply
the offline status.

FIGURE 2.9
GroupWise can be set to work offline when you're in cache or remote modes.

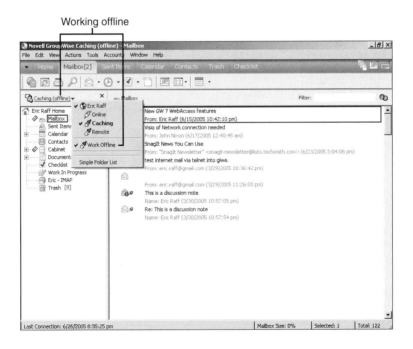

Unicode Support

GroupWise 7 now supports Unicode in the Subject, Message body, and Attachment fields. This allows for greater support for other languages and attachment names. For example, you can now attach files with filenames that contain extended or foreign characters to an email message.

Management

The following sections describe features and enhancements that provide new capabilities in organizing and accessing information. More effective information management with GroupWise is the goal of these features.

Home View/Panel Management

The Home view is a completely new component of GroupWise 7. It includes the use of panels that allow you to display any content inside them. The Home view can contain multiple panels in one or two columns. This provides a central place to display information such as your calendar items, unread mail, checklist items, follow-up items, and so on. The Home view is highly customizable; you can leverage it to meet your specific work style. Figure 2.10 displays a customized Home view with panels for unread mail, follow-up items, and a summary view of the calendar.

NOTE

Chapter 11 explains in detail how to work with the Home view and manage your panels.

Edit Corporate Distribution Lists

Have you ever noticed that a system distribution list may not be accurate or needs to be updated? In previous versions of GroupWise, only the GroupWise administrator could update system distribution lists. With GroupWise 7, you can now update system distribution lists from within the GroupWise Address Book. This allows the administrator to delegate the management to you, the user, because you usually know more about what the distribution list contents should contain anyway. Figure 2.11 displays the Address Book with a system distribution list selected. Notice the active Add and Remove buttons to the left. They allow you to keep the distribution list updated from the client. For you to be able to manage a system distribution list, the GroupWise administrator has to define you as a distribution list administrator. When this is done, you can then manage the distribution list membership.

FIGURE 2.10
GroupWise customized Home view.

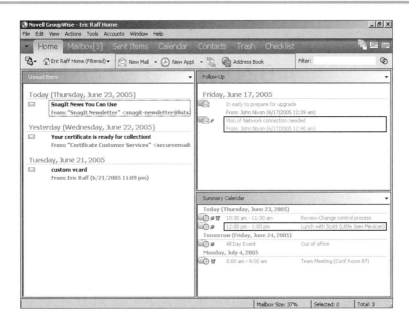

FIGURE 2.11
Editing GroupWise system distribution lists from the address book.

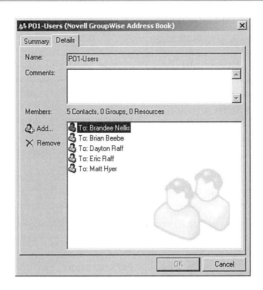

NOTE

Chapter 4, "The GroupWise Address Book," explains how to manage system distribution lists.

Speed Enhancements for Cache or Remote Mode

When you're running GroupWise in cache or remote mode, the update process is now faster. You don't need to configure anything for this to work. Novell has made speed enhancements to the way the client applies updates and works with the cache or remote databases.

WebAccess Client

The GroupWise WebAccess client contains several new features. Chapter 13, "GroupWise WebAccess," discusses each of these enhancements. We decided to describe the new features here as well so that you are aware of some of the exciting new features that you can leverage when using the GroupWise WebAccess client.

Updated Look to Match Windows Client

The WebAccess interface has a completely new look. This look better matches the GroupWise 7 client interface, making it more consistent with the client. Figure 2.12 displays the new WebAccess client interface.

Drag-and-Drop Support

You can now drag and drop messages between folders in the WebAccess client. This makes moving and managing items between multiple folders much simpler. You can also select multiple items using the check boxes and drag and drop several messages at one time.

Right-Click Context-Sensitive QuickMenus

Just as the Windows client supports right-click QuickMenus, the WebAccess client now supports right-click context-sensitive QuickMenus. This feature allows you to quickly access the possible actions that you can perform on a selected item. Figure 2.13 displays this feature in WebAccess.

FIGURE 2.12
GroupWise 7 WebAccess client interface.

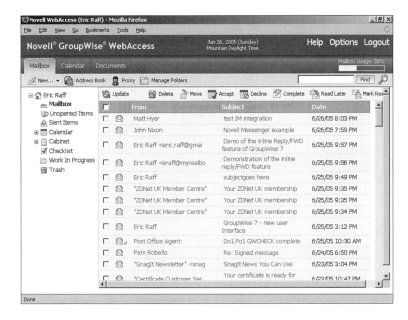

Support for Posted Items

You can now create any type of posted item through WebAccess. To create a posted item, click the down arrow next to the New button and select the desired posted item type.

Access to Full Message Properties

GroupWise provides a comprehensive set of properties for each item. You can now view the complete properties of a message through WebAccess. The properties are also divided between basic and advanced properties. Usually, the basic properties contain the information you use most often. Figure 2.14 displays the basic properties of a sent appointment through WebAccess.

Manage Folders and Shared Folders

The GroupWise 7 WebAccess client provides a central interface to manage all your folders. Through this interface, you can add, delete, or share any of your GroupWise folders. Figure 2.15 displays the WebAccess folder management interface.

FIGURE 2.13
The WebAccess right-click options for messages.

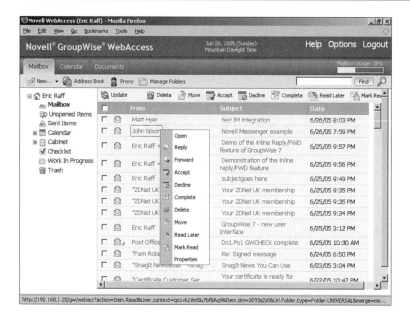

FIGURE 2.14
The properties of a sent appointment as viewed through WebAccess.

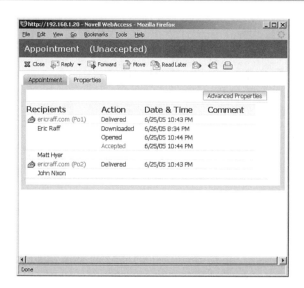

FIGURE 2.15
The folder management interface for WebAccess.

Quick Find Feature

The WebAccess client now supports a quick find interface. This allows you to quickly search for items in the WebAccess client. When you issue a quick find, the results are displayed in the main WebAccess window. Figure 2.16 highlights the quick find interface.

Auto-Name Completion

WebAccess now supports auto-name completion. This feature has been available in the Windows client for years, and Novell has now exposed this technology through the WebAccess client. The auto-name completion works off your Frequent Contacts/Contacts folder of names. Figure 2.17 displays a new mail message with auto-name completion in use.

Mark Unread Support

You can now mark an already read message as unread through the WebAccess client. This option is available as a right-click option on a message as well as the Read Later toolbar option.

FIGURE 2.16

The WebAccess quick find option.

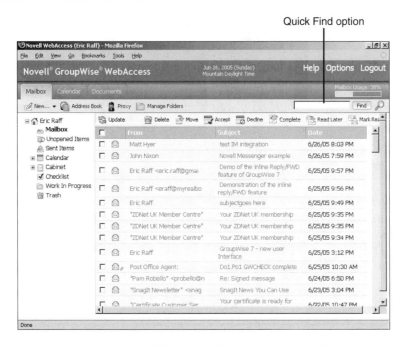

Access and Save to Work In Progress Folder

You can now begin composing a message through the WebAccess client and then save it to your Work In Progress folder. You can also see any saved messages in the Work In Progress folder that were saved by the Windows client.

View Mailbox Size Usage

If the GroupWise administrator has set a size limit on your mailbox, the WebAccess client will now report how much space you have used in the upper-right corner of the main WebAccess screen, as shown previously in Figure 2.16.

FIGURE 2.17
The WebAccess auto-name completion feature dynamically checks for email address matches against your Frequent Contacts.

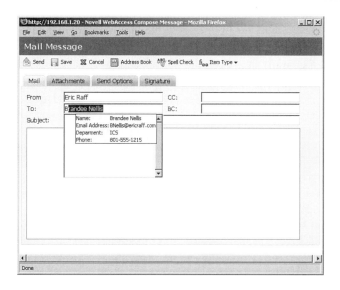

Summary

In this chapter, we looked at the new look and feel, functionality, and organizational features and enhancements of GroupWise 7. We covered them briefly to expose you to what is new. We also looked at the new features of the WebAccess client. Chapter 3, "Messaging Fundamentals," walks you through the fundamentals of using GroupWise as a powerful email messaging client program.

CHAPTER 3

Messaging Fundamentals

This chapter introduces messaging fundamentals. This information will allow you to understand the core features and concepts that the GroupWise client provides. You will then be able to use these core concepts to meet your various messaging needs as you work with and interact with the GroupWise client.

GroupWise Modes

The GroupWise client can be run in three different modes (a *mode* is what defines how the GroupWise client functions). Each of the following three modes provides various benefits:

- Online
- Cache
- Remote

Each is discussed in the sections that follow.

Online Mode

Online mode is the default mode that the GroupWise client operates in when first loaded. When in online mode, your GroupWise client establishes a network connection with the GroupWise server. (The GroupWise server hosts a GroupWise post office, which your client actually connects to.) This session is always connected, and as you compose, read, or send items, the client communicates in real time with the GroupWise post office. Online mode depends on the GroupWise post office being accessible all the time. If the GroupWise post office becomes inaccessible, your client will lose its connection, and you will not be able to run the GroupWise client.

Cache Mode

In cache mode, the GroupWise client loads and runs against a local copy of your mailbox. This means that when the GroupWise client is running in cache mode, it does not depend on the GroupWise post office being accessible 100% of the time. Cache mode implies that the GroupWise client *does* have a readily available connection to the GroupWise post office whenever it needs to connect. Therefore, the GroupWise client in cache mode can connect at any time and synchronize the local mailbox with the online mailbox. Such is the case when you send a message—it is sent immediately.

NOTE

When you are using GroupWise in cache mode, as you send messages, the number of unsent messages appears in red parentheses next to the Sent Items folder for a brief moment. If the client can connect to the GroupWise post office, this number will appear for only a few seconds, whereupon the message is sent. If you see a number in red next to your sent items in cache mode for several minutes, this could indicate that the GroupWise post office is not responding. Usually, you can simply wait, and the messages will be automatically sent when the post office is available. During this time, you can continue to read and compose other messages as you normally would.

The benefit of cache mode is that your GroupWise client can continue to function and stay up even if the GroupWise server becomes temporarily inaccessible. When the GroupWise server is once again accessible, the GroupWise client automatically establishes a connection, and the user is not interrupted.

Remote Mode

Remote mode is similar to cache mode in that the GroupWise client loads and runs against a local copy of your mailbox. In remote mode, however, the GroupWise client may *not* have a readily available connection to the GroupWise server whenever it needs to connect. Therefore, when in remote mode, the GroupWise client will queue up any outgoing mail and synchronize it only when a scheduled or manual Send/Retrieve operation is issued. Additionally, in remote mode, some features such as Proxy and Busy search are not available. Remote mode also allows you to have very granular control over what you choose to synchronize between your local mailbox and the online mailbox.

Identifying Your Client Mode

There are two ways to identify what mode the GroupWise client is running in. The first is to look under the Mailbox tab to see the mode currently in use.

Figure 3.1 shows the client in online mode.

FIGURE 3.1
Identifying the current mode of the client.

The second way to identify the mode is to display the Main menu and then choose File, Mode. Then the current mode of the GroupWise client will be checked.

Message Types

When we refer to message types in GroupWise, there are many different meanings, and different message types have different purposes. Six different message types can be created by the GroupWise client. (Additional message types are available if you have an enhanced system, such as voice-mail messages and fax messages. Check with your system administrator if you are not sure whether your system has enhanced capabilities.) Each message type is indicated by a unique icon. Message types include

- Mail
- Appointment
- Task
- Reminder Note
- Discussion Note
- Phone Message

Figure 3.2 displays several of these message types.

FIGURE 3.2
Several different message types appear, as denoted by the various icons representing them.

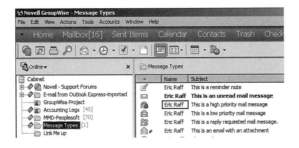

TIP

The Help option in the GroupWise client contains a complete list of icons and their functions. To access this information, choose Help, Help Topics. Then, on the Index tab, type **icons**. From here, you can see all the icons that will appear next to various message types and their meanings.

Each message type is discussed in the sections that follow.

Mail Item Type

The mail item type, also known as an email item, is the most commonly used item type in GroupWise. It contains a sender and at least one recipient. There may also be Carbon Copied (CC) or Blind Copied (BC) recipients of an email.

You can attach files to mail items also. Mail messages can be received from users inside your GroupWise system (internal email messages) or from users outside your system (email from the Internet or another mail system).

Appointment Item Type

Two types of appointments can be created in the GroupWise calendar: posted appointments and regular appointments (also referred to as meeting notices). Posted appointments are entries you make in your calendar to keep track of your personal engagements and to block out time periods within your calendar when you are busy with important tasks or tentative appointments. You cannot send a posted appointment to another user.

Regular appointments are group appointments that you can use to schedule meetings with other GroupWise users. By default, when you compose an appointment, you are automatically listed as a recipient of the meeting.

When another user sends you a request for an appointment and you accept it, the meeting automatically moves to your calendar. If you decline a meeting request, the message status information in the sender's Sent Items folder tells the sender that you have declined the meeting. From the status information on your sent item, you can also tell if the user accepted the appointment as busy, free, tentative, or out of the office. Chapter 8, "Advanced Features," discusses how to set sending options for additional alerts when meetings are accepted or declined.

GroupWise meetings include information such as the date, place, start time, and duration of the meeting. If you send a request for a meeting to a user outside your GroupWise system, it may be received as an appointment for the external user. How it is received depends on how both your GroupWise system and the recipient's mail system are configured. Check with your GroupWise administrator to see whether your GroupWise system has been configured to allow appointments to pass to external (Internet) users as appointments using the iCal standard.

NOTE

The iCal standard allows disparate email systems to send appointments between each other and retain the appointment item type. You can find detailed information about the iCal standard at www.faqs.org/rfcs/rfc2445.html.

Figure 3.3 displays an Internet recipient receiving an appointment sent from a GroupWise user.

FIGURE 3.3

Using Novell NetMail to accept an appointment sent from GroupWise.

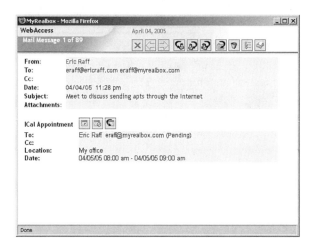

When appointments are sent, the time of the appointment should be from the sender's perspective. For example if you schedule a meeting with a GroupWise user, you do not have to worry about what time zone the recipient(s) may be in. Simply create the appointment at the time that is relative to you, and the GroupWise system will take care of making sure that each recipient sees the appointment at the correct time relative to his or her time zone.

To create a posted appointment, double-click the time in your calendar that you want to place the appointment. Alternatively, click the small down arrow next to the New Appointment icon and select Posted Appointment. Notice that there are no To, CC, or BC fields because posted appointments will exist only on your calendar.

NOTE

Creating a posted appointment does not prevent others from scheduling you for meetings at that time; however, this action will display a scheduling conflict for the senders if they perform a "busy" search on your calendar prior to sending the appointment item.

Task Item Type

You can use a task message to delegate or assign tasks to other GroupWise users. You can also create posted tasks for your personal Task List.

TIP

Instead of using email messages to delegate assignments, send a task. Tasks automatically appear in the recipients' Task Lists, and you can conveniently specify a priority, a start date, and a due date for each task.

When someone receives and accepts a task, the task appears in the task section of the recipient's Calendar view. The task is carried forward each day until that person marks it as completed. If the recipient does not mark a task completed by the specified due date, the task turns red in the Calendar view.

NOTE

Tasks and the Checklist folder are somewhat related: You can use both for keeping track of items you need to deal with. Tasks are not displayed in the Checklist folder unless they are placed there, via drag and drop. The Checklist folder is discussed in Chapter 5, "Message Management."

To create a task, choose File, New, Task. This allows you to create a group task to send to other users. To create a posted task (a task for yourself), double-click in the task area of your calendar.

Reminder Note Item Type

You can use reminder notes to create notes for yourself or to send reminders to other GroupWise users. When someone receives and accepts a reminder note, the reminder note automatically moves to the Notes area in the recipient's Calendar view. Unlike a task, however, a reminder note is not carried over from day to day. You enter reminder notes into the calendar only on the date specified.

NOTE

If you want to create a reminder note that appears regularly—for example, to remind yourself when payday comes around—you can use the Auto-Date feature. When creating a new note, select Actions, Auto-Date and then click the dates for the recurring note. Auto-Date is further explained in Chapter 6, "Personal Calendaring and Task Management."

To create a personal reminder note, open your Calendar view and double-click inside the Notes field. To send someone else a reminder note, choose File, New, Reminder Note.

You can send reminder notes to members of your workgroup notifying them of
days and times when you are away from your desk, in meetings, or on vacation. This action reminds the people in your workgroup where you are on the
specified days.

Discussion Note Item Type

Discussion notes are primarily used in shared folders or when working with
newsgroups. Discussion notes are discussed in further detail in Chapter 8.

Phone Message Item Type

You use phone messages to inform other GroupWise users about phone calls
you have taken for them. A phone message is similar to an email message. The
Phone Message window includes fields for caller information (such as name,
company, and phone number) and a description of the call (Urgent, Please Call,
Returned Your Call, and so forth). GroupWise phone messages are basically
electronic versions of preprinted phone message forms.

To create a phone message or "while you were out" message, choose File, New,
Phone Message.

Because phone messages are so similar to regular email messages, with the
exception of the fields in the view, we do not need to discuss them further.

Message Formats

The GroupWise client supports two message formats: HTML and plain text.
Plain text provides limited functionality for formatting messages. HTML provides a much richer set of options for formatting messages, including the ability
to insert pictures, tables, bullets, numbers, and so on. If users send mail to you
in different formats, the client can read messages in either format. Be aware that
if a user sends you an HTML-formatted message and your default read view is
plain text, you may not see all the formatting options that the sender applied to
the message. You can easily switch between formats as you read or compose
items if you suspect a formatting mismatch. You may also set a default
format for composing and reading messages to one of these two specific
options. Chapter 11, "Customizing GroupWise," discusses how to set up your
default message format. Figure 3.4 shows an example of composing an HTML-
formatted message.

FIGURE 3.4
GroupWise allows you to enhance mail messages using the HTML format.

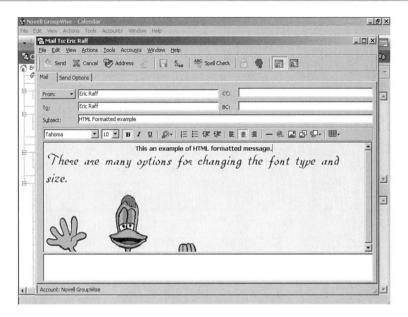

TIP

When composing mail in HTML view, you can press Ctrl+Z to undo and Ctrl+Y to redo any action performed while typing your message. This capability is helpful if you paste content into the message body and then want to undo the paste operation. Pressing Ctrl+Y would redo the paste operation as well.

Sending Messages

You can send a message in several ways in GroupWise: You can click on the new mail icon on the Toolbar; press the hotkey Ctrl+M; or select File, New, Mail.

TIP

When selecting the new mail icon, you see a small down arrow. Clicking this arrow allows you to create a simple mail item or a posted mail item. The simple mail item hides the CC and BC fields. The posted mail item will be delivered only to you; there are no recipients to a posted item.

Fill out the To, Subject, and message body fields of the new message. Note that when you're entering a GroupWise user in the To field, the GroupWise auto-name completion feature automatically completes the name of the desired recipient. It also pops up a brief window with the user's email, title, department, and phone information in it. This information allows you to quickly determine or verify that you are sending the message to the desired recipient. Figure 3.5 shows an example of the auto-name complete in action.

FIGURE 3.5
GroupWise will auto-complete GroupWise addresses as you type them.

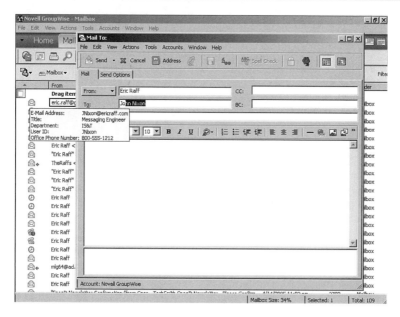

When you're sending messages, it is courteous to enter a short, descriptive subject. Once you are ready to send your new message, click the Send button in the upper left of the message window. You may be prompted to spell check or attach a signature depending on any send options that you may have set. (These send options are discussed in Chapter 8 in further detail.) The message will then be sent to the destined recipient(s) .

Attaching a File to a Message

You can attach files to messages in several ways. While composing any item type, you can click the paperclip icon on the Toolbar and browse to the file. You can also drag and drop a file or files into the attachment window or message body window. Not only can you attach files to an email, but you can also attach other GroupWise item types to a message. For example you could compose a new message and then attach any other item type (mail, appointment, task, note, and so forth) to the message.

TIP

If you attach files frequently, you can press Ctrl+L to open the attach window.

The From Drop-Down List

As you compose various item types, you may see a small drop-down arrow next to the From field. This arrow allows you to specify who this particular message will be from. The options you have as you select the drop-down arrow include any user(s) that you have proxy rights to and any additional POP or IMAP accounts that you have defined.

NOTE

The Send button will not be available if you do not have the write privilege granted via Proxy from another account, even though the name will appear in the list.

Figure 3.6 displays a new mail message with the option to choose a different sender selected.

Using Internet Addresses

When composing messages, you can choose to send messages not only to internal GroupWise users, but also to Internet mail recipients. This is as simple as typing in an Internet-style address in the To, CC, or BC field in a message (for example, bob@yahoo.com). Chapter 4, "The GroupWise Address Book," provides more information about creating contacts with Internet addresses in your personal GroupWise Address Books.

Saving Draft Messages in the Work in Progress Folder

Have you ever been working on a message and been interrupted? GroupWise provides a quick and easy way to save any item type into a Work in Progress folder. This way, you can complete the message at a later time and send it. When composing any item type (mail, appointment, task, note, and so on), you can save the message by clicking on the floppy disk icon, navigating to the File menu, and choosing Save Draft, or pressing Ctrl+S. When saving a message, you are prompted for the folder to save it in. The default is the Work in Progress folder. After saving the message, you can close the email, and your content is safely saved in the Work in Progress folder. You can open the item later, finish composing it, and then send it. When it is sent, the item in the Work in Progress folder is removed.

FIGURE 3.6
GroupWise allows you to change the From field to send the message from different users or accounts.

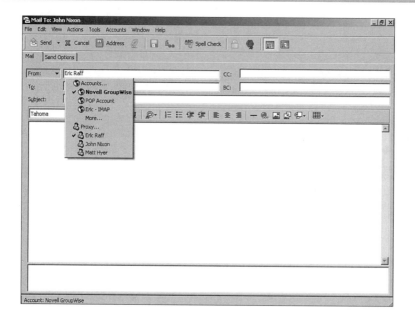

NOTE

If you cancel or close a message before sending it, you will be prompted to save the item. You can then save it to the Work in Progress folder and not lose your work.

TIP

The Work in Progress folder is visible from the GroupWise WebAccess client. This feature allows you to save items to the Work in Progress folder using the GroupWise client and then complete the item through GroupWise WebAccess while you are out of the office if needed. Using WebAccess to access your mailbox is discussed in Chapter 13, "GroupWise Access."

Reading Messages

As messages are sent to your GroupWise account, they appear in your mailbox. New or unread items show up in bold. To read an item, you double-click on it, and the item opens where you can read it. After an item is read, it is no longer bolded. However, you can mark messages as Read Later, so they once again appear as new, bold items. To mark mail as Read Later, simply select the item(s), right-click, and select the option Read Later.

If your organization is running the GroupWise Instant Messenger, when you read mail you can see the status (online, busy, away, and so on) of the GroupWise user who sent you the email. This makes it convenient to initiate an Instant Message chat session rather than replying to the sender, if appropriate. Figure 3.7 shows an example of reading a message with the GroupWise Instant Messenger integrated into GroupWise. Note the Novell Messenger presence icon next to the From field shows the user online. To start a chat session with the user, simply click the user icon.

FIGURE 3.7
Reading mail with GroupWise Instant Messaging integrated so you can see the status of the sender.

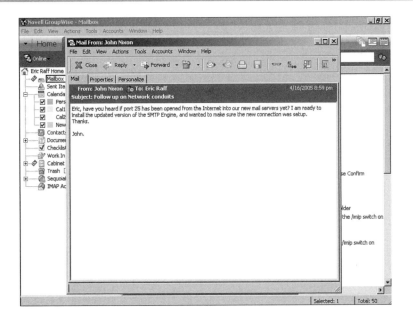

Working with the QuickViewer

The GroupWise client has a built-in viewer, called the QuickViewer, that can be used to view item types and various attachment types. To enable the QuickViewer, select View, QuickViewer. (You can also press Ctrl+Q to toggle on and off the QuickViewer.) To configure various aspects of the QuickViewer, select View, QuickView to expand the options to the QuickViewer. The QuickViewer can be placed horizontally across the bottom of the client or vertically on the right side of the client—whichever you prefer. If you place the viewer at the bottom of the client, you can also enable the Long Folder List. It shifts the viewer window so that you can see the entire folder list if it has been displayed. Figure 3.8 depicts the Quick Viewer enabled on the right side of the screen.

FIGURE 3.8
GroupWise with the QuickViewer enabled on the right side of the screen.

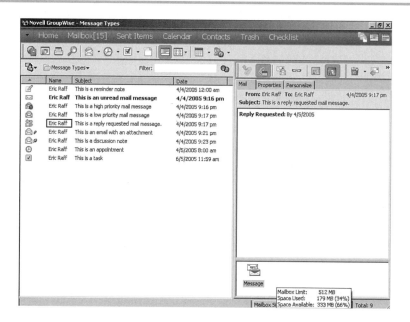

TIP

When you're using the QuickViewer or reading email, a Personalize tab is available at the top of the window. This tab allows you to quickly change the subject of the message to meet your needs. You can still see the original subject if you read the email, but you see the personalized subject from the item list view. If you are searching for email, the search will look at the original subject as well as the personalized subject. So, instead of a subject being something like "for your review," you can customize it to display as "ACME Contract."

Working with Attachments

When you receive a message with a file attachment, you have several options: You can view the attachment's contents, open the application associated with the attachment, save the attached file to your hard drive, or print the attachment.

Viewing Attachments

You can easily view an attachment's contents by simply clicking the attachment. The message window will then display the contents. To return to the original message, click the Message icon in the attachments area.

NOTE

If the attachment is an email message itself (for example, a series of forwarded emails), GroupWise 7 allows you to select whether you want each forwarded message to open in a single window or in its own window. You will be prompted to select this option the first time you open a message that is attached. You can adjust this selection using the Default Actions tab from the Options selection under the Tools menu.

To open the attachment in its own window, double-click the attachment icon. The first time you view an attachment by double-clicking it, GroupWise prompts you to indicate what function you want double-clicking to launch, as shown in Figure 3.9.

You can choose to have attachments open in their default application or in the GroupWise viewer. If you change your mind later, you can adjust this setting under the Default Actions tab from the Options selection under the Tools menu.

If you decide to use the GroupWise viewer, a new window opens, displaying the contents of the attachment. GroupWise supports numerous attachment types for viewing. This greatly simplifies your ability to read attachments even if you may not have the associated application installed on your computer.

FIGURE 3.9
You select the default action the first time you double-click an attachment.

NOTE

The first time you view a file attachment in this way, GroupWise generates the viewers for all supported file formats. GroupWise generates the viewers only the first time you view an attachment after GroupWise is installed (or if you have installed updated viewer files), and generating them usually takes less than a minute.

From a viewer screen, you can launch the associated application or save the attachment.

Finally, you can choose to open an attachment in its default application. Double-clicking the attachment opens the application with the file open and ready for you to begin work.

Saving File Attachments

When you receive a file attachment, you can easily save it to your file system. The following methods can be used to save attachments:

- Right-click the attachment icon, choose Save As, and specify the location where you want to save the file.

- From the File menu, choose Save As, select the attachment, and specify the filename (in the Save File As field) and location (in the Current Directory field).

NOTE

To change the default location for Current Directory, choose Tools, Options, Environment. On the File Location tab, modify the Save, Check Out path.

- Open Windows Explorer and arrange the open message window so that you can also see Windows Explorer. Click the file attachment and drag it to the target folder in Windows Explorer. With a little practice, you should find this to be a powerful method of saving files and inversely attaching files.

TIP

You can change the view of the attachment window by right-clicking in it and selecting the View option, which expands to several view types. For example, if you want to see the size and date of the attachment(s), you could select the Detail view. The attachment view that you select will be applied to all attachment windows for any item type. It also applies when you read items with attachments.

Printing File Attachments

You can print attachments either directly from GroupWise or from the associated application. You need to experiment with both methods to find out which one works best for you. Here are two methods to print an attachment:

- Right-click the attachment icon, choose Print, click the attachment in the Items to Print list (shown in Figure 3.10), and click Print. To use the associated application to print the attachment, select the Print Attachment with Associated Application check box.
- From the File menu, choose Print, highlight the attachment in the Items to Print list, and click Print. To use the associated application to print the attachment, select the Print Attachment with Associated Application check box.

TIP

Use the Page Setup button to configure page orientation, margins, paper size, and paper source.

FIGURE 3.10
The Print dialog box allows you to print the message and/or any attachments.

Replying to Messages

When you respond to another person's message, you can reply to the sender only or reply to all recipients of the message. You can also include the original message in your reply. When you include a copy of the original message, you can insert your comments at the top of the message or at various points throughout the message. Figure 3.11 shows the message reply options.

To reply to a message, follow these steps:

1. While the message is open, select a reply option from the drop-down list next to the Reply button on the Toolbar. You can also choose the Reply option from the Actions menu.

2. Choose either Reply to Sender or Reply to All, and specify whether you want the original message included.

3. By default, the Include Message Received from Sender option is selected. Deselect this option if you do not want to include a copy of the original message in your response.

FIGURE 3.11
The Reply dialog box lets you select the recipients for your reply.

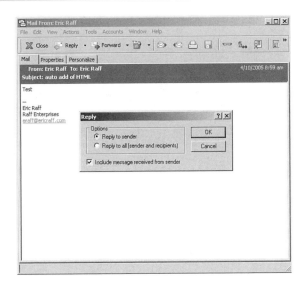

NOTE

Use the Reply to All option judiciously. Make sure that everyone who received the original message really needs to see your reply.

When you select the Reply to All option on a reply, the sender's name is automatically placed in the To field, along with any other recipients that the message was sent directly to. Users who were copied on the original message are placed in the CC field. The original message's Subject field is retained, with the abbreviation Re: in front of it. If you left the Include Message Received from Sender option selected, the original message text appears in the reply message. When you type your reply, by default it appears below the original message unless you move the cursor to another location. After you complete your reply, click the Send button on the Toolbar.

Reply messages do not automatically include the file attachments from the original message. You can, however, attach files to a reply as you would to any other message.

TIP

You can change the format of the reply message layout. For example, you can place your reply at the top rather than the bottom of the original message, and you can adjust the indent and format of the reply. Chapter 11 explains this in more detail.

Forwarding Messages

If you want to pass along a message—and any file attachments—to someone else, you should forward the message. When you forward a message, you send a new message with the old message either embedded in the new message or as an attachment. The original message remains intact, along with its file attachments, as shown in Figure 3.12. It is a good idea to always include your own introductory message when you forward a message.

FIGURE 3.12
Forwarding a message sends the entire contents, including attachments, to additional people.

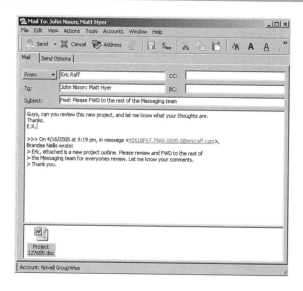

You can easily forward messages that you receive to other recipients by using one of the following options:

- From the mailbox list of messages, right-click a message (or select multiple messages via Ctrl+click or Shift+click) and choose Forward as Attachment. This creates a new email message with the selected messages attached.

- From an open message, select an option from the drop-down list next to the Forward button on the Toolbar.

NOTE

Forward places the contents of the forwarded message into the body of the new message. Attachments are always included when forwarding. Forward as Attachment leaves the new message's body blank and places the forwarded message as an attachment.

- From the mailbox list of messages, select a message (or select multiple messages via Ctrl+click or Shift+click) and choose either Forward as Attachment or Forward from the Actions menu.

NOTE

You can also create a new email and drag and drop any item from the mailbox or other cabinet folder into the attachment portion of the item creation window.

Regardless of the method you choose, a new message will be sent with the contents of the forwarded message. Enter the recipient names in the To, CC, and BC fields, as appropriate, and type your subject line (the default subject line is the original message's subject with Fwd: in front of it). Then type an introductory message and click the Send button on the Toolbar.

When you forward a message, you actually create a new message that contains a copy of the original message *and* its file attachments. A copy of the original message remains in your mailbox. You can delete the original message if you don't need it, or you can store it in a folder.

When a recipient opens the forwarded message, he or she accesses the original message and its file attachments by double-clicking the mail message icon in the Attach field.

Deleting Messages

When you no longer need a message, you can delete it from your mailbox or any folder. After you delete it, the message goes to the Trash folder. The message remains there until you empty the Trash manually or until the Trash is emptied automatically, according to settings you chose in GroupWise Options (see Chapter 8) or based on any organizational policies.

NOTE

Your GroupWise administrator may have configured the users' Trash to be purged automatically after a certain number of days. Check your organization's policy to see whether Trash is being purged automatically by the GroupWise server.

To delete a message, select the message and press the Delete key. Alternatively, you can click the message and drag it to the Trash folder. You can also right-click the item and choose the Delete option from the menu that is displayed.

You can delete messages from any location (for example, from the Mailbox folder, from the Sent Items folder, or from any Calendar view).

Restoring Messages

When you delete a message, it goes to the Trash folder and stays there until you empty the Trash—or until your Trash is automatically emptied according to the default options that are set for your GroupWise account. While the message is stored in the Trash, you can undelete or restore the message to its original location.

To restore a message to the location it was deleted from, follow these steps:

1. Open the Trash folder.
2. Highlight the message.
3. Choose Undelete from the Edit menu.

Alternatively, you can right-click the message and choose Undelete. The message is restored to its previous location.

Purging Messages

To permanently delete a message, you can open the Trash folder and delete the message. You can also empty all messages from your Trash by right-clicking your Trash folder and selecting Empty Trash.

You can recover a purged item from your Trash if your administrator has made proper backups of your mailbox. If you run GroupWise in cache or remote mode, you can configure it to automatically back up your cache or remote mailbox after a number of days you set. You can then access this backup and restore mail if needed. If you run in online mode, the GroupWise administrator will need to restore your post office; you can then open the restored post office and recover the items needed.

Summary

In this chapter, we discussed the fundamental methods of sending, reading, replying to, and performing other actions on messages. We covered different message types as well as saving, printing, deleting, restoring, and purging messages. These features allow you to manage messages as you create and receive them. In Chapter 4, we dive deep into the GroupWise 7 Address Book.

CHAPTER 4

The GroupWise Address Book and the Address Selector

The GroupWise Address Book is your GroupWise "yellow pages"; it's your master directory for looking up information about other users. Using the Address Book, you can find other users' phone numbers, fax numbers, departments, and much more. It is also the primary tool for managing your contacts.

The Address Book is actually an independent software application that is tightly integrated with the GroupWise client. It can be launched independently of GroupWise to function as a corporate directory tool.

NOTE

When we refer to the *Address Book* (capitalized), we mean the Address Book program that is part of GroupWise. When we refer to *address book* (lowercase), we are referring to one of the individual directories—such as the system address book or the Frequent Contacts address book—that contains lists of users.

GroupWise 7 also utilizes a feature called the *Address Selector*, which is a simplified display of the Address Book that's shown when you are working with GroupWise messages (for example, when you are creating an email message).

Both the Address Book and the Address Selector pull their data from the same source in the GroupWise system.

In this chapter, we first discuss the functionality of the Address Book and the most common tasks you will perform therein. Then we discuss the Address Selector and explain the techniques you can use when addressing messages.

You can use the Address Book and the Address Selector components of GroupWise 7 to do the following:

- Send messages to groups of users (for example, to all members of a specific department)

- Create personal groups that list the users who are working on a particular project or receive common communications

- Look up information about other GroupWise users, such as phone numbers

- Create personal address books that contain addresses of users both inside and outside the GroupWise system, such as people you commonly correspond with on the Internet

- Add or remove users from System Distribution Lists (if you have been defined as a group administrator by the GroupWise administrator)

Introducing Address Book Features

To access the Address Book from within GroupWise, click the Address Book icon on the GroupWise Toolbar, or click the Tools menu and select Address Book. To access the Address Book outside GroupWise, choose Start, Programs, Novell GroupWise, GroupWise Address Book. The Address Book appears as shown in Figure 4.1.

The GroupWise Address Book is streamlined for easy navigation and efficiency in locating users, contacts, and resources. Here are the address book's main components:

- Address book list
- Menus
- Search fields
- Information field headings
- Address book membership list

Figure 4.2 shows the GroupWise Address Book with its main components labeled.

FIGURE 4.1

The GroupWise Address Book displays information about users.

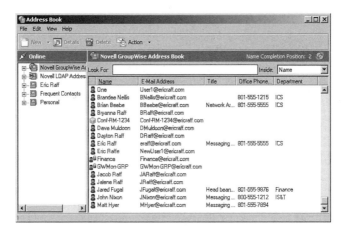

FIGURE 4.2

The GroupWise Address Book components provide access to the main Address Book features.

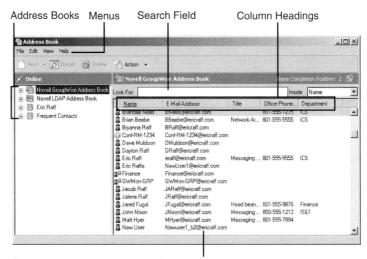

Notice in Figure 4.2 that, by default, the Address Book has four address books:

- Novell GroupWise address book
- Frequent Contacts address book
- Novell LDAP address book
- An address book with your name

The Novell GroupWise address book (the system address book) is the master address book for your GroupWise system. All users, groups, and resources in the system are visible in this address book (unless the administrator has purposely hidden some of them).

The Frequent Contacts address book lists all the users to whom you have previously sent messages or from whom you have previously received messages. These users are listed in alphabetical order. The Frequent Contacts address book lets you send messages quickly to the people with whom you correspond most often.

NOTE

By default, the Frequent Contacts address book is also tied to the Contacts list visible from the home page. Hence, if you click on the Contacts link from the Home folder or the folder list, you will see the contents of the Frequent Contacts address book. You can change the address book that is tied to the Contacts list by right-clicking on the Contacts folder or link and selecting Properties. Under the Address Book selection, you can select what personal address book is tied to the Contacts folder or link.

The special Novell LDAP address book lets you look up information about users from a source other than GroupWise. This feature may be useful if your organization provides an LDAP-compliant directory of users. You can configure the Novell LDAP address book to query this LDAP directory for users' email addresses, phone numbers, and so on. After you locate an individual using LDAP services, you can add him or her to your other GroupWise address books.

The address book with your name on it is a personal address book that you use to add names, email addresses, and other personal information about people with whom you correspond. The users, groups, resources, and organizations listed in your personal address book do not have to be individuals within the GroupWise system (or even email users, for that matter). You can use your personal address book to store all your contact information. Later in this chapter, we explain how to create additional personal address books.

To switch between the various address books, simply click an address book in the left pane. If you don't want one of the default address books to display, you can highlight the address book and choose File, Close Book. This action does not delete the book, but hides it. To display the book again, choose File, Open Book and then select the book that you want to display.

You can change the way the address book membership information is displayed by moving or modifying the column headings. To move a column heading from one location to another, simply click and drag the column heading to a new location. To remove a column heading, click and drag the column heading off the headings bar. To replace a column heading that has been deleted, right-click the headings bar and select the column heading you want to add. You can resize column headings by clicking and dragging the line that separates two column headings.

You can use two methods to obtain more information about an individual listed in an address book. First, you can simply move your mouse pointer over the name and let it rest for about a second, and a pop-up window will display details about the user. Second, you can right-click a name and select Details. A separate window will open, giving extensive details about the individual, as shown in Figure 4.3. (If some information is not displayed, the GroupWise system administrator has not populated all the available fields in the master directory.)

FIGURE 4.3
The Address Book user details dialog box provides information about individuals in the address book.

Configuring the Address Book Service

Two very common concepts are important to understand when you are working with the address book. They are *name format* and *name completion search order*.

Name format controls how names are displayed in your address books. You can select to display names in "First, Last" or "Last, First" format.

Name completion search order defines what address books are searched and in what order as you begin typing an address into a new mail message.

When you understand what the name format is and how the name completion search order is set up, you control the format for how you address messages and what address auto-completes first.

To configure the name format option, open the Address Book and choose View, Name Format. By default, GroupWise shows names in the "First, Last" format. When you adjust the name format, that format will automatically be applied to the system address book as well as any personal address books selected. Figure 4.4 displays the interface used to adjust the name format.

FIGURE 4.4
Changing the name format used in the address books.

NOTE

If you change the name format, you may be prompted to change the format of some personal address book entries. This is normal, and you simply need to review that the proposed change is correct if you receive this prompt.

TIP

The Name column displays both the first and last names of users combined into one field. If you adjust the name format setting, the contents of the Name field are switched accordingly. Changing the name format does not affect the First or Last name columns in the address book.

To configure the name completion search order, open the Address Book and choose File, Name Completion Search Order. Figure 4.5 displays the Name Completion Search Order interface.

FIGURE 4.5
Changing the name completion search order.

By default, your Frequent Contacts address book is searched first for name completion. If you want to have your personal address book searched first, you can add it to the Selected Books column and move it to the top of the list.

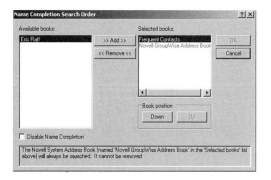

NOTE

Remember that, by default, any item sent from your account has the address added to the Frequent Contacts address book. When you're composing new mail, if the Auto-Name completion feature completes the address with an incorrect or undesired address, you may need to review your Frequent Contacts address book for incorrect addresses.

TIP

When you're selecting an address book, look in the upper-right corner to see what order this particular address book is in the Name Completion Position. For example, if you select the Novell GroupWise Address Book, you may see that the Name Completion Position is set to 2. This indicates that the system address book will be searched second as you begin typing names into address fields when you are composing items.

Addressing Messages with the Address Book

You can use the Address Book to initiate GroupWise messages to others. (Usually, you initiate messages from the GroupWise client and use the Address Selector to address the message, which is explained later in this chapter.)

To initiate a GroupWise message from the Address Book, highlight the user or users in the membership list and click the Action button on the Toolbar to launch a preaddressed email message. Alternatively, you can click the down arrow next to the Action button to select a different message type.

Managing Groups

A GroupWise *group* (also known as a *distribution list* in previous versions of GroupWise) is a list of users to whom you can send messages. Two group types exist: public groups and personal groups.

A public group is a list of users defined by the system administrator for convenient message addressing. All GroupWise users have access to the system's public groups, unless the system administrator has limited access to particular public groups. An example of a public group may be that your system administrator creates a group called Sales that includes all members of the sales organization. Public groups are located in the system address book.

GroupWise 7 introduces the ability for you to manage and update public groups in the system address book. The GroupWise administrator creates the group initially and then defines a user or users as a group administrator for this group. As the group administrator, you can then add or remove users from this system group from within your GroupWise client. These updates are then applied to the public group and replicated through the GroupWise system for other users to see. To perform this task, open the Address Book or the Address Book Selector, locate the system group that you have rights to (as enabled by the GroupWise administrator) and go to the Details of the group. To add a user or users to the system group, click the Add button and then select the user or users from the list of users in the system. To remove a user or users, select one or more users and click Remove. Figure 4.6 shows the interface for modifying a system group.

FIGURE 4.6
Managing system groups from within the GroupWise system address book.

A personal group is a list of users you create to automate message addressing. For example, you can create personal groups that include the members of each project you work on. (Personal groups are displayed only in personal address books. They are not displayed in the system address book.)

Groups are listed in the Address Book along with individual users. They are distinguished from users by a group icon, as shown in Figure 4.7.

Notice in Figure 4.7 that you can expand the address book in the left pane to reveal all the groups available. If you highlight one of the groups in the left pane, the group members are displayed in the membership area.

Addressing Messages to Groups

To address a message to a group from within the Address Book, follow these steps:

FIGURE 4.7

Groups in the Address Book are represented by a special group icon.

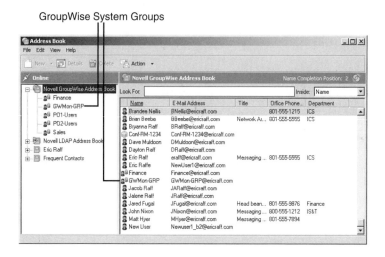

GroupWise System Groups

1. Open the Address Book.

2. Highlight the group in the membership list (right pane).

3. Click the Action button on the Toolbar, or click the down arrow next to the Action button and select a message type.

To search for groups, simply begin typing the group's name in the Look For field. When GroupWise finds the group you want, it will complete the name and you can stop typing. This feature, known as *Name Completion*, is available in several areas of GroupWise, including the To line when you are composing a message.

If you want to send a message to most, but not all, group members, expand the address book listing in the left pane and highlight the group. Then Ctrl+click to select individuals in the group (in the right pane) and click the Action button.

Creating Personal Groups

You can create personal groups that appear in your personal address book or in your Frequent Contacts address book. To create a personal group, follow these steps:

1. Right-click your personal address book or your Frequent Contacts address book in the left pane and then select New Group. Enter a name for the group.

2. Click the address book that contains the users you want to add to this group (most likely the Novell GroupWise address book).

3. Locate the first user you want in the group and then click and drag that user into your new group. Repeat with all additional users.

You can include users from different address books in one group.

Creating Personal Address Books

Personal address books give you additional flexibility in organizing lists of individuals you correspond with most often. Personal address books can contain users who are in the GroupWise system address book or contacts who are external to the GroupWise system, such as Internet users. (Remember, the Novell GroupWise address book is a system address book, and only the administrator can add to or modify the users and resources in this book.) You can create an unlimited number of personal address books within the Address Book to organize your contacts.

By default, GroupWise creates one personal address book for you. Your personal address book has your name on the address book line.

To create a new personal address book, do the following:

1. With the Address Book open, choose File, New Book.

2. Name the new address book and click OK. The address book name appears in the left pane.

3. Click the New button.

4. Choose Contact, Group, Resource, or Organization.

5. Fill in the fields for the entry.

6. Click OK.

TIP

To quickly add users from the Novell GroupWise address book to a personal address book, Ctrl+click to select multiple users; then right-click, choose Copy To, and select your personal address book as the destination. You may also simply drag and drop users into personal address books. This method copies the contact(s) into the selected address book.

Keep in mind the following points about personal address books:

- You can create, edit, and save any number of personal address books.
- You can add and delete names and address information for any person, resource, or organization in your personal address books.
- The same name can be included in multiple address books. If you copy an entry from one address book to another and then later modify the entry, the entry is updated in all address books that contain it.
- Internet addresses can be included in personal address books.
- You do not have to display all address books in the Address Book main window. To choose which books you want open, use the Open Book and Close Book options in the File menu to specify which address books appear. Closing a book does not delete it, but simply hides it.
- You can define custom fields for your personal address books. See the topic "Create My Own Fields and Columns" in the Address Book Online Help system for instructions.

TIP

To send a message to everyone in a personal address book, click the address book tab to make the address book active. Then choose Edit, Select All (or press Ctrl+A), and click the Action button.

To edit an entry in a personal address book, simply double-click the entry. You can edit the fields of the entry and click OK to save the changes.

Here's how to delete a personal address book:

1. Choose File, Delete Book.
2. Highlight the book or books you want to delete.
3. Click OK.
4. Click Yes to confirm the deletion.

Remember, the deletion of a personal address book is permanent, and it cannot be restored once deleted.

Searching the Address Book

You can search for Address Book information by using the Search List box, by using a predefined address filter, or by defining your own filter.

Using the Search List

To search for an address using the Search List, follow these steps:

1. Select the address book that you want to search.

2. In the Look For box, begin typing what you are searching for. GroupWise places information that matches your search criteria in the resulting search box.

Figure 4.8 shows the Search List box.

FIGURE 4.8
Address Book search fields allow you to quickly find individuals in the address book.

Search Window   Search inside selector

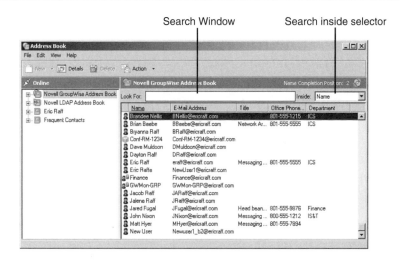

When searching the address book, pay careful attention to the Inside field, as shown in Figure 4.8. This field controls what *visible* columns are being searched as you type in the Look For field. For example, if your name format is Show First

Name Then Last Name and you want to find someone by his or her last name, you must select the Last Name option for the Inside field as you begin searching for the last name. You can look inside four columns: Name, Last Name, First Name, and Department. To add a column, right-click and check the column(s) you want to add to the address book interface.

Predefining Address Filters

In GroupWise, a *filter* is a set of conditions that removes unspecified items from being displayed in a list. For example, you can use a message filter to stop unopened messages from appearing in your mailbox, or you can use an address book filter to display only resources or groups. You learn more about using filters in Chapter 5, "Message Management."

By default, address books display all entries that have been incorporated into them. Consequently, in large address books, individuals and groups can be difficult to locate. By using a predefined filter, you can display only the information you are looking for.

The Address Book has four predefined filters: Filter for Groups, Filter for Contacts, Filter for Resources, and Filter for Organizations. In addition, you can define your own customized address filters.

To use a predefined filter while using the Address Book, follow these steps:

1. Click View.

2. Click one of the predefined filters displayed in the menu.

After you enable a predefined filter, a dot appears next to the selected filter in the View menu, and a filter icon appears in color near the upper-right portion of the Address Book display. Only the individuals, groups, organizations, or resources specified in the filter appear in the address list.

Figure 4.9 shows the GroupWise Address Book filtered to show only groups. Notice that the filter icon appears next to the Name Completion Position text in the upper-right portion of the Address Book.

To return to the regular (nonfiltered) Address Book view, choose View, Filter Off.

Learning About User-Defined Filters

You can design customized filters to help you with common address book searches. For example, if you often send a message to all managers in a company, you might define a filter that searches for all managers. By using this filter to send a message to managers, you ensure that the message is sent to people with that title.

FIGURE 4.9
Address books can be filtered to show only groups.

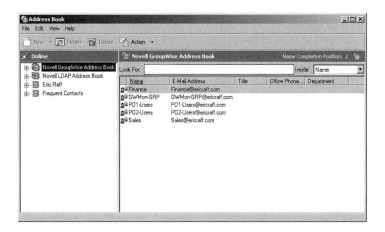

Using customized filters is often more efficient than creating personal groups because groups quickly become outdated. A filter ensures that only current users in the address book receive your message.

To create a filter, follow these steps:

1. Choose View, Define Custom Filter. The Building a Filter dialog box appears. The first column lists the filter criteria available in the address book.

2. Click a criterion.

3. Click the Operator drop-down box to select an operator.

4. Type a parameter in the Parameter text box. By default, the Parameter drop-down box displays End.

5. If you want to choose additional parameters, click the Parameter drop-down box and choose an operator.

6. Repeat Steps 2 through 5 to establish additional filter criteria.

7. After you have defined the filter, choose End in the final parameter's drop-down box and then click OK.

An *operator* is a symbol that represents a mathematical operation. A *parameter* is a variable used with a command to indicate a specific value or option. For example, to create a filter that lists only users with the last name Williams, click the Last Name column, click the equal sign (=) button, and then type **Williams**. In this example, = is the operator and Williams is the parameter.

Here is another example. Suppose you want to create a filter that addresses a message to everyone in your company's sales department. Follow these steps:

1. Choose View, Define Custom Filter.
2. Click the Column drop-down list and select Department.
3. Click the Operator box and choose =.
4. Enter the department's name (for example, Sales) in the Parameter box.
5. Click OK to apply the filter.

Figure 4.10 shows the Building a Filter dialog box for the preceding example.

FIGURE 4.10
Custom filters allow you to select only specific items for display in the address books.

TIP

As you define a custom filter, the filter is saved so that you can use it any time. To apply the filter, select it from the View menu or select the two interlocking circles in the upper-right corner of the Address Book. To edit an existing custom filter, select it and then choose Define Custom Filter from either the View menu or from the two interlocking circles drop-down list.

Sharing Personal Address Books

You can easily share an address book you create with other GroupWise users, who can then use the address book themselves.

Suppose you maintain an address book for a specific department. You can share the department address book with other users by following these steps:

1. Create the custom address book and populate it with the user information.

2. Right-click the address book and select Sharing. The Sharing dialog box appears.

3. Click the Shared With option, as shown in Figure 4.11.

FIGURE 4.11
Personal address books can be easily shared with other GroupWise users.

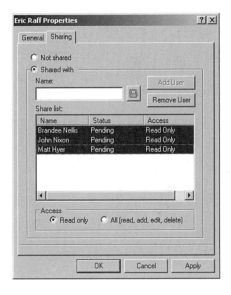

4. Enter the names or groups with which this address book should be shared in the Name field.

5. Specify the access rights the user should have. In most cases, the recipients of your shared address book need only read access.

NOTE

If you grant full access rights to the shared address book, the recipient can read, add, edit, and delete entries in the address book.

6. Click OK. In the dialog box that appears, you can customize the message that the recipient of the shared address book receives.

7. Click OK to share the address book. The recipients receive a message indicating that you have shared an address book with them. They have the opportunity to accept or decline the shared address book.

After you share an address book, the people you share it with can see all the items within it—no other steps are necessary. If you add, change, or delete entries, the users you shared the address book with also see those changes.

As an alternative to sharing an address book, you can use the Address Book's export and import features to share specific items within any address book with other users. This capability is handy for sharing this information outside your organization because you can share address books only within the GroupWise system.

Here's how to export an address book:

1. Open the address book you want to export.

2. Choose File, Export.

3. Choose Entire Address Book (exports all entries in an address book) or Selected Items (exports only the selected entries in a particular address book).

4. Name the address book file. (Address book export files have a .nab file extension.)

5. Choose Save.

You can now send this file to other users as an attachment to a message. They can then import the file.

To import a personal address book file, follow these steps:

1. Highlight the personal address book into which the group is to be imported, or create a new personal address book to contain the imported users.

2. Choose File, Import.

3. Locate the NAB file and choose Open.

NOTE

You cannot import users into the system address book.

Integrating This Address Book with Other Systems

GroupWise supports integration with other messaging vendors' address books. For example, if your organization supports another email program, you might be able to use that email program's address book along with the GroupWise Address Book.

Here's how to integrate another vendor's address book in GroupWise:

1. Open the Address Book.
2. Choose File, Services.
3. Select Add.
4. Follow the prompts to add the vendor's address service.

You should contact your system administrator to determine whether you can use another vendor's address book with your GroupWise program.

Using the Address Selector

The Address Selector's functionality is similar to the Address Book's functionality. Many of the same tasks can be accomplished in the Address Selector. The Address Selector is simply a modified view of the Address Book, optimized to perform the tasks most commonly used when addressing messages.

The Address Selector appears only when you are generating a message in GroupWise, when you select the Address function from the Toolbar or from the Actions menu, and in other areas within the GroupWise client program when you need to select users. The Address Selector is shown in Figure 4.12.

The Novell GroupWise address book is displayed by default. You can select any of your other address books by clicking the drop-down menu.

TIP

When addressing a message, if you are sure of how to spell a user's name and don't want to use the Address Selector, you can simply begin typing the user's name in the To, CC, or BC field, and GroupWise uses the Name Completion feature to make a best guess about which user you want. When the correct name appears, simply tab to the next field.

FIGURE 4.12

The Address Selector appears when you click the Address button from within the compose window.

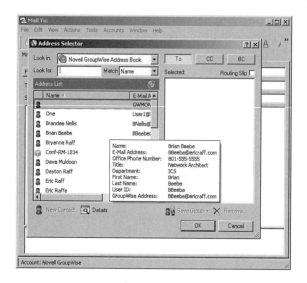

To address a message with the Address Selector, use the arrow keys or the scrollbar to locate an addressee and then double-click the user's name to insert that name in the Address Book's To field. Insert any additional names and then click OK to return to your message. The recipients are inserted in the message's To field.

Instead of trying to scroll through a long address book, you can quickly find an addressee by simply beginning to type the person's name. The address list quickly highlights the name that most closely matches what you type. Remember that you may need to change the Match field to look in the proper column for the name you are looking for.

The right column (where the users are listed when you select them from the Address Book) defaults to the To field. GroupWise assumes that most users you send the message to are the primary recipients and should be added to the To field of the message. Consequently, when you select users from the address list, they are listed in the To field by default. To add BC or CC recipients, click the corresponding button before adding users.

If you have a user in the To field who needs to be moved to either the CC or BC field, you can right-click the username and choose the appropriate field from the QuickMenu. Alternatively, you can hold down the Ctrl button, select multiple names that need to be moved to either CC or BC, and then click the CC or BC button. You can also select a user from the Selected list and then change the user to a CC or BC recipient.

Finally, you can drag and drop usernames from one field to another within the item creation window.

TIP

If you want to route the message to the recipients in a sequential order, click the Routing Slip check box above the To field in the address book. You can then click and drag the recipient names to your desired routing order. This lets you create a simple workflow for messages or documents that should go to recipients in a specific order. (If the Routing Slip option is selected, you cannot create new personal groups, as explained in the next subsection.) You also can choose Routing Slips from the Actions menu off the item creation window.

Creating a New Personal Group with the Address Selector

After you have selected the individuals to whom you will send the message, it is common to want to save that distribution list for future use. The Address Selector allows you to save the group you have built to one of your personal address books.

To save a group, follow these steps:

1. Use the Address Selector to populate the To, CC, and BC fields.

2. Click the drop-down list in the Look In field to select a personal address book where you want the group to be saved.

3. Click the Save Group button at the bottom and then name the group and add any comments.

4. Click OK.

NOTE

By default, the group will be listed in your Frequent Contacts address book. You will probably want to select a personal address book for the new group.

Summary

This chapter explained how to use the GroupWise Address Book and the GroupWise Address Selector to automate mail message addressing and to organize information about people with whom you frequently correspond. In the next chapter, you learn how to effectively manage messages using GroupWise.

CHAPTER 5

Message Management

Electronic communication, once thought of as basic email, has now become the mission-critical application for many organizations. The use of collaboration systems such as GroupWise is definitely on the rise, as is the amount of information that users send and receive on a daily basis.

In addition, as messaging technology advances, more and more message types are being created. In a standard GroupWise 7 system, the mailbox displays mail messages, phone messages, discussion notes, contacts, appointments, tasks, notes, and documents. In addition to the messages in your corporate GroupWise system, you might be using GroupWise as a mail client for additional Internet mail accounts, such as an email account through your Internet service provider (ISP). With GroupWise add-on products, the mailbox can also display other kinds of messages, such as fax messages, voice-mail messages, and workflow action items.

With all these different message types available, you need some way to manage your messages, prevent information overload, and eliminate clutter from your GroupWise mailbox. In addition, locating information quickly is a key need. This chapter explains how to use the different GroupWise features to organize, manage, and locate your messages.

We've organized this chapter into three main areas: working with folders in the Cabinet (creating, sharing, and using folders); working with messages you receive (finding, filtering, saving, archiving, printing, deleting, and organizing using the Checklist and Categories); and working with the messages you send (checking the properties, resending, and retracting).

Organizing Messages Using Folders

You can create folders to organize and store your messages. Usually, you create folders under the Cabinet folder, but you can also create folders at the same level as your Mailbox and other system folders. You can organize folders in the Cabinet the same way you organize directories or folders on a Windows, Linux, or Mac workstation.

The folders you create fall into five categories: personal folders, shared folders, find results folders, IMAP folders, and NNTP folders.

You create personal folders for your own private use. Use them to organize your messages and documents into separate groups. For example, you can create folders for information pertaining to certain projects, for specific message types, or for messages from certain individuals.

You can also create shared folders containing messages that can be viewed by other users. A shared folder's creator determines the access rights to the folder. For example, when you create a shared folder, you can decide who is permitted to read the messages in the folder, who can add messages to that folder, and so forth.

Find results folders are used to display a fresh listing of items that are the results of a Find session. For example, a High Priority Items folder can do a fresh search of your entire mailbox for messages that have a priority of high. Each time you click this folder, the search is performed again, so the listing is updated. The Find tool is covered in "Finding Messages," later in this chapter.

NOTE

The Sent Items and Checklist folders are system folders and cannot be deleted.

IMAP folders are used when accessing an IMAP mail account on the Internet with the GroupWise client. Enabling this feature is discussed in Chapter 8, "Advanced Features."

NNTP folders are used to store messages received from Internet newsgroups. Setting up NNTP access with the GroupWise client is also discussed in Chapter 8.

Creating Folders

GroupWise folders work the same way as the subdirectory structure of your computer's hard drive. When you open GroupWise 7, you may choose to display the folder list as a simple list, which shows any of your folders that exist under the cabinet; or the full list, which shows all your folders including the system folders of sent items, contacts, work in progress, trash, and so on. Your name should automatically appear on the top-level folder (your home folder). In addition to your home folder, nine default GroupWise folders exist: Mailbox, Sent Items, Calendar, Contacts, Documents, Checklist, Work In Progress, Cabinet, and Trash.

You can add new folders under your home folder, in the Cabinet, in the Documents folder, and in the Work In Progress folder. You cannot create subfolders under any find results folder (such as Sent Items or Checklist) or under the Contacts, Calendar, Trash, or Mailbox folders. We recommend that you store most of your GroupWise messages in Cabinet folders. You can organize the folders and subfolders in your Cabinet any way you like.

NOTE

In GroupWise, folder names can include punctuation and spaces.

Figure 5.1 shows some typical folders. A button with a plus sign to the left of a folder indicates that the folder contains hidden subfolders. A button with a minus sign to the left of a folder means that the folder has been expanded to show all its subfolders. Click a + or − button to show or hide the substructure beneath a particular folder.

To create a folder, follow these steps:

1. If you want to create a folder that extends directly from the Cabinet folder, highlight the Cabinet folder. (If you want to create a subfolder under another folder, select the folder under which you want to create the subfolder.) You can also highlight the Work In Progress folder to create subfolders underneath it.

2. Click the Nav Bar Options drop-down arrow. Then choose File, New, Folder.

TIP

Alternatively, you can right-click the folder and choose New Folder from the QuickMenu.

FIGURE 5.1

You can create folders to help organize messages.

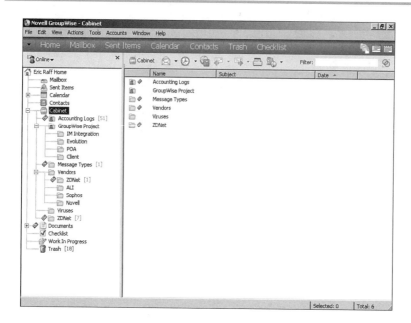

3. Select the type of folder you want to create from the list—Personal, Shared, or Find Results—and then click Next. IMAP and NNTP folders are discussed in Chapter 8.

4. Enter a folder name that describes the folder. You can use the Position area and the buttons at the right of the dialog box (Down, Left, and so on) to adjust the placement of the folder, as shown in Figure 5.2.

    If you want to move a folder later, simply click it from the main screen and drag it to where you want it.

5. Click Next to continue creating the folder. You see the settings dialog box, as shown in Figure 5.3.

6. You can change the description, item source and type, default view and sort, and column information for the folder. After you have personalized these choices, you can save them by clicking the Save As button and naming the folder configuration. Clicking the More Display Settings button allows you to further customize how the contents of the folder are displayed.

FIGURE 5.2
You can enter a lengthy description of new folders as they are created.

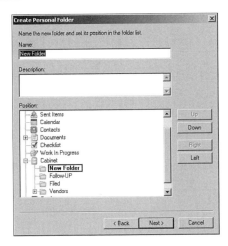

FIGURE 5.3
Folders can be highly customized using the options in this dialog box.

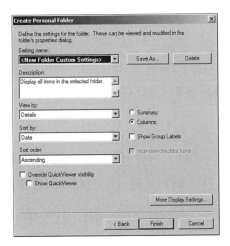

TIP

You can choose from a list of predefined folder settings in the Setting Name drop-down list.

7. If you are creating a personal folder, click Finish to create the folder. (Shared folders are discussed in the next section.)

8. If you are creating a find results folder, you see the Find dialog box, as discussed later in this chapter. Enter the Find criteria and click Finish to create the find results folder.

After you create folders, you can change the settings later by editing the properties of the folder. Highlight the folder, click the right mouse button, and choose Properties.

NOTE

We explain more about how to customize the Cabinet and its folders in Chapter 11,"Customizing GroupWise."

Sharing Folders

When you create a folder in GroupWise 7, you can easily share it (and its contents) with other people in your system. This feature, called *shared folders*, is an excellent way to manage information that pertains to many people. For example, you may need to create a shared folder to share information within a workgroup of users. When you share the folder, each user can view the contents of the shared folder.

As mentioned before, the creator of the shared folder controls access to it. In the workgroup example, a few key people might receive Add privileges (to add messages to the folder), and everyone else would be given Read privileges. Table 5.1 explains the different kinds of access privileges.

TABLE 5.1
Shared Folder Access Privileges

ACCESS PRIVILEGE	DESCRIPTION
Read	View and read messages in a folder
Add	Add messages to a folder
Edit	Modify items in a folder
Delete	Delete items from a folder

To share a folder, follow these steps:

1. Highlight the folder you would like to share. (If you select a folder that has subordinate folders, only the selected folder is shared, not the folders underneath it.)

2. Choose File, Sharing. The Sharing tab opens, and the Not Shared option is highlighted. Alternatively, right-click and choose Sharing from the QuickMenu.

TIP

When you create a new folder, you can choose Shared Folder as the type of folder you want to create.

3. Select Shared With and enter the names of the users you would like to share the folder with, or click the Browse button next to the Users field to open the Address Selector. If you open the Address Selector, double-click the users or groups you want to share this folder with. (Choosing a group means sharing with all members of the group. You can set the permissions for each person, as described next.) Click OK.

4. From the Sharing properties page, highlight a user from the list (or select multiple users by either Shift+clicking or Ctrl+clicking) and choose the access privileges you want that person to have. All users added to the Sharing list receive Read access by default. (Add allows users to place items in the folder, Edit enables users to change the items in the folder, and Delete enables users to erase items from the folder.)

TIP

If a user has Delete rights and deletes mail from a shared folder, the item will be removed from all users' view of the shared folder.

5. Click OK.
6. The Shared Folder Notification screen appears. All new participants are displayed, and a mini message screen appears. Fill in the Subject line, enter a short message, and click OK.

Your Shared Folder Notification message automatically is sent to the participants, informing them about their access to the shared folder. The people you shared the folder with receive a Shared Folder Notification message in their mailbox. Each recipient needs to install the shared folder. To do this, follow these steps:

1. Double-click the Shared Folder Notification message in your Mailbox folder. You see the Install Shared Folder Wizard start (see Figure 5.4).

FIGURE 5.4
Recipients of a shared folder receive this notification to install the folder.

2. Read the summary information and note the rights that you have been granted to this shared folder. Click Next.

3. The Install Shared Folder Wizard lets you name the folder whatever you would like and place it in your individual structure of folders wherever you would like. Use the Up, Down, Right, and Left buttons to move the folder. Click Finish to install the shared folder.

TIP

When you are the recipient of a shared folder, it is represented with a red person on the right side of the folder. If you share a folder (so you are the owner), it is represented with a blue person on the left side of the folder.

You can use shared folders to move mail from one user to another. This capability would be useful for directly exchanging a large group of messages, rather than forwarding them individually. Following are the steps involved (for this example, we define the *source user* as the one whose mail is to be moved and the *target user* as the user who is to become the new "owner" of that mail):

1. The source user shares a folder (or folders) containing the mail to be moved. The target user is added to the access list and granted all rights.

2. The target user accepts the shared folder or folders.

3. The target user drags all items from these shared folders to other folders in his or her own mailbox.

4. After waiting for the move-to-folder operation to complete (usually just a minute or two), the target user deletes the shared folders.

5. The source user may now delete the shared folders. Note that when the source user looks in these folders (before deleting them), all the items in them are gone.

The items would be gone from the source user's folders because the recipient moved them out of the shared folder. This equates to deleting the messages from the shared folder. This procedure allows you to easily transfer messages to a different user. The messages retain their original formatting and information as if you had forwarded them, and they're still listed as coming from the original sender.

Deleting Folders

To delete a folder, follow these steps:

1. Select the folder to be deleted.

2. Choose Edit, Delete. (Alternatively, you can right-click the folder and choose Delete from the QuickMenu or simply press the Delete key on the keyboard.) A summary of the messages in the folder appears, as shown in Figure 5.5.

FIGURE 5.5
When you delete a folder, you see a summary of its contents.

3. Choose whether to delete only the messages or both the folder and its messages.

4. Click OK.

When you delete a folder, you see exactly what the contents of the folder contain. You can also use this technique to delete all items in a folder without deleting the folder itself. If you are deleting a lot of items, completing the deletion process may take a few minutes.

Renaming Folders

To rename a folder, follow these steps:

1. Select the folder to be renamed, right-click it, and then choose Rename from the QuickMenu.

2. Edit the folder name and press Enter.

TIP

You can use the Folders option under the Edit menu to determine which folder opens in the main GroupWise screen when you start GroupWise. This allows you to see your calendar by default when you launch the client, for example, rather than the mailbox. You can also use this dialog box, as shown in Figure 5.6, to move folders up or down in the listing of folders, create new folders, and rename folders.

FIGURE 5.6
The Folders dialog box provides an alternative method of managing your folders.

NOTE

You can sort the folder list manually using the Folder Manager, or you can click the folder you want to move and drag it to its destination.

Managing Messages Using Folders

You can place a message in a folder in two different ways: move it there or link it to the folder. When you move a message to a folder, the message is actually stored in that folder.

To move a message into a folder, do the following:

1. Expand folders (if necessary) by clicking the button with a plus sign (+) to the left of the folder. The target folder needs to appear in the folder tree.

2. Click the message in the Items Area and drag it into the target folder. The message is now stored in that folder. If the message was previously stored in a different folder, it no longer appears there.

When you link a message to a folder, a copy of the message is placed in the destination folder. When this is done, you can see the message in the original folder and in the folder to which the message has been linked. Any modifications to the original message (for example, changes in the appearance of the message icon) are reflected in the folder to which the message has been linked.

Follow these steps to link a message to a folder:

1. If necessary, expand the folders by clicking the plus sign to the left of them.

2. Hold down the Ctrl key on your keyboard, click the message, and drag it from the original folder into the target folder. The message is now stored in both the original folder and the folder to which the message has been linked.

You can also use the dialog box shown in Figure 5.7 to move and link your messages to folders. To access this dialog box, highlight a message and choose Edit, Move/Link Selections to Folders.

FIGURE 5.7
Use this dialog box to move or link messages to folders.

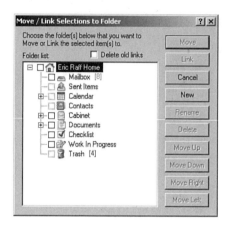

Using Message Threading in a Folder

When you use message threading, you can view the whole history of messages and replies behind a particular message. Message threading has many uses. You can follow workflow as it develops and see the development of collaboration. You can also go back and review certain steps in a long process. Figure 5.8 shows message threading.

Follow these steps to enable message threading in a folder:

1. Open a folder by clicking it.
2. From the View menu, select Display Settings, Discussion Threads.

Now you see all the messages and their replies in a particular folder.

TIP

Message threading is particularly useful when viewing *discussions* in a shared folder. Shared folders were discussed earlier in this chapter, and discussions are covered in Chapter 8.

FIGURE 5.8
Message Thread views allow you to see the replies to messages in a historical fashion.

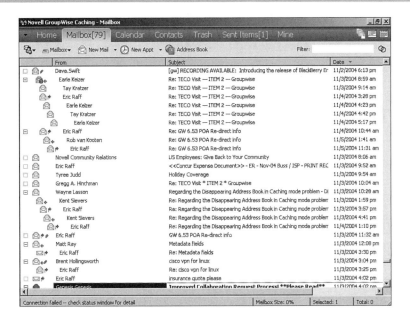

Finding Messages

The GroupWise Find is another tool used to look for and locate messages and documents throughout your mailbox and any document-management library you have rights to. Documents are different from other message types in that they are stored in libraries and are accessed using the program, document, spreadsheet, or graphics file the documents are associated with. Using Find to look for documents is covered in Chapter 9, "Document Management."

Find is a simple yet powerful utility that returns a results window; this is similar to any lookup system, such as locating a book by a particular author on a website. The Find operation looks at the message body as well as attachment text for possible matches. The results from the search can then be read, deleted, moved to a folder, saved, printed, or archived, just like any other message.

To start a Find session, simply click the Find option in the Tools menu or click the magnifying glass icon on the Toolbar. The Find tab is opened first.

There are two tabs available to search from: the Find and the Find by Example tabs. The Find tab provides a more advanced interface for locating items, and the Find by Example tab provides a simpler way to find items. For instance, the Find by Example request shown in Figure 5.9 looks for mail messages that have the word *resume* in the Subject line or anywhere in the message's contents (that is, a *full text* search).

FIGURE 5.9
The Find by Example tab is used to search for messages based on criteria you enter.

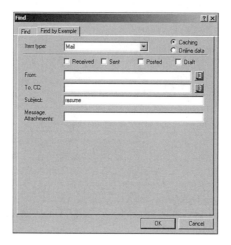

TIP

Pressing Ctrl+F is a quick way to start a Find. Also, if you're running in cache mode, you can select whether to look at the cache or online data from the Find or Find by Example tabs.

TIP

The From and To, CC search fields in the Find by Example tab use the Name Completion feature and the Address Book (discussed in Chapter 4, "The GroupWise Address Book and the Address Selector") to complete the names for the search.

All folders and libraries are searched. After specifying the Find criteria in this screen, click OK to execute the search. The GroupWise Find Results screen appears (see Figure 5.10), listing the messages and items that are found.

FIGURE 5.10
Find results are displayed and can be acted on in this screen.

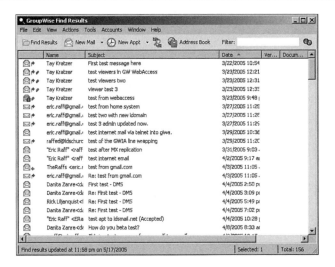

After the results have been displayed, you can act on the messages just like you would normally, or you can perform any other action, such as moving the messages to a folder.

TIP

As you see in "Finding Messages," later in this chapter, you can save the results of a Find operation as a find results folder, which performs the search every time you access the folder's contents.

A more in-depth search can be created using the Advanced Find tab and filters, which are discussed in depth later in this chapter. Figure 5.11 is an example of using the Find tab for a Find session that looks for all phone messages sent to Matt Hyer. Notice that the mailbox (and any folder underneath) can be selected in the Look In area of this screen, as well as libraries.

FIGURE 5.11
Find is highly customizable to meet any search requirements.

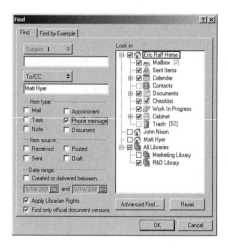

To add more criteria to the Find session, select other items, such as message type, who the message was from, the disposition of the message (sent, received, and so on), and a date range for the age of the message. To add advanced search criteria beyond what is available in this dialog box (such as message priority of high), click the Advanced Find button, and you can craft a search that can boggle the mind.

The Advanced Find dialog box (see Figure 5.12) is exactly like the Filter dialog box, which we cover next.

FIGURE 5.12
Advanced Find allows you to make a complex search for messages.

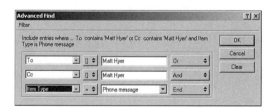

Using Filters to Manage Your Messages

The Filter option is a quick way to filter the items that are displayed in whatever folder you are in. An example of using the filter would be that you know you have received a message that indicated *SPAM* in the subject line. By typing **SPAM** into the Filter box, you can instantly see all items in the folder you have selected that have *SPAM* as a part of the subject.

There are two methods of using filters in GroupWise 7. The first is to begin typing what you are looking for in the Filter box. This method of using a filter is considered a basic filter operation. It is applied dynamically as you type the characters and will search most of the available columns for information that matches the filter. It will not search the message body or attachment fields of messages. To apply a filter, begin typing characters and then press Enter or pause momentarily to see the results. Pressing Esc clears the filter. Figure 5.13 shows an example of filtering for the word *Agenda*.

FIGURE 5.13
The Filter option allows you to quickly filter for items.

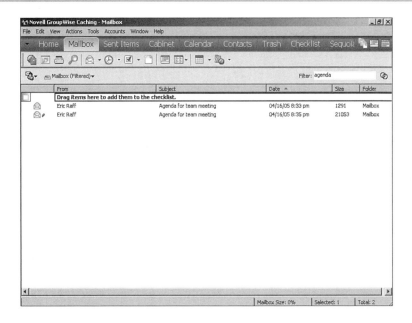

TIP

When using the filter, you can type a few characters and then pause to see the results. This feature allows you to search for *Agen* and get all email with the word *Agenda*, *agent*, and so on, in them. If you continue typing, the filter is applied immediately. Also note that the Filter option is not case sensitive.

Using the quick filter option will be the most common method you use to filter for items. Here are some situations in which a quick filter can be very useful:

- You want to see only messages you received from or to a specific person.
- You want to see only messages that contain a certain keyword in the Subject field.

TIP

You can use filters to locate messages. For example, if you know that John Smith sent you a message, but you can't find it among your many messages, simply type **John Smith** in the quick filter window, and the filter will screen out all messages except those from John Smith. This technique works only if you know what folder the message is in. Otherwise, you are going to be better served with a Find operation that allows you to look across all folders.

The second method of using filters allows you to create a filter that is much more advanced and can be active on any folder you select in GroupWise. Think of this type of a filter as a more advanced filter with numerous options that you may filter on. You access this filter feature by clicking on the two interlocking circles next to the Filter box in the upper-right corner of your mailbox.

You can use the advanced filter to screen out certain messages when viewing them in any GroupWise folder. For example, you can apply a filter to your mailbox that displays only your mail and phone messages, or a filter that displays only your unopened messages. You can save the filters you create and use them again later.

Here are some situations in which an advanced filter can be very useful:

- You have a lot of messages in your mailbox, and you want to see only unopened messages.
- You want to see only messages that were received during a specific period of time (for example, from January 1, 2005, to February 1, 2005).

- You want to see only high-priority messages.

- You want to be able to apply the filter to any folder you click on, or leave the filter on as you move around your account.

A filter does not remove messages from your mailbox; it only determines which messages are displayed. When you close a filtered display, the filter is automatically removed. The next time you open the same folder, all the messages appear again. The exception is if you used a filter from the predefined list of filters. In such a case, the filter stays active.

NOTE

Remember, a filter limits the messages displayed in a folder based on your criteria. Find uses a filter to generate a list (Find Results) of messages that meet the criteria.

Filter Terminology

You should understand five key terms before you begin working with advanced filters:

- Filter topic
- Filter qualifier
- Filter variable/constant
- Filter group
- Filter terminator

Each is discussed in the following sections.

FILTER TOPIC

The *filter topic* is the part (or parts) of a message you want considered when GroupWise determines which messages to display. The following list shows the various filter topics from which you can choose:

- Account
- Annotation
- Assigned Date
- Attachment List
- Attachments

- Author
- Caller's Company
- Caller's Name
- Caller's Phone Number
- Category

- CC
- Copy Type
- Created
- Date Opened
- Delivered
- Document Created Date
- Document Creator
- Document Number
- Document Type
- Due/End Date
- Filename Extension
- From
- Item Source
- Item Status
- Item Type
- Library
- Message
- Mime-Precedence
- Mime-Received
- Mime-Return Path
- My Subject
- Number Accepted
- Number Completed

- Number Deleted
- Number Opened
- Number Replied
- Opened By
- Place
- Posted By
- Priority
- Send Options
- Size
- Started
- Subclass
- Subject
- Task Category
- Task Priority
- Thread State
- To
- Total Recipients
- Version Created Date
- Version Creator
- Version Description
- Version Number
- Version Status
- View Name

FILTER QUALIFIER

The *filter qualifier* is the logic component of a filter; it indicates the selections to be made. Each filter topic has a different list of available qualifiers. For example, Less Than applies to the filter topic Size, whereas Begins With is applicable to the filter topic From, but not to Size.

The following list shows the different filter qualifiers:

- Contains
- Begins With
- Matches

- Includes
- Does Not Include
- Equal To

- Not Equal To
- Less Than
- Less Than or Equal To
- Greater Than
- Greater Than or Equal To
- Equal To Field
- Not Equal To Field
- Less Than Field
- Less Than or Equal To Field
- Greater Than Field
- Greater Than or Equal To Field

- On
- Before
- On or After
- After
- On or After Date
- On or Before
- On Date
- On or Before Date
- After Date
- Before Date

FILTER VARIABLE/CONSTANT

A *filter variable* is the input on which GroupWise bases message filtering, such as a user's name. A filter constant sets the parameters of the filter topic. For example, High is a filter constant for the filter topic Priority; Phone Message is a filter constant for the filter topic Item Type.

FILTER GROUP

A *filter group* is a single, complete decision line in one filter. The formula for filter groups is explained in the section "Building a Filter," later in this chapter.

FILTER TERMINATOR

The *filter terminator* determines what kind of action GroupWise takes after it has made the proper selections. Table 5.2 explains the different filter terminators available.

TABLE 5.2
Filter Terminators

TERMINATOR	ACTION
And	Adds an "And" condition to a single filter group
Or	Adds an "Or" condition to a single filter group
Insert Row	Adds an additional condition row in a single filter group
Delete Row	Deletes a condition row in a single filter group
Insert Group	Adds an additional filter group
End	Terminates the filter

Building a Filter

When you build a filter, you specify the criteria GroupWise uses to determine which messages to display. The formula for this decision appears in the Advanced Filter dialog box, as shown in Figure 5.14.

FIGURE 5.14
The Advanced Filter dialog box allows you to build filter scenarios.

The formula for building a filter is as follows:

Include entries where <Filter Topic> <Qualifier> <Variable/Constant>

Here's an example:

Include entries where Items Type = Phone Message

This filter displays only phone messages in the folder.

A *simple filter* is a single-decision filter. A *complex filter* is one in which multiple decisions can be evaluated. The Filter Terminator field on the far-right side of the Advanced Filter dialog box enables you to add more than one decision.

The filter in Figure 5.15 displays only high-priority messages received from Eric.

FIGURE 5.15
This is a more complex filter with multiple conditions.

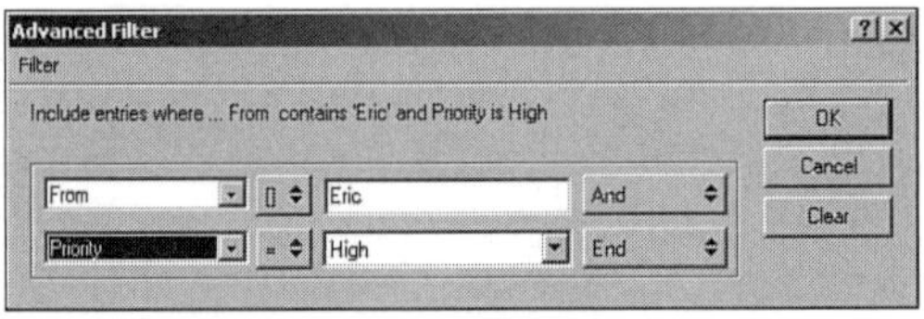

To apply a filter to a folder, follow these steps:

1. Open the folder and choose View, Filter, Edit/Create.

2. Select the display criteria and choose Save (if you want to use this filter again). You need to specify a filter name and click the Put On menu option to add this filter to the menu.

   If your filter does not display any items, you see the dialog box shown in Figure 5.16.

FIGURE 5.16
If no items match your filter criteria, you will see this notification.

3. Click OK to apply the filter.

If you want to use a previously created filter, follow these steps:

1. Choose View, Filter.

2. Select the filter you would like to use and click OK. The folder now displays only the filtered messages.

To return to your normal, unfiltered view, right-click in the filtered folder and choose Clear Filter from the QuickMenu.

Archiving Messages

The primary method for storing messages indefinitely is called *archiving*. An archived message is not stored in your master mailbox (which is on a GroupWise server); rather it is stored on your local hard drive or in your user directory on the network. Archiving messages gives you access to your old messages without cluttering up your master mailbox. You can archive messages that have been sent to you as well as messages you have sent to others. The process of archiving messages is fairly easy. In fact, you can set up the

GroupWise 7 client so that archiving happens automatically when messages have been sitting in your master mailbox for a certain period of time.

NOTE

You can archive messages when using GroupWise in online, remote, or cache modes. However, you cannot archive items using GroupWise WebAccess.

Before you can archive messages, you must specify a location where your archived messages will be stored. This location is usually on your hard drive. If you have questions about your archive directory's location, ask your system administrator. Here are the steps to follow:

1. Choose Tools, Options.

2. Double-click the Environment icon and choose the File Location tab, as shown in Figure 5.17.

FIGURE 5.17
The archive path specifies the location for archive files.

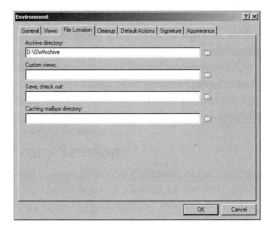

3. Enter a directory path in the Archive Directory field or browse to a directory on your hard drive by clicking the file symbol next to the Archive Directory field.

NOTE

If the Archive Directory field is grayed out, the system administrator has locked down this setting, preventing you from changing it. This may be desired to keep all users' archives in a common, manageable location.

4. Click OK. You are prompted that archiving mail will remove these items from your online mailbox and asked whether you want to enable archiving. Click Close after this prompt.

To archive messages, follow these steps:

1. From a folder (for example, the Mailbox or the Sent Items folder), select a message or group of messages. (You can select a range of messages by pressing Shift and clicking the beginning and end of the range. You can select multiple, nonadjacent messages by pressing Ctrl and clicking the messages.)

2. Choose Actions.

3. Choose Move to Archive.

The selected messages move to your local archive storage file.

TIP

Optionally, you can right-click the message or group of messages you want to archive and choose Move to Archive from the QuickMenu.

To have GroupWise automatically archive messages after a certain length of time, choose Tools, Options, Environment, Cleanup (see Chapter 11 for customizing these options). You can adjust the period of time that mail messages, phone messages, appointments, tasks, and notes remain in your mailbox before they are automatically archived. Automatic archiving then takes place as needed each time you start GroupWise.

Viewing Archived Messages

To view an archived message, follow these steps:

1. Choose File, Open Archive. The messages stored in the Archive mailbox are listed. As Figure 5.18 illustrates, the text (*Archive*) appears on the title bar to indicate that you are looking at archived messages. If you view the File menu again, you see that a check mark appears next to the Open Archive option. The check mark indicates that the archive is currently open.

2. Double-click the message you want to read. If you are using the QuickViewer (see Chapter 1, "Introduction to GroupWise 7"), the contents of the archived message appear in the QuickViewer.

FIGURE 5.18
The GroupWise window's title bar displays *(Archive)* to denote archive access.

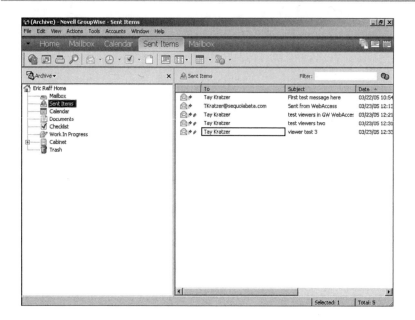

NOTE

The folders you have created in your master mailbox for organizing your messages are replicated to the archive storage when a message in those folders is archived. This includes the replication of nested subfolders. We discussed creating folders earlier in this chapter.

To return to your mailbox from an archive, click File and then deselect Open Archive. The active folder and its contents appear. If you look at the File menu again, you see that no check mark appears next to the Open Archive option. The check mark disappears when the regular mailbox is active, and *(Archive)* disappears from the title bar.

Unarchiving Messages

To unarchive a message or group of messages, do the following:

1. With your Archive mailbox open, select the message or group of messages you want to move back to your active mailbox.

2. Click Actions and then deselect Archive. (The Archive option is a toggle switch. When a message is archived, a check mark appears next to the Archive option in the Actions menu.) You can also use the QuickMenu to unarchive items.

The selected messages are removed from your hard drive on a GroupWise server. You should now be able to see the messages in their original folder.

Saving Messages

Saving messages is different from archiving. When you save a message, you transfer the message information into a separate file.

TIP

You can also save a message to a GroupWise library. Document management is covered in Chapter 9.

This file can then be used in a word processing program or other application. When you save a message, the message is not deleted from your mailbox; GroupWise merely saves a copy of it in a separate file.

To save a message, follow these steps:

1. From the Mailbox folder, select the message and then choose File, Save As.

2. Highlight the message listed in the Items to Save box, as shown in Figure 5.19. You can save the message to disk or a GroupWise library from the options in the first drop-down box. Next, select the Saved Message format as Plain Text, Rich Text (RTF), Internet Mail (MIME), or GroupWise Classic. Review the filename and note the directory that the message will be saved to. Click Save to save the message as a file. A default filename is created from the Subject field, or you can define your own filename.

NOTE

When you save a message as an individual file, it does not maintain the properties of the item (such as priority or who sent it), and the formatting is similar to what you get when you print the message.

You can define the default directory where files are saved. To do so, choose Tools, Options. Then, on the File Location tab, choose Save and enter the location in the Check Out field.

FIGURE 5.19
You can save GroupWise messages to your file system or a GroupWise library using this dialog box.

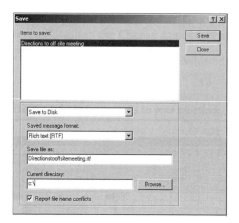

Saved GroupWise messages in the DOC or RTF formats are best used by the GroupWise client to retrieve the message contents into a new mail message. To do this, open a new mail message and choose File, Retrieve (or press F11). Then select the saved message file. The contents are added to the new mail message. This capability is very handy for frequently used communications, such as a weekly corporate email. Of course, you can also open the saved messages into Microsoft Word, edit the email messages, save them back to the disk, and retrieve them into GroupWise, as discussed. You can also begin composing a message and then save the message view. This allows you to create a mail template view that has predefined information already in it. To save a message view for later use, go to the compose window and select File, Save View and then provide a name of the view file. You can simply double-click a view file to open it and then send the message. The saved view file can be used again to send additional messages with the saved formatting.

Printing Messages

The Print option under the File menu enables you to specify custom print settings. To select paper type, fonts, and other options, follow these steps:

1. Choose File, Print.

2. Click the Page Setup button in the lower right of the window. The dialog box shown in Figure 5.20 appears.

FIGURE 5.20
You set up your printer's options using this dialog box.

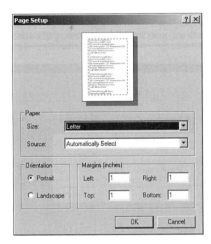

3. Select the desired options and click OK.

To print messages, follow these steps:

1. Select the messages you want to print.

2. Choose File, Print (or press Ctrl+P).

3. Select either the message or the attachment you would like to print.

4. Click the Print button.

Using the Checklist

One of the most convenient features of GroupWise 7 is the Checklist. The Checklist folder allows you to simply place any message—using drag and drop—into the Checklist folder for action at some point.

NOTE

The message retains its original type after you move it and does not become a task. Tasks are not contained in the Checklist folder unless placed there on purpose.

Figure 5.21 shows messages in the Checklist folder.

FIGURE 5.21
The Checklist folder contains messages requiring some type of action.

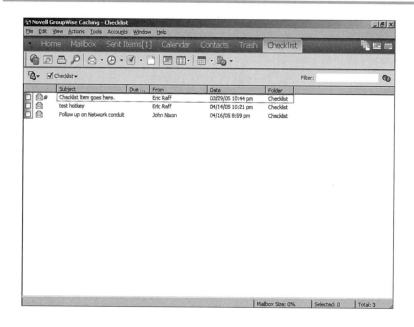

After a message is placed into the Checklist folder, a box is displayed next to the item, allowing you to "complete" it with a single mouse click.

To move an item into the Checklist folder, select the message (or messages) with a single mouse click (or Ctrl+click or Shift+click to select multiple messages) and drag it to the Checklist folder.

NOTE

To keep a copy of the message in its original folder, hold down the Ctrl key while performing the drag and drop steps.

Optionally, you can select messages as described, right-click, and choose Move to Checklist Folder from the QuickMenu.

TIP

You can view items in any folder as Checklist items. That way, you can work within the same folder. With any folder selected, choose View, Display Settings, As Checklist. To make this change permanent on a particular folder, right-click the folder, click Properties, click the Display tab, choose Checklist from the View By drop-down list, and click OK.

Using Categories

Another powerful feature of GroupWise 7 is the ability to add *categories* to messages. You can create unlimited color-coded categories for your messages based on anything you would like. There are four default categories to get you started: Follow-up, Low Priority, Personal, and Urgent. You can add categories for projects that you are working on, assign a color to them, and be able to quickly tell if any message pertains to that project.

To assign a message or group of messages to a category, select a message with a single mouse click (or Ctrl+click, or Shift+click to select multiple messages), right-click, and select the category from the pop-up list of categories from the QuickMenu. Optionally, you can select Categories from the Actions menu.

To create additional categories, choose Actions, Categories and then choose More. You see the dialog box shown in Figure 5.22.

At the bottom of this dialog box, enter the name of the category you would like to create and then click Add. To change the color associated with any category, select the category, choose Edit Color, select your new color from the palette, and click OK.

From this same dialog box, you can rename or delete a category; the primary category is the color that will display on an item with more than one category associated with it. For example, if you have associated Urgent and New Project to the same item, and Urgent is set as the primary category, the item will be displayed in red in the folder (if red denotes the Urgent category).

FIGURE 5.22
The Categories dialog box lets you create and customize your own categories.

Managing Outgoing Messages

The Sent Items folder stores all the items that you send from your account. You retain access to these sent items for three purposes: to track the status of the messages, to edit and resend the messages, and to retract the messages.

Checking the Status of Sent Items

GroupWise offers the distinctive feature of tracking the status of sent messages. With status types, you can find out the disposition of any message you have sent.

You can get some information about the message simply by looking at the icon to the left of the message in the Sent Items folder. For example, if the recipient has not opened the item, the envelope is closed. If the recipient has opened the message, the envelope icon is open. If the message is shown in bold, it has not yet been delivered.

The status information in GroupWise corresponds to specific message types. For example, you can check to see whether a Phone message has been read or a task you sent has been completed. However, you can't see whether an email message has been completed because you can only mark a task completed. Table 5.3 lists the different status types, and Table 5.4 shows how they correspond to each message type.

TABLE 5.3
Description of Status Messages

STATUS	DESCRIPTION
Delivered	The message has been delivered to the recipient's mailbox.
Replied	The recipient has replied to the message.
Opened	The recipient has opened the message.
Retracted	The message has been retracted from the recipient's mailbox.
Deleted	The message has been moved to the recipient's Trash.
Emptied	The message has been purged from the recipient's Trash.
Completed	The task has been completed.
Accepted	The recipient has accepted the appointment, note, or task.
Declined	The recipient has declined the appointment, note, or task.
Downloaded	A remote client has downloaded the message.
Transferred	The message has been transferred to the gateway.

NOTE

The only status information you can obtain about a message sent outside your GroupWise system (such as an email message sent to the Internet) is Transferred. You can also get a return notification email when the Send Notification to My Mailbox option is checked under the Send Options of new mail. The recipient's mail system must support Delivery Status Notifications back to your GroupWise system for this feature to work properly.

TABLE 5.4
Message Type/Status Information Correlation

STATUS	EMAIL MESSAGE	PHONE MESSAGE	MEETING REQUEST	TASK ASSIGNMENT	REMINDER NOTE
Delivered	X	X	X	X	X
Replied	X	X	X	X	X
Opened	X	X	X	X	X
Retracted	X	X	X	X	X
Deleted	X	X	X	X	X

TABLE 5.4

Message Type/Status Information Correlation (continued)

STATUS	EMAIL MESSAGE	PHONE MESSAGE	MEETING REQUEST	TASK ASSIGNMENT	REMINDER NOTE
Emptied	X	X	X	X	X
Completed				X	
Accepted			X	X	X
Declined			X	X	X
Downloaded	X	X	X	X	X
Transferred	X	X	X	X	X

To check the status of a message, follow these steps:

1. Click the Sent Items folder.

2. Double-click the message for which you want the status and choose the Properties tab. (Alternatively, you can select a message, right-click it, and choose Properties from the QuickMenu.)

   The two styles of properties you can view are Basic Properties and Advanced Properties. The Basic Properties view shows the basic information about the recipients of an item. To view a detailed list of information about the properties of a sent item, select the Advanced Properties from the Style setting in the upper-right corner of a sent item.

TIP

The default for double-clicking a message in the Sent Items folder is set the first time you run GroupWise and double-click the item. You are prompted to either view the properties or open the message. To change this, choose Tools, Options. Then double-click Environment and select the Default Actions tab. Sent Items default actions are in the upper-left corner.

Figure 5.23 shows a typical message with Basic status properties displayed.

Retracting Messages

Retracting a message is extremely useful if you have regrets about a sent message or if you have any other reason to recall a message you have sent. As long as the message has not been opened, you can retract it.

FIGURE 5.23
The properties of a sent message display delivery information.

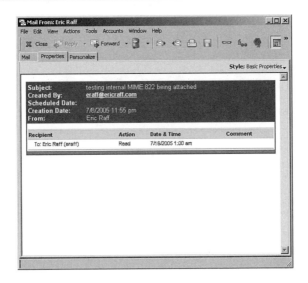

NOTE

You cannot retract messages sent through a gateway to another mail system, such as messages you send to Internet users.

To retract a message, follow these steps:

1. Click the Sent Items folder.

2. Click the message you want to retract and press the Delete key, or choose Edit, Delete. (As a shortcut, right-click a message and choose Delete from the QuickMenu.)

3. From the Delete Item dialog box, shown in Figure 5.24, make a choice about which mailboxes you want to remove the message from:

   - **My Mailbox**—Removes the message from your Sent Items folder only, leaving a copy in the recipient's mailbox

   - **Recipient's Mailbox**—Removes the message from all recipients' mailboxes, leaving a copy in your Sent Items folder

   - **All Mailboxes**—Removes the message from all recipients' mailboxes as well as from your Sent Items folder

FIGURE 5.24
The Delete Item dialog box allows you to determine the options for the retraction of a message.

NOTE

If you are using GroupWise in remote or cache mode (discussed in Chapter 10, "Remote Access"), you see an additional option: Delete from Remote and Online Mailbox or Delete from Caching and Online Mailbox.

4. Click OK and the message is retracted.

If you send a message to several recipients, you can retract the message from all recipients who have not opened the item. If a recipient has opened the item, and you attempt to retract it, it will be retracted from all users who have not yet opened the item. You can check the status of the sent item to see the status of a retract request. When you see Retracted and Purged, you know the message has successfully been retracted. You can also see the status of the retraction per recipient.

NOTE

You can retract a message only if the recipient has not opened it. The Delete from Recipient's Mailbox option is the safest way to retract because you still keep a copy of the item in your Sent Items folder (for status tracking, resending, and so on).

Resending Messages

If you have ever sent a message to the president of your company, only to read it later and find a glaring typo, or you forgot to attach the file you were going to send, you should appreciate being able to resend messages with GroupWise.

From the Sent Items folder, you can edit a message you have sent and resend it—with an option to retract the original message.

To resend a message, follow these steps:

1. Click the Sent Items folder.

2. Click the message you want to edit; then choose Actions, Resend. (As a shortcut, right-click a message and choose Resend from the QuickMenu.)

3. Edit the message, click the Send button, and answer Yes when you are prompted with the question, Retract Original Item? (see Figure 5.25).

FIGURE 5.25
When you resend a message, you see the Resend dialog box, which allows you to remove the old message from the recipients' mailboxes.

Managing the Trash

Do you know someone who likes to keep every possession, supposing that someday he might need it, only to clutter up an attic or basement? Well, GroupWise is like that. Deleted messages stick around in the Trash folder until you manually empty it, or until trash day rolls around. Trash day is set up just like it is in your neighborhood—once a week. However, you can change the default setting for emptying the Trash folder. (We explain how to change the default setting in Chapter 11.)

You saw how to delete messages in Chapter 3, "Messaging Fundamentals." After messages have been deleted, you can perform one of two actions: undelete the messages or purge them from the Trash.

Here's how to undelete a message:

1. Highlight the Trash folder. All deleted items appear in the Items Area.

2. Select a message or group of messages from the Items Area.

3. Select Edit and Undelete. (Alternatively, right-click the message or group and choose Undelete from the QuickMenu.)

The message returns to its original location.

To purge the Trash, simply choose Edit, Empty Trash.

Summary

In this chapter, we discussed the features of GroupWise that enable you to organize, find, sort, and manage the messages you receive. With the incredible increase of email and its many uses, GroupWise provides these features to allow you to build complex searches for messages meeting certain criteria, to share folders with your co-workers, and to track the status of the messages you send. In Chapter 6, "Personal Calendaring and Task Management," we look into managing time using the personal calendaring aspects of GroupWise.

CHAPTER 6

Personal Calendaring and Task Management

In this chapter, we show you how to use GroupWise 7 to replace your old-fashioned calendar or daily planner. The time-management features of GroupWise are extraordinarily useful; after you start using these features, you'll wonder how you ever got by without them.

GroupWise 7 also allows you to create multiple calendars. This makes it simple to create different classifications of calendars. For example, you may want to create a separate calendar for personal items, a separate project, or your team of coworkers. You will see how you can use multiple calendars to help simplify and manage your time for personal or other needs.

Working with Calendars

When you showed up for work this morning and turned on your computer, one of the first things you probably did was check your email. After that, you likely checked your calendar to see what appointments you had for the day. With GroupWise, the integration of the email interface with the Calendar system makes it very easy to do most of your communications and scheduling with one program. As you saw in Chapter 1, "Introduction to GroupWise 7," switching from email to the calendar is as simple as clicking the Calendar folder.

With the calendar's built-in views, you can instantly display calendar items, such as appointments and tasks. Later in this chapter, you learn how to change your view to one that suits your needs.

To use the GroupWise Calendar system most effectively, you need to understand the difference between the various calendar items. The calendar keeps track of three different kinds of personal reminders: posted appointments, posted reminder notes, and posted tasks.

Table 6.1 explains the different calendar items.

TABLE 6.1
GroupWise 7 Calendar Items

ITEM	DESCRIPTION
Posted appointments	Personal meetings and events on a certain date with a start time and an end time (duration)
Posted reminder notes	Personal reminders for a certain date
Posted tasks	Personal task entries that appear as check box entries in your calendar from the start date through the due date, with a priority level

Note the distinction between personal calendar items (posted) and group calendar items. Posted items are not sent to anyone; you post them to your own calendar. Group items are sent to other people in much the same way you send email messages. Group calendaring is discussed in Chapter 7, "Group Calendaring and Task Management." Also remember that you can create these calendar items on any of your multiple calendars.

Using the Calendar Interface

When you click the Calendar folder, a default view of your GroupWise Calendar appears on the right side of the main GroupWise screen, as shown in Figure 6.1.

New to GroupWise 7 is the Multiple Calendar feature. This feature lets you create multiple calendars that you can then display in one summary view.

The Categories feature lets you group and organize the various GroupWise message types in categories of your choosing. For example, you might create categories called Work, Personal, and Family. Depending on your current activity, you might want only messages that fall into a particular category to appear. The category selector is located in the status bar at the top right of the GroupWise Calendar display.

Below the status bar is another row that contains several calendar control buttons. The date selector displays the current date. The button next to the date selector displays a pop-up display of the current month. The button with the sun icon returns your calendar display to the current day (today). Using the number buttons, you can quickly advance your Calendar view by one day, seven days, one month, or one year.

FIGURE 6.1

The GroupWise Calendar helps you manage your appointments, tasks, and notes.

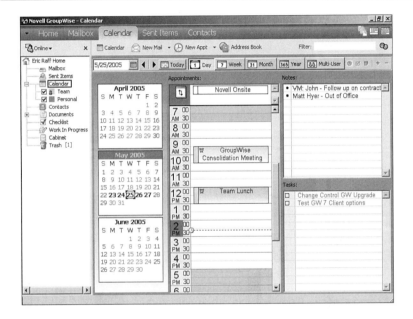

By default, five numbered buttons appear at the top-right corner of the calendar display. These buttons allow you to quickly display your favorite view of your calendar information. If you place your mouse pointer over each button, you will see a pop-up explanation that indicates Day, Week, Month, Year, or Multiuser view. (Multiuser view allows you to view calendars of other GroupWise users who have granted you "proxy" access. Proxy access is explained in Chapter 8, "Advanced Features.")

To the right of the view buttons are five more buttons that are not active in the default Calendar view. These buttons are used in other Calendar views to display item types that are not displayed in different views. For example, in the Week view, tasks are not displayed by default. You can click the check box to open a display of your tasks.

NOTE

All your calendar items—both personal and group—appear in your calendar. This chapter discusses personal items only. Chapter 7 discusses group items.

TIP

You can change the function of the view buttons by right-clicking any of the buttons and choosing Properties. You can edit the buttons, change the order in which they appear, add new ones, or delete the buttons you don't use in the Calendar folder.

Working with Multiple Calendars

In previous versions of GroupWise, you placed all of your calendar items on one calendar. You could not create a separate calendar for other purposes or projects. GroupWise 7 now allows you to create additional calendars and easily manage items between various calendars you may have created. To create an additional calendar, right-click on your calendar and select New Calendar. You will see a new calendar appear beneath the master calendar, where you can provide a name for it. This new calendar is treated totally independent of the system calendar.

When dealing with multiple calendars, you can view each calendar independently of each other or combine the contents from each calendar into one master view. This view is accessible from the topmost calendar. The check marks next to each calendar define whether or not this calendar's items will display in the Master Calendar view. This allows you to see all appointments across multiple calendars in one interface. You can also color code each calendar's appointments so that you can visually identify what appointments are on each calendar when viewing the master calendar. Clicking on the square next to the calendar pops up a color window, allowing you to quickly change the color that represents a calendar. To move appointments between calendars, simply drag and drop them onto the calendar where you want them. They will preserve their date and time information and be moved to the desired calendar. Figure 6.2 displays two new calendars named Team and Personal. The system calendar is highlighted, and each calendar is checked so you can see their appointments from the master calendar.

FIGURE 6.2
Multiple GroupWise calendars can be created and color coded.

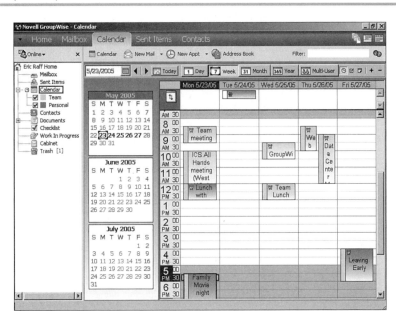

To manage each calendar, right-click on it and select Properties. From this interface, you can change the color, define whether the calendar contents are displayed in the Mail calendar, adjust display settings, and even share the calendar with other users. The capability to share calendars is new with GroupWise 7, and it allows you to collaborate better in team environments. For example, you can create a team calendar and share it with all teammates. Each user would then see the team calendar. Figure 6.3 displays the properties of a calendar, allowing you to modify its settings.

Day View

The Day view (shown previously in Figure 6.1) displays your appointments, reminder notes, and tasks in separate panes in the items area, along with multiple months (two to four months usually, depending on your computer's resolution and the size of the GroupWise window). The subject line of each calendar item also appears. To see the details of an item in the Day view, simply double-click the heading bar button (Appointments, Reminder Notes, or Tasks) for the item.

FIGURE 6.3
Properties of a GroupWise calendar.

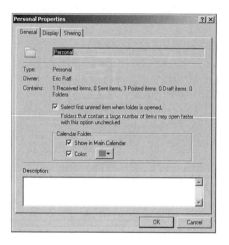

TIP

If you have enabled the QuickViewer, the message contents of each calendar item will appear in the QuickViewer pane at the bottom of the screen.

Notice that the current (approximate) time is displayed in the Appointments field with a small clock icon and a dashed line.

TIP

You can quickly adjust the duration of a posted appointment by clicking and dragging the appointment border.

Week View

The Week view displays your calendar items for several consecutive days, as shown in Figure 6.4.

You can add or subtract days from the view by clicking the plus (+) or minus (–) sign in the top-right corner of the display. (The maximum number of days/weeks you can see depends on your computer's resolution and the size of the GroupWise window.) You can also navigate forward in the calendar by clicking the right arrows to move ahead or the left arrows to move back. You can also click the Appointments, Reminder Notes, or Tasks buttons in the upper right to determine whether these items are displayed.

FIGURE 6.4

The Week view displays your appointments for several consecutive days.

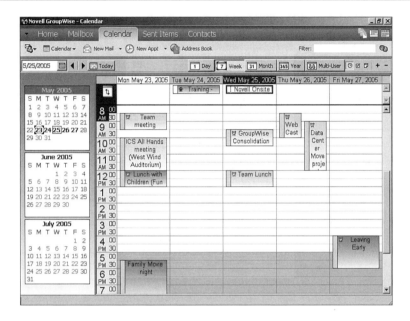

TIP

Leave your mouse pointer over a calendar item to see a quick view of the details of the item, or you can double-click the item to open the full appointment.

Month View

The Month view displays your calendar items for the entire month, as shown in Figure 6.5. You can use the arrows at the top of the display to change the month. You can use the Appointments, Reminder Notes, and Tasks buttons to change what information is displayed in the Month view.

TIP

Right-click any day to create a new calendar item quickly. You can also double-click any day to see a larger display for that date.

FIGURE 6.5
The Month view allows you to see an entire month's appointments in a single window.

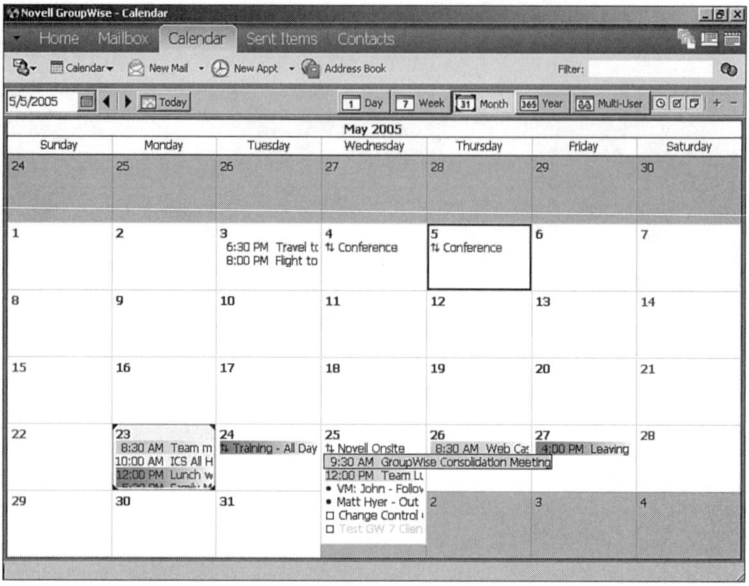

TIP

To quickly insert a posted item in any of the calendar item panels, simply click and begin typing the subject.

Year View

The Year view shows an entire year's worth of items, as shown in Figure 6.6. Note that days in boldface are days for which you have calendar items set. You can use the arrows next to the year to change the year being displayed.

TIP

Double-click any day in the Year view to see details about that day.

Multiuser View

The Multiuser view is used to view more than one person's calendar information at a time. We cover the Multiuser calendar in Chapter 7.

FIGURE 6.6
The Year view allows you to see your entire year calendar at a glance.

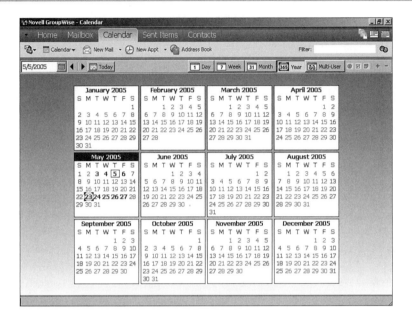

Changing Dates and Views

From any of these views, if you want to see the calendar items for a different day, click the calendar icon in the upper left of the Calendar view and go to the date you want to see. You can also choose View, Go to Date from the drop-down menu.

To return to the current day's calendar items quickly, click the Go to Today button (the one with the sun on it) or choose View, Go to Today from the drop-down menu.

In addition to the Calendar folder views previously discussed, you can choose from 15 different views of the calendar, which are available from the Window, Calendar drop-down menu. These views open the calendar in its own window, separate from the main GroupWise view. These views are listed in Table 6.2. Experiment with them until you find the one that best suits your work style.

TIP

You can add any of the alternate Calendar views to the Calendar folder buttons at the top right of the Calendar view by right-clicking any of the buttons, choosing Properties, selecting New, picking your view from the drop-down list, giving the view a name, and then clicking OK.

TABLE 6.2
Calendar Views Available from the Drop-Down Menu

NAME	FEATURES
Day	Displays appointments, reminder notes, and tasks for a single day. Monthly calendars are displayed, allowing you to quickly move to a specific date.
Week	Displays appointments several days at a time. You can also view tasks and reminders with the control buttons.
Week & Calendar	Displays appointments, reminder notes, and tasks five to seven days at a time, with a month at a glance.
Month	Displays appointments, reminder notes, and tasks a month at a time.
Month & Calendar	Displays appointments, reminder notes, and tasks a month at a time, with several months at a glance.
Year	Displays the entire year. Boldface dates on the calendar contain scheduled items.
Desk Calendar	Displays daily appointments and tasks one month at a time.
Notebook	Displays reminder notes and tasks for one day.
Day Projects	Displays expanded Cabinet folders, group appointments, tasks, and reminder notes, with multiple months at a glance.
Day Planner	Displays tasks, appointments, and reminder notes, with multiple months at a glance.
Project Planner	Displays tasks and reminder notes, with all folders expanded and multiple months at a glance, as shown in Figure 6.7.
Appt (sm)	Displays appointments for one day.
Note (sm)	Displays reminder notes for one day.
Task (sm)	Displays tasks for one day.
Multiuser	Displays appointments, reminder notes, and tasks for multiple users.

FIGURE 6.7

The Project Planner view is 1 of 15 optional Calendar views available from the drop-down menu.

To open a Calendar view, click Window, Calendar and then select the view from the list.

TIP

After you have found a view that you like, you can set it as the default by choosing Tools, Options, Environment, Views. (Setting default options and customizing the Toolbar are explained in Chapter 10, "Remote Access.")

Task List

The task list is separate from the Checklist folder. Tasks are really an older feature of GroupWise that still exists. The Checklist folder is more comprehensive and functional than the former Task List folder. However, the Calendar view still includes a task list that you can create and use to help manage daily tasks. When you create a task, if it is not checked off as complete, the GroupWise system will automatically move that task to the next day so that you can keep track of tasks and they are not forgotten. You can move a task to the Checklist folder by simply clicking and dragging it from the Calendar view to the Checklist folder.

NOTE

Any type of GroupWise message can be placed into the Checklist folder. When a message is placed in the Checklist folder, it has a new task-focused tab when you open it. The Checklist tab in the message allows you to prioritize the item and assign it a due date.

The Checklist folder is very useful for storing email messages you have received that require a follow-up action. The Checklist folder was explained in more detail in Chapter 5, "Message Management."

Making Posted Appointments

A large part of time management involves scheduling appointments, and GroupWise provides an easy-to-use interface for creating and managing your personal engagements. Posted appointment messages appear only on your calendar; you don't send them to other people. Figure 6.8 shows an example of a posted appointment.

FIGURE 6.8
Using the Posted Appointment screen, you can manage your personal appointments.

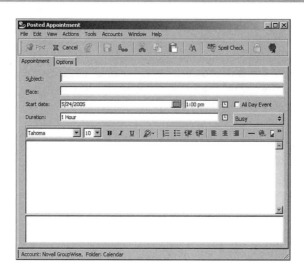

As you can see in Figure 6.8, a posted appointment includes the following information: appointment date, start time, duration, and place. The time increment (default of 15 minutes) can be changed, as well as the date format. You can also set the appointment as an all-day appointment. In addition, you can customize GroupWise to use military date and time as well as other formats. (See Chapter 10 for more information on customizing your GroupWise environment.) The Subject line of an appointment appears in the calendar.

TIP

One of the best uses for a personal posted appointment is to block out time on your own schedule that will show as "busy" when other individuals look at your schedule or do a Busy Search to try to schedule a meeting. This allows you to clear a portion of your schedule to work on projects that require you to be distraction free.

To create a posted appointment, follow these steps:

1. Click the down arrow next to the New Appt button on the Toolbar and choose Posted Appointment from the list. Alternatively, in the Calendar view, double-click the time for which you want to make the posted appointment, and you will achieve the same result.

TIP

If your Calendar folder is open, you can also click the start time in the Appointments field, drag the mouse pointer to the end time of the appointment, release the mouse button, and simply start typing the subject of the posted appointment. When you use this method, the appointment's subject line will also be the same text as the message body.

2. Enter a subject for the appointment and place more detailed information in the message area.

3. Fill in the appointment's date, start time, and duration, and choose Post to add the appointment to your calendar. (If the appointment will apply all day, check the All Day Event option.)

You can also set alarms for your appointments. Here's how to set an alarm:

1. Right-click an appointment in your Calendar view.

2. Choose Alarm from the QuickMenu. The Set Alarm dialog box appears.

3. Specify, in hours and minutes, how much advance notice you want. The maximum is 99 hours and 59 minutes. You can also set up a variety of sounds for the alarm. (See Chapter 10 for information on how to customize the alarm.)

4. Click SET. Notice the alarm clock icon next to the appointment.

NOTE

After you set an alarm, you can change the time or remove the alarm by right-clicking the appointment, selecting Alarms, and then clicking the Clear button.

Creating Posted Tasks

Posted tasks are very useful, reminding you to finish assignments or projects that may last for several days. Your posted tasks appear in the Tasks field in your Calendar views.

NOTE

If you want a task to appear in your Checklist folder, you need to either create the posted task with the Checklist folder active (selected) or click and drag the task from the Calendar view's Tasks field into the Checklist folder.

Each task has a start date, a due date, and a priority level, as shown in Figure 6.9. The priority level determines the order in which tasks appear in the list, based on an alphabetic and numeric code. For example, a task with a priority of A1 appears before A2, and A2 appears before B1. The code you assign to a task is completely up to you. You can use only letters or only numbers if you prefer.

The Subject line of each task you create appears on the starting day's calendar and will carry forward each day until you mark the Task Completed check box. If a task is not marked completed by the due date, it will continue to be carried forward, but it will appear red in the Task List.

To create a posted task, follow these steps:

1. Click the arrow next to the New Task button on the Toolbar and choose Posted Task from the list.

FIGURE 6.9
The Posted Task screen allows you to manage your personal to-do list.

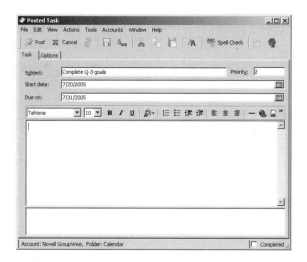

TIP

You can also double-click in the task area of your calendar to create a new posted task.

2. Enter a subject for the task. You can place more detailed information in the message area.

3. Enter a priority level for the task (or leave the priority setting blank if you like).

4. Enter a start date (which must be today's date or later) and then enter an end date in the Due On field.

5. Click Post to enter the task in your calendar.

To mark a task completed, click the Task heading button in the Calendar folder. Click the box next to the task in the Task List. Notice that a check mark appears in the box.

Posting Reminder Notes

Reminder notes can be added to your calendar and linked to certain dates, as shown in Figure 6.10. The Subject line of each note appears in your Calendar view. You can use reminder notes to remind yourself about anything you like—for example, picking up your dry cleaning. You might also use a recurring note to mark paydays on your calendar, just in case you forget what day you get paid.

FIGURE 6.10
The Posted Reminder Note screen allows you to link a reminder to a specific date.

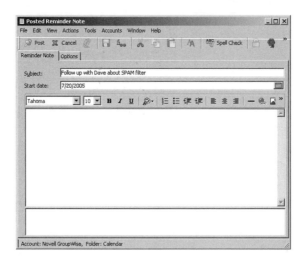

To create a reminder note, follow these steps:

1. Double-click the Note pane under your appointments.

TIP

If your Calendar folder is open, simply click an empty line in the Reminder Note box and start typing the subject of your note. Click elsewhere to enter the note into your calendar.

2. Enter a subject for the note. If you like, you can place details about the note in the message area.

3. Fill in the date for the note and click POST to add the note to your calendar.

Remember, reminder notes do not carry from one date to the next. Reminders are specific to the day for which they were created.

Rescheduling Appointments, Tasks, and Reminder Notes

Rescheduling a posted appointment, task, or reminder note requires only a simple click and drag of the mouse. Here's how to move an appointment, task, or reminder note to a different day:

1. Open your Calendar folder.

2. If the day you need to move the item to does not appear, use either the Week or Month button on the Calendar folder view or open the Day view of the calendar. (See the "Using the Calendar Interface" section at the beginning of this chapter for instructions on changing views.) The Day view displays multiple months at a glance.

3. Click the appointment, task, or reminder note you want to reschedule and drag it to the new day.

To change the time of a posted appointment, follow these steps:

1. Open your Calendar folder and click the appointment you want to change.

2. With the mouse button held down, drag the appointment to a new time on the same day, and the appointment will move.

The preceding steps show you how to move a posted appointment, task, or reminder note from one day to another. You can also *copy* a posted appointment from one day to another by holding the Ctrl key as you click and drag the posted appointment from the current date to another date. You can also move calendar items by dragging them to a different calendar if you want.

Changing Calendar Item Types

Suppose you are over halfway finished with a new posted appointment, only to realize that you should be making a posted task instead. Instead of canceling and starting over, you can change one message type into another, on the fly. For example, you can keep all the information about the appointment (subject, message body, and so on) and change it into a new task, retaining all the information.

There are two ways to change a calendar item from one type to another. The first method is best to use after the item has been created: Simply click the calendar item and drag it to another area in the calendar display. For example, you could click a posted appointment and drag it to the task area, and the item will change to a posted task. The second method is best to use while the item is being created: Any time you create a new calendar item, click the Change Item Type button on the Toolbar (it has an arrow with two dots). Then click the desired new calendar item type and click OK. The screen changes to the new item type.

NOTE

When you use the first method, the mouse pointer changes to represent what you are doing, using the item icons with an arrow in between.

TIP

You can also use the Edit, Change To menu option to change the item type.

Summary

In this chapter, you saw the many features of GroupWise as they relate to your own calendar. The use of multiple calendars provides additional flexibility in managing your various appointments. Posted appointments, reminder notes, and tasks that you create to manage your time can also be used to invite people to meetings, remind them of events on a certain day, and delegate tasks. The next chapter shows you how to make the most of the GroupWise 7 group scheduling and workflow features.

CHAPTER 7

Group Calendaring and Task Management

In Chapter 6, "Personal Calendaring and Task Management," you learned how to manage your personal calendar items, such as appointments and tasks. In this chapter, we show you how to use the GroupWise 7 workgroup and collaboration features, including group calendaring and task management.

Scheduling Meetings

When you want to schedule a meeting with other people, you send an appointment message.

NOTE

Appointment messages that you send to other people are sometimes referred to as *meetings* or *meeting requests*.

In some cases, you may need to schedule a meeting for someone else, such as your supervisor. GroupWise enables you to schedule meetings for others (in other words, meetings that you don't plan to attend).

You can use the GroupWise Proxy feature to view and manage others' calendars. (Chapter 8, "Advanced Features," explains the Proxy feature.)

Sending Appointments

You send appointments to other GroupWise users to schedule meetings—either for yourself or for someone else. When you want to send an appointment, you must set a start date, start time, and duration—just like you do for posted (personal) appointments. The only difference is that you are sending the appointment request to others, not just adding the appointment to your calendar.

To create and send an appointment, follow these steps:

1. Choose File, New, Appointment or click the New Appt button on the Toolbar. You see the screen shown in Figure 7.1.

FIGURE 7.1
The New Appointment screen provides many fields to designate details about the meeting, such as place and duration.

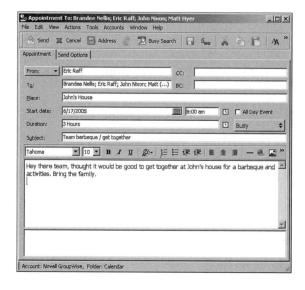

2. Address the appointment message just as you would any other type of GroupWise message—by entering the names in the To field or by using the Address Book. If you plan to attend the meeting, make sure you include your own name in the To field. If you do not include your own name, the appointment will not appear in your calendar. (By default, GroupWise inserts your name in the To field when you create an appointment.)

3. Enter the location of the meeting in the Place field.

TIP

If your system administrator has added the meeting place to the GroupWise system, it will appear as a resource (for example, a certain conference room). You can schedule the room at the same time you send the appointment. Open the Address Book and choose View, Filter for Resources. Select the room from the list of resources. If the room has not been defined as a resource, you can describe the meeting place in the Place field, but GroupWise will not reserve the room.

4. Enter a subject in the Subject line. (Be descriptive because only the Subject line appears in the recipients' calendars.)

5. Enter detailed information about the meeting in the Message field. If you like, you can attach a file, such as the meeting agenda.

6. Set the date of the meeting by typing the date in the Start Date field or by clicking the small calendar icon to the right of that field. If the appointment is an all-day event, check the All Day Event option.

NOTE

If you want to create a recurring appointment, you can use the Auto-Date feature, explained later in this chapter.

7. Set the time of the meeting by typing the time in the field to the right of the small calendar icon or by clicking the small clock icon next to that field.

8. Enter the duration of the meeting in the Duration field (or set the duration by clicking the small clock icon to the right of the Duration field).

9. Click Send.

The appointment appears in the recipients' mailboxes and calendars.

When you schedule meetings, you can use the Busy Search feature to find a time when all invitees are available. The Busy Search feature automatically sets the date, time, and duration of the meeting. Busy Searches are explained in the next section.

Busy Search

The Busy Search feature is a very powerful GroupWise scheduling tool. You no longer need to call people in advance of a meeting to find a time when everyone can meet. GroupWise takes care of that chore for you.

To perform a Busy Search when scheduling a meeting, follow these steps:

1. Open a new appointment message and use the Address Book to place the invitees' addresses in the To field.

2. Click the Busy Search button on the Toolbar. GroupWise searches the users' calendars and displays the Choose Appointment Time dialog box, as shown in Figure 7.2.

FIGURE 7.2
Busy Search displays the availability for invitees to your meeting.

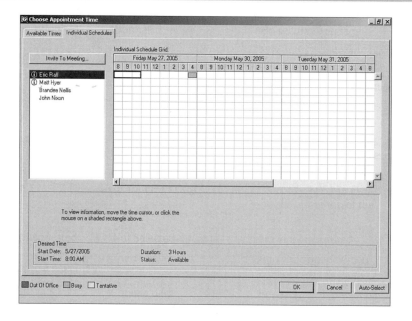

NOTE

If an *i* with a circle around it appears next to some users' names, this indicates that you can click on their appointments and see their details. These users must have granted the View Proxy right to their calendar to you for this feature to work.

The Choose Appointment Time dialog box presents a grid showing the schedule of each user you specified. An empty space across from the username indicates that the user is available for that time.

If you want GroupWise to show you the times when all users are available, click the Available Times tab (see Figure 7.3) .

FIGURE 7.3
The Available Times tab can help you select the best time for the meeting.

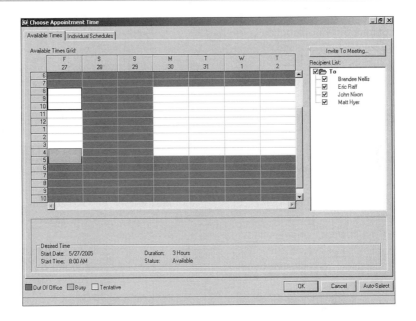

You can select the appointment time from either of the Choose Appointment Time tabs. To set the appointment time, follow these steps:

1. Click the highlighted box in the grid and drag it to a time the invitees are available. You can click and drag the sides of this box to increase or decrease the duration of the meeting.

2. Click OK. The date and time of the meeting appear in the appropriate fields of the appointment message.

Here are some handy Busy Search tips:

- If there isn't a time when all invitees are free, you can extend the search to include more days by clicking the Invite To Meeting button and increasing the value in the Number of Days to Search field.

- When the Choose Appointment Time dialog box shows that some users are busy, you can find out what a user has scheduled by clicking the box representing that timeslot. (You can see the person's schedule only if the user has granted you access rights to his or her calendar via Security Proxy settings.)

- The Auto-Select button selects a time when all the selected users are free for the duration you have specified.

- You can exclude a user from the Busy Search without removing the user from the To field by choosing the Available Times tab and then clearing the check mark that appears next to the user's name on the right side of the dialog box. (This exclusion feature is useful when someone should be invited but that person's attendance is not absolutely necessary.)

- To perform a Busy Search before creating your appointment message, choose Tools, Busy Search. Enter the usernames in the dialog box that appears.

- You can add names to the Busy Search by clicking the Invite To Meeting button. You can delete names from the Busy Search by clicking usernames and pressing the Delete key.

- If you are busy searching for multiple users, GroupWise may take awhile to return the results on all users. You can minimize the Busy Search dialog box and work on other tasks while GroupWise receives the Busy Search results. A status box appears on your Windows taskbar, showing you the search progress.

- You can do a Busy Search for a resource (such as a conference room, company car, or projector) to find out times when the resource is not reserved.

Here's how to change Busy Search defaults:

1. Choose Tools, Options.
2. Double-click the Date and Time icon.
3. Choose the Busy Search tab.

NOTE

The Busy Search feature is useful only if all GroupWise users keep their calendars up to date. Remember also that recipients can delegate appointments. Check the status of the message to see whether any of the intended attendees have delegated the appointment to another person.

Busy Search is a very good tool to make sure the meetings you are scheduling work with the schedules of the intended attendees.

iCal Appointments

iCal is a relatively new standard for calendar information sent to Internet recipients.

When you are sending a new appointment to an Internet recipient and that person's system can work with iCal messages, the appointment will be displayed in his or her native system's calendar.

NOTE

In GroupWise 7, the iCal feature works only if your GroupWise system administrator has enabled it or you are sending appointments from POP3/IMAP4 accounts (discussed in Chapter 8).

To enable iCal appointments, verify that you are in either cache or remote mode and then choose Accounts, Account Options, General Options. Select the option Use iCal when Sending Appointments via SMTP and then click OK.

Sending Tasks

You can use GroupWise task messages for assigning projects to other GroupWise users. Tasks are also useful for large projects that involve many people.

To send a task, follow these steps:

1. Choose File, New, Task or click the New Task button on the Toolbar. The task message screen shown in Figure 7.4 appears.

2. Address the task message by typing in the recipient's name or by using the Address Book.

3. Enter a priority code for the task. The task priority can be a character, number, or character followed by a number. For example, valid priority codes include A, B, C, 1, 2, 3, A1, B1, B2, and so on.

4. Enter the subject and message in the appropriate fields.

5. Select a start date. The start date is the date when the task will first appear in the recipient's calendar, after the recipient accepts the task from his or her mailbox.

FIGURE 7.4
A task can be delegated to another GroupWise user.

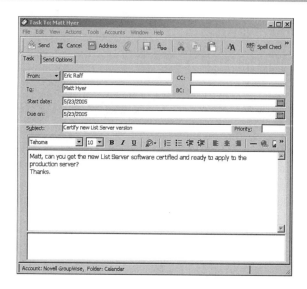

6. Select a due date. Tasks that are not completed before the due date turn red in the recipient's calendar.

7. Click Send.

In addition to the priority code you enter in the task message screen, you can also set a priority for the task itself. Here's how:

1. While you are composing a new task message, choose the Send Options tab.

2. Select High, Standard, or Low priority.

3. Click Send.

Sending tasks allows you to electronically delegate activities to co-workers.

Sending Reminder Notes

Use reminder notes to send reminders to people. Reminder notes are very useful as meeting reminders because notes appear on specific days in the recipients' calendars. Often, notes are used to remind others about specific assignments for upcoming meetings. You can also send reminder notes to co-workers when you are out of the office.

To send a reminder note, follow these steps:

1. Choose File, New, Reminder Note.
2. Enter the information in the To, Subject, and Message fields.
3. Specify a date for the note in the Start Date field.
4. Click Send.

Figure 7.5 shows a typical reminder note.

FIGURE 7.5
A reminder note can be sent to other users for items that pertain to a particular date, such as payday reminders.

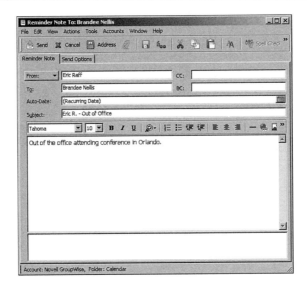

As you can see, reminder notes add items to your calendar to track daily activities.

Monitoring Appointments, Tasks, and Notes

Users often fail to keep their calendars up to date, and even though a Busy Search may show that they are available, they may not be. After you send an appointment, you should monitor the status of the message to find out whether it has been accepted, declined, or delegated (or simply ignored).

If a recipient has declined the message and has provided a comment explaining why, that comment appears in the message status information, not as a message in your mailbox. (See Chapter 5, "Message Management," for more information on checking the status of sent items.)

To see whether the recipients have accepted, declined, or delegated a message, and to view their comments, follow these steps:

1. Open your Sent Items folder.

2. Right-click the appointment item and choose Properties. (You can also open the message and click on the Properties tab.)

You can use these steps to see whether users have accepted, declined, or completed the items you have invited them to and delegated to them.

Retracting Appointments, Tasks, and Notes

You can retract appointments, tasks, and notes after the recipients have opened them, unlike regular email messages. When you retract an appointment, task, or note, it is removed from the recipients' calendars and mailboxes.

To retract an appointment, task, or note, follow these steps:

1. Open your Sent Items folder and highlight the message to be retracted.

2. Press the Delete key (or right-click the message and select Delete).

3. Select Recipient's Mailbox or All Mailboxes and then click OK.

Here's how to reschedule or resend a calendar entry:

1. Right-click the message in the Sent Items folder and select Resend.

2. Change the message information, if necessary, and click Send.

3. If you want to retract the original entry, choose Yes when prompted.

4. Because the recipients receive no warning (the item simply disappears from their calendars), it is good messaging etiquette to let them know you have retracted the item.

The ability to retract items you send allows you to take back or edit these items.

Acting on Received Appointments, Tasks, and Notes

The appointments, tasks, and notes you receive from other GroupWise users appear in your mailbox along with other email messages. Appointments, tasks, and notes also appear in your Calendar folder or in your Calendar view on the specified date. In the calendar, they appear in italics until you accept them, indicating that these items are tentative and have not been accepted.

Figure 7.6 shows an opened Calendar folder with accepted and unaccepted appointments, tasks, and notes.

FIGURE 7.6
Unaccepted calendar items are displayed in italics until you accept or decline them.

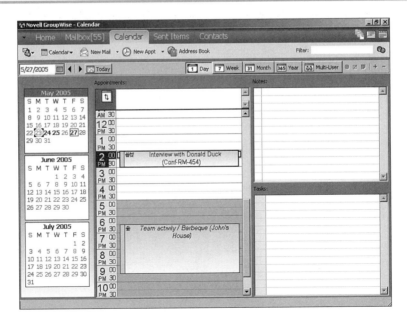

You have several options when you receive an appointment, task, or note from someone else. You can accept the entry, and it will convert the tentative (italicized) entry to a regular (nonitalicized) entry. Alternatively, you can decline the message, and it will move to your Trash folder.

Accepting

To accept an appointment, task, or note from the Mailbox or Calendar folder, double-click the icon to open it and choose the Accept button. Alternatively, you can right-click the item and choose Accept from the QuickMenu.

TIP

To accept an appointment, task, or note with options, select the down arrow next to Accept and choose Accept with Options. A dialog box appears, enabling you to send a comment to the message's sender. This comment will appear in the sender's message properties.

Either at the time of acceptance, or even after the appointment has been accepted, you can change how the item is displayed in your calendar. Free, Busy, Tentative, and Out of Office are the options that appear as different color shadings in the calendar.

To change how an appointment is displayed in your calendar, right-click the appointment, choose Show Appointment As, and select an option.

Declining

To decline an appointment, task, or note from the Mailbox or Calendar folder, double-click the icon to open it and choose the Decline button (or right-click the item and choose Decline from the QuickMenu). When declining an entry, if you want to provide a note to the sender, you can decline with options. Click the down arrow next to Decline and select Decline with Options. You are given the option to comment about why you have declined. If you enter a comment, the sender can see it when he or she checks the status of the message you declined.

Delegating

If you receive an appointment that you cannot attend or a task you cannot complete, but you desire that someone else attend in your place or complete the task for you, you can delegate the message.

When you delegate an appointment or task, you pass it along to someone else without necessarily keeping a copy for yourself. To delegate an appointment or task, right-click the item and choose Delegate from the QuickMenu.

Here's how to delegate an appointment or task when the item is open:

1. Select Actions.

2. Select Delegate. A new message is created, identical to the message you received, except that the word *Delegated* is appended to the subject line.

3. Address the message to the person to whom it is being delegated.

4. Click Send. You are asked whether you want to keep a copy of the item in your mailbox.

5. Answer Yes or No.

The person who sent you the message can find out that you have delegated the item by checking the message status. The Delegated status appears along with the name of the person to whom you delegated the appointment or task.

Creating Recurring Items Using Auto-Date

The GroupWise Auto-Date (Recurring) feature enables you to send recurring appointments, tasks, or note messages. Auto-Date enables you to send one message that applies to many different days. For example, you can use an appointment Auto-Date to schedule a staff meeting that occurs every Wednesday at 9:00 a.m., or you can use a task Auto-Date to make sure staff members turn in a report on a certain day each month. You can also send a note configured with Auto-Dates to remind employees which day is payday.

There are three different ways to create Auto-Date messages:

- By dates
- By example
- By formula

For the most part, the by-example method makes the by-formula method obsolete. Therefore, we do not discuss the by-formula option.

By Dates

The by-dates Auto-Date method is the easiest to use and understand. When you choose this method, a calendar opens for the current year, and you click the dates on which you want the appointment, task, or note to appear. You can click the Year button to advance the calendar to the next year.

To create an Auto-Date Calendar entry using the by-dates method, follow these steps:

1. Open a new appointment, task, or note message.
2. Fill in the To, Subject, and Message fields.
3. Click the Actions pull-down menu.
4. Select Auto-Date. The Auto-Date dialog box appears, as shown in Figure 7.7 (the Dates tab is active by default).

FIGURE 7.7
You can use the Dates tab of the Auto-Date feature to set up recurring appointments, notes, or tasks.

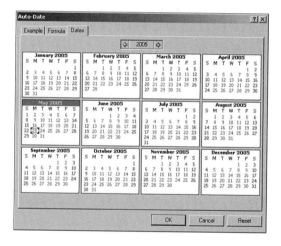

5. Click all dates when the appointment, task, or note should appear. They become highlighted.
6. Click OK.
7. Click Send to send the message.

The by-dates method of setting recurring calendar items is the most flexible and easy to use of the three methods.

By Example

Use the by-example Auto-Date method when you want to send appointments, tasks, or notes for dates that follow a regular pattern. For instance, a by-example Auto-Date could be used to schedule a meeting that occurs on the third Tuesday of every month.

The by-example Auto-Date requires some experimenting to get the hang of it. The following example should help you get a sense of how it works.

One of the most common ways people use Auto-Date is to create personal notes reminding themselves when it's payday. The following steps show how to use Auto-Date to create a personal note for a payday that occurs on the 1st and 15th day of every month, unless the payday falls on a weekend. If the 1st or 15th falls on a weekend, the payday occurs on the preceding Friday. Here is what you would do:

1. Navigate to your calendar.

2. Double-click in the Reminder Notes field to open a new posted reminder note message.

3. Click Actions.

4. Click Auto-Date.

5. Choose the Example tab.

6. In the Start field, enter the date when the Auto-Date period should begin.

7. You can either define how many occurrences of the item there should be or an end date. In this example, change it to End by clicking the arrow next to Occurrences and selecting End. Enter the date when the Auto-Date period should end.

8. Click all months in the Months field to indicate that the paydays occur every month.

9. Click the drop-down list box named Days of the Week and select instead the Days of the Month setting. The dialog box changes, enabling you to specify certain days in the month for the note.

10. Highlight Monday, Tuesday, Wednesday, Thursday, and Friday to indicate that the note should appear only on a weekday.

11. Choose On/Before from the drop-down list located below the days you have highlighted. The On/Before option tells GroupWise that the note can appear only on or before the day you specify. For example, if the 15th of the month falls on a Saturday, the note should appear on the previous Friday.

12. Click 1 and 15 in the calendar to indicate the dates when the note should appear. Figure 7.8 shows how the Auto-Date dialog box should look at this point.

FIGURE 7.8
The Payday note will create a note in recipients' calendars for the whole year.

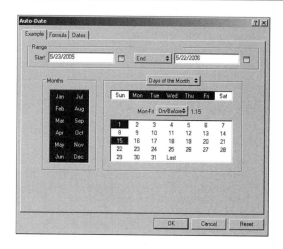

13. Click OK.

14. Fill in the remaining message fields in the reminder note and click Send.

A note appears in your calendar on each day that meets the Auto-Date criteria during the period you specified in the date range fields.

When you send an appointment message or note created using Auto-Date, The GroupWise system creates and sends one message for every date that meets the Auto-Date criteria. If you send an Auto-Date appointment message that occurs every Friday during a year interval, 52 separate appointments will appear in each recipient's mailbox. The recipient will be given the option to accept all instances at once or to accept or decline each message individually.

The Online Help system includes a guide for using the Auto-Date feature. To access the guide, follow these steps:

1. Choose Help, User's Guides.

2. Choose the GroupWise Basics option.

3. Select the Schedule a Recurring Event guide.

The by-example method allows you to create regularly recurring calendar items.

Multi-User Calendars

GroupWise provides for an office administrator to manage calendars for several other GroupWise users. Before you can manage another GroupWise user's calendar, the other user must give you proxy access to his or her GroupWise calendar. The instructions for granting proxy access are provided in Chapter 8.

To manage multiple users' calendars, you use the Multi-User button on the Toolbar that appears when you open your Calendar folder, as illustrated in Figure 7.9.

FIGURE 7.9
The Multi-User button allows you to see others' calendar information.

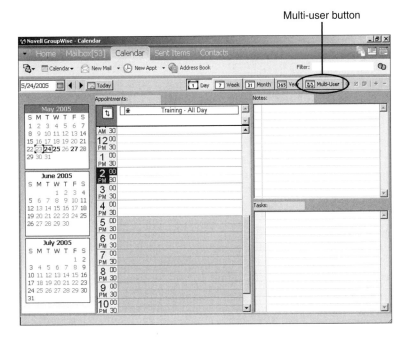

Here's how to add users to the multi-user calendar display:

1. Verify that the users you want to add have granted you proxy access to their calendars.

2. Click the Add User button. The Multi-User List dialog box appears (see Figure 7.10).

FIGURE 7.10
You can select the users to display in the Multi-User Calendar view with this dialog box.

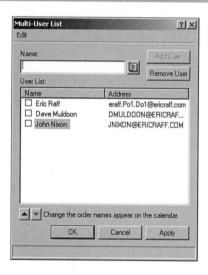

3. Enter the users' names in the Name field or use the Address Book to select the users.

4. Click the up- and down-arrow buttons to change the order in which the users appear in the calendar.

5. Click OK. You see multiple users' calendars displayed, as shown in Figure 7.11.

TIP

You can alter the Multi-User Calendar view display by clicking the message type buttons that appear on the calendar's Toolbar. You can choose to display any combination of multiple users' appointments, reminder notes, and tasks. You can also choose the order in which the tabs appear in your Calendar view by right-clicking the Toolbar and choosing Properties.

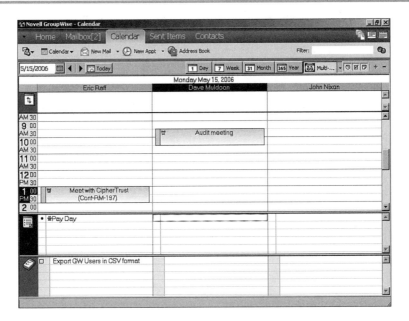

Printing Calendars

GroupWise provides powerful calendar printing capabilities. You can choose from several popular formats, including formats familiar to users of the Franklin Quest day planners.

Here's how to print your GroupWise calendar:

1. Open the Calendar folder in the main GroupWise screen.

2. Choose File, Print Calendar. The Print Calendar dialog box, shown in Figure 7.12, appears.

3. In the Format field, select from Day, Week, Month, List, or Multi-User.

4. In the Available Forms field, select your desired form.

5. Select a form size and a form orientation.

6. Click the Content tab.

7. Select the starting date, the number of weeks (if the Week format is selected), the content, and the display option.

FIGURE 7.12
You can print your calendar items using this dialog box.

NOTE

Step 7 depends on the Print format you have selected. If you are printing the Day calendar, it will display as the number of days; if months, the number of months.

8. Click the Options tab.

9. Specify the custom options. Among the options you can select are headers, footers, and page numbers.

10. Click Print when you're done.

Figure 7.13 shows the preview screen for the popular Franklin Quest Day-planning calendar printing format.

The print options for the GroupWise Calendar provide several different styles, options, and content configurations. You should try several to see which works best for you.

FIGURE 7.13
The Franklin form can be used to print your calendar information.

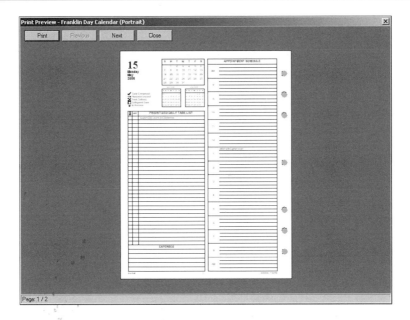

Summary

In this chapter, we discussed the appointments, notes, and tasks that make up the group calendaring features of GroupWise. We also discussed using the Busy Search feature, tracking items you send to others, and printing calendar items. In Chapter 8, we get into the advanced features of GroupWise 7 that will make you a true power user.

CHAPTER 8

Advanced Features

This chapter introduces you to the advanced features of
GroupWise. We call this our "kitchen sink" chapter because of the
variety of topics covered here. After you master the concepts of this
chapter, however, you will likely become known as the GroupWise
Guru among your co-workers.

We have divided this chapter into two halves. The first deals with
the features for using GroupWise day to day that will make you
more productive, such as rules and Proxy. The second covers
advanced mailbox configuration and maintenance features, such as
using Internet accounts and repairing your mailbox.

In the first half of the chapter, we cover the advanced features that
add to your productivity. The following advanced features are covered in this section:

- Rules (automatic actions on messages)
- Proxy (allowing access to your mailbox or accessing someone
  else's mailbox)
- Send options (such as status tracking or notification)
- Advanced security (using encryption)
- My Subject (customizing a received message)
- Discussions (threaded, posted messages around one topic)
- Notify (alerts on received messages)

GroupWise Rules

GroupWise is capable of managing most of your messages for you (even while you are not logged in to the system) through GroupWise rules. Rules enable you to move messages to folders, generate automatic replies, forward messages, and delete messages. You can also set up rules to manage your calendar items automatically. For example, you can create a rule that accepts all the tasks your boss sends you (always a good idea) or a rule that automatically declines appointments scheduled after 5:00 p.m. (an even better idea) .

This chapter doesn't list all the possible rules you can create, but it does explain the basics for setting up rules and show you a few useful examples.

To access the rule-creation process, from the main window of the GroupWise client application, choose Tools, Rules, New. The New Rule dialog box, shown in Figure 8.1, appears.

FIGURE 8.1
This sample rule automatically accepts any new reminder notes that are sent to you.

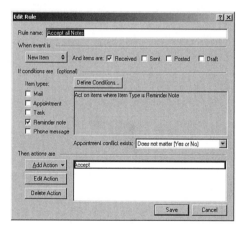

The rule is added to your *Rules List* and is automatically activated (the check mark in the box next to a rule indicates that the rule is activated, as shown in Figure 8.2).

FIGURE 8.2
Your Rules List shows all the rules you have saved, both active and inactive.

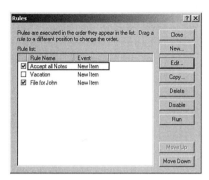

You can use the Rules dialog box to change a rule in the following ways:

- To modify a rule, select the rule and then click the Edit button. You can then change any of the parameters of the rule. Choose Save to complete your changes to the rule.

- To copy or delete a rule, select the rule and then click the Copy button or the Delete button. You can use the Copy feature to create additional rules, based on the original rule. For example, if you create a rule that routes all messages from a specific user to a specific folder, you could copy this rule for messages from another user that you want routed to a different folder (without having to create a new rule from scratch).

- To activate or deactivate a rule, click the check box next to the rule or use the Enable/Disable button to the right of the Rules List.

- To run a rule, select the rule in the list and then click the Run button. You need to use the Run button only when you create a new rule that acts on messages already in your mailbox.

TIP

Your rules are executed in the order in which they appear in the Rules List (see Figure 8.2). This is important when, for example, you have a "delete" rule before a "reply" rule. To change the order in which the rules are executed, click a rule in the Rules dialog box and drag it to a new position, or use the Move Up and Move Down buttons to change the rule position.

Figures 8.3, 8.4, and 8.5 show examples of commonly used rules.

FIGURE 8.3

This commonly used *vacation* rule will reply to the sender during specific dates you are out and only if the message is from internal GroupWise users.

FIGURE 8.4

This rule automatically accepts appointments, tasks, or notes from a specified person.

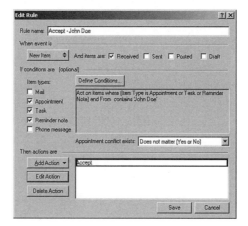

FIGURE 8.5
This commonly used rule marks the message read and then automatically moves it to a folder based on the subject of the message.

Table 8.1 describes the available actions that you can assign to a rule, under the Add Action button. It also describes the information needed to completely specify the action.

TABLE 8.1
Actions Assignable to a Rule

ACTION	DESCRIPTION	INFORMATION NEEDED
Send Mail	Generates a new mail message	Complete the Mail Message dialog box (recipient, subject, message, and so on)
Forward	Forwards a copy of the message with a comment	Identify the recipient of the forwarded message, along
Delegate	Delegates the appointment, reminder, note, or task to another individual	Complete the Delegate dialog box with a comment to both the sender of the original message and the person to whom you are delegating this item

TABLE 8.1
Actions Assignable to a Rule (continued)

ACTION	DESCRIPTION	INFORMATION NEEDED
Reply	Generates a reply to the sender the original message, and	Specify the recipient (sender or all recipients), indicate whether to include enter a reply message (subject and message body)
Accept	Accepts the appointment, reminder, or note	Select whether to show the accepted item as Free, Busy, Tentative, or Out of the Office, and enter a comment to the sender
Category	Categorizes item	Specify the desired category to apply to items that the rule fires upon
Delete/Decline	Deletes the message or declines the calendar event	Enter a comment for the sender's Sent Items folder
Empty Item	Purges the item from the Trash folder	N/A
Move to Folder	Moves the message to a folder	Select the folder and click Move
Link to Folder	Places a copy of the message in a folder	Select the folder and click Link
Mark as "Private"	Places a "Private" lock on the item	N/A
Mark as "Read"	Changes the status of the item to "Opened"	N/A
Mark as "Unread"	Changes the status to "Unopened"	N/A
Stop Rule Processing	Ends the processing of a rule	N/A

The highly customizable Rule feature allows you a significant amount of automation for your mailbox.

TIP

To see how other users have employed GroupWise rules, see the GroupWise Cool Solutions Community at www.novell.com/coolsolutions/gwmag/ or choose Help, Cool Solutions Web Community.

Using the Proxy Feature

The Proxy feature allows you to access other users' GroupWise messages and calendars. With this feature, you can also permit others to view your GroupWise messages.

Remember, your mailbox contains all your GroupWise information: email messages, calendar items, sent items, deleted messages, personal folders, rules, and so forth.

There are two general steps to setting up the Proxy feature:

1. Specify access to a mailbox. Decide who can access what information and how it can be accessed (Read, Write, or both).

2. Start a Proxy session. This is the process of opening up someone else's mailbox.

You cannot access others' mailboxes until they have given you access privileges to their mailboxes. Likewise, others cannot access your mailbox until you have granted them access privileges. Attempting to do so without this privilege produces an access denied error message.

NOTE

Be sure you completely understand the available access privileges before granting them to others. If you are too liberal when granting rights to your mailbox, other users can send messages that appear to be from you. They could possibly modify your setup and grant other individuals Proxy rights.

Setting a Password

To provide the highest level of security for your mailbox, we strongly recommend setting a password and thereafter keeping that password secure.

NOTE

If you use Proxy to access someone else's mailbox, the password is not required to gain access. The password feature protects against unwanted access by someone who has not been granted any access rights.

Setting a password is an option you establish through the Tools menu. (We discuss how to set other options and defaults in Chapter 11, "Customizing GroupWise.")

To set a password on your mailbox, follow these steps:

1. Choose Tools, Options and double-click the Security icon.

2. Enter a password in the New Password field and in the Confirm New Password field. Click OK to set the password. The next time you start GroupWise, you will need to type in your password. If you select the No Password Required with eDirectory option, you will not be prompted to enter a password when you access your own mailbox if you are logged in to eDirectory.

NOTE

Your administrator may have enabled LDAP authentication for your GroupWise account. If this has been done, you may not be able to change your password from this interface, and it could be grayed out. Pay attention to any warnings or notes from within the change password screen for more information on how your GroupWise system may be configured.

Granting Access to Others

To grant other GroupWise users access rights to your mailbox, follow these steps:

1. Choose Tools, Options and double-click the Security icon.

2. Choose the Proxy Access tab.

3. Click the Address button next to the Name field to start the Address Selector. Double-click the username you want to grant access to. Click OK to add the user to the access list (see Figure 8.6).

NOTE

The All User Access entry in the Access List box allows you to grant blanket rights to all other GroupWise users. This capability may be useful if you want everyone to be able to see your calendar items. Use extreme caution when selecting this option.

4. With the username in the Access List highlighted, select the appropriate access (see Table 8.2 for a description of the access rights). Click OK and then Close to apply the rights.

5. To remove a user from the Access List, highlight the username in the Access List and click the Remove User button.

FIGURE 8.6
The Proxy feature allows you to grant others access to your GroupWise mailbox.

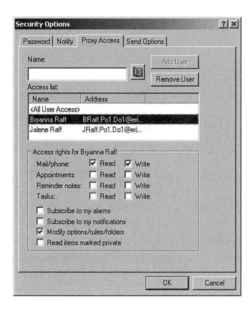

6. To change someone's access, highlight the username in the Access List, change the rights, click OK, and then click Close to complete the change.

TABLE 8.2
Proxy Access Fields

ITEM TYPE	ACCESS RIGHT
Mail/Phone	Read: Read messages in your Mailbox folder. Write: Write email and phone messages in your stead.
Appointments	Read: Read posted and group appointments from your calendar. Write: Create posted appointments and invite others to meetings in your stead.
Reminder Notes	Read: Read personal and accepted notes from your calendar. Write: Create personal notes and send notes in your stead.

TABLE 8.2
Proxy Access Fields (continued)

ITEM TYPE	ACCESS RIGHT
Tasks	Read: Read posted tasks and assigned tasks from your calendar or to-do list. Write: Create posted tasks or send tasks to others in your stead.
Subscribe to My Alarms	Enable users to have alarms for your appointments.
Subscribe to My Notifications	Enable users to have notifications for all messages you receive displayed on their computers.
Modify Options/Rules/Folders	Enable users to change your preferences (pass word, rules/folders, mailbox access, defaults, and so on), create rules for your mailbox, and change your folder structure.
Read Items Marked Private	Enable users to read any item (mail message, appointment, task, or note) that is marked "Private."

NOTE

You should grant Modify Options/Rules/Folders rights only to very trustworthy individuals. These rights enable users to change your password and grant others access to your mailbox.

Starting a Proxy Session

With the Proxy feature, you can access a person's entire mailbox and perform other activities within the parameters allowed by the permissions the other GroupWise user has granted to you. Having full access to someone else's mailbox does not mean you can only view the person's messages and calendar items. You can also send mail messages as that user; access the user's sent items, personal folders in the Cabinet, and deleted messages in the Trash; and edit the user's rules and preferences.

After you are through viewing someone else's mailbox, you need to end the Proxy session to view your mailbox again. Optionally, you can open an additional GroupWise window for the other user while keeping your mailbox open (this technique is explained in more detail in the next section).

To start a Proxy session and view someone else's mailbox, follow these steps:

1. Choose File, Proxy or click the icon next to the online status indicator and select Proxy. (You can also select the drop-down arrow next to the mode and select the Proxy option.)

2. Type in the username of the user whose mailbox you want to access. Alternatively, you can click the Address Book icon next to the Name field, double-click the username from the Address Selector, and click OK.

The Proxy session starts. Note that the status changes to Proxy and the name of the user whose mailbox you are accessing appears in the GroupWise title bar, as shown in Figure 8.7.

FIGURE 8.7
The GroupWise main screen indicates Proxy access.

Status

Title Bar indicates proxied user

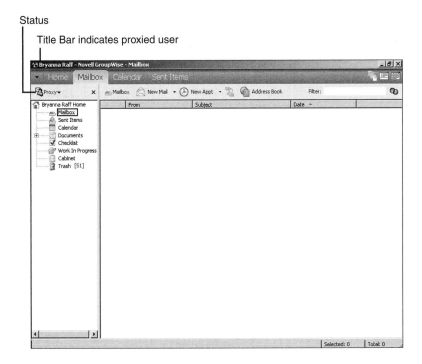

To end the session and view your mailbox again, click the Proxy icon and select your name. Your mailbox opens.

Opening Multiple Windows

By default, your main GroupWise window changes to the mailbox you are accessing with the Proxy feature. This default can be tedious if you need to view multiple mailboxes. In this case, it is useful to open a different GroupWise window for each active Proxy session. This multiple-window feature enables you to view many different mailboxes from your workstation.

TIP

There are other reasons to open multiple GroupWise windows. For example, you can have one window for viewing the new messages in your mailbox, another one showing your open calendar, and a third window for viewing documents in the document library.

To open an extra GroupWise window (with your mailbox open), follow these steps:

1. Choose Window, New Main Window. A new, complete GroupWise window appears on your screen.

2. Click the Proxy icon and start a Proxy session with another mailbox. This new window displays the mailbox you are accessing.

3. You can access any of the open windows by choosing that window from the Window menu. Each window is labeled with the name of the user whose mailbox is open.

NOTE

As discussed in Chapter 7, "Group Calendaring and Task Management," you can use the Multi-User tab in the Calendar folder view to see multiple users' calendar information on one screen.

Specifying Send Options

When you create any type of message—from mail messages to tasks—you can specify a number of different send options (in other words, options that affect the way GroupWise sends the message). These options fall into three categories: General, Status Tracking, and Security.

To apply one of the send options to a message you are creating, follow these steps:

1. Choose the Send Options tab before you click Send. The Send Options page appears, as shown in Figure 8.8.

2. The general send options are displayed by default. Choose the Status Tracking or Security buttons to display those advanced options.

3. Select the desired options and then click the Mail tab to return to the message.

This message is sent with the options you selected.

General Send Options

General options, shown in Figure 8.8, allow you to configure your outgoing messages, such as requesting a reply to a message within four days.

FIGURE 8.8
The General Send Options page allows you to control your message delivery.

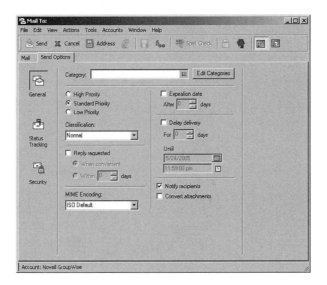

NOTE

You can set any of these send options as the default. Setting defaults is covered in Chapter 11.

Table 8.3 lists the general send options (asterisks denote the default options). These options enable you to configure your outgoing messages.

TABLE 8.3
General Send Options

OPTION	AVAILABLE CHOICES	DESCRIPTION
Category	Dependent on configured categories	Allows you to select a pre-established category for the message
Priority	High	Delivered before other messages
	*Standard	Normal delivery
	Low	Deliver after standard priority messages
Classification	*Normal	No security message
	Proprietary	"Security: Proprietary" placed at the top of the message
	Confidential	"Security: Confidential" placed at the top of the message
	Secret	"Security: Secret" placed at the top of the message
	Top Secret	"Security: Top Secret" placed at the top of the message
	For Your Eyes Only	"Security: For Your Eyes Only" placed at the top of the message
Reply Requested	*Not Selected	No reply requested
	When Convenient	Reply requested when convenient
	Within n days	Reply requested within n days (up to 99)
MIME Encoding	*ISO Encodes	Converts attachments using ISO MIME
	UTF8	Use Unicode Transformation Format to encode/convert attachments
	(Other options are available depending on system configuration.)	
Expiration Date	*Not Selected	Message deleted from mailbox by the recipient
	After n days	Message deleted from mailbox after n days (up to 999)

TABLE 8.3

General Send Options (continued)

OPTION	AVAILABLE CHOICES	DESCRIPTION
Delay Delivery	Delay *n* days	Deliver after *n* days
	Until date/time	Delay message delivery until specified date and time
Notify Recipients	On/Off	Use the Notify program to tell recipients that this message has been delivered
Convert Attachments	On/Off	Convert file attachments that pass through a gateway

Status Tracking Options

The status tracking options, shown in Figure 8.9, allow you to select the amount of information you want made available to you as the sender of a message, such as tracking all information versus just the delivery date and time of the message.

FIGURE 8.9

The Status Tracking page allows you to control your message delivery.

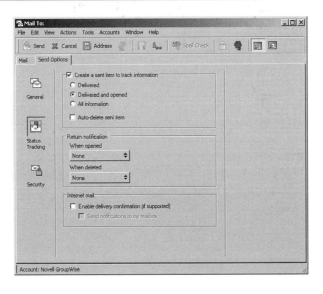

Table 8.4 summarizes the Status Tracking options (asterisks denote default options).

TABLE 8.4
Status Tracking Options

OPTION	AVAILABLE CHOICES	DESCRIPTION
Create a Sent Item to Track Information	*On/Off	Create an item in your Sent Items folder (or not)
Delivered	On/Off	Status for Delivered date and time
*Delivered and Opened	*On/Off	Status for Delivered and Opened
All Information	On/Off	Delivered, Opened, Deleted, Accepted, Declined, Completed, Downloaded, Transferred, Retracted, Replied, and Emptied
Auto-Delete Sent Item	On/*Off	Delete the message from the sender's Sent Items folder after all recipients have deleted it from their mailboxes
Return Notification When Opened, When Accepted, When Declined, When Completed, or When Deleted (The options differ depending on item type.)	*None	No notification or mail
	Mail Receipt	New message in mailbox
	Notify	Notification
	Notify and Mail	Notification and new message in mailbox
Internet Mail	Enable Delivery Confirmation (If Supported)	Allows you to receive a delivery confirmation in your Message Information screen for messages sent through the Internet when the receiving system supports delivery confirmation
	Send Notifications to My Mailbox	Allows you to receive a delivery confirmation mail message if confirmation is supported

Security Options

The Security page relates to the security aspects of the messages you send, as shown in Figure 8.10.

FIGURE 8.10
The Security page enables you to add security to your message.

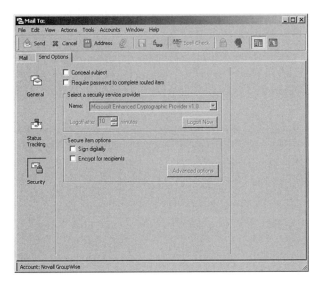

The Conceal Subject security option hides the message subject when viewing the mailbox. The subject is visible only when the recipient opens the message.

The Require Password to Complete Routed Item option causes each recipient of a routed item to enter his or her GroupWise password after marking a routed item "Completed." The message is not forwarded to the next recipient unless the password is entered correctly.

TIP

You may turn a mail message into a routing slip that allows you to create a chain of recipients. The message is delivered to each recipient in the order that his or her name is entered in the Route field. (You can drag and drop names to change the route order also.) To turn a message into a routing slip, from the standard email compose window, choose Actions, Routing Slip. Enter the recipient names in the Route field in the desired order.

The Select a Security Service Provider option is available only if you have installed a supported security provider. If this option is not available, either you have not installed a security provider or your security provider does not support the options.

GroupWise works with security software available from third-party companies. The following security products are supported:

- Entrust 4.0 or higher from Entrust Technologies Inc.
- Gemplus GemSafe Card CSP v1.0.
- Infineon SICRYPT Base Smart Card CSP.
- Microsoft Base Cryptographic Provider version 1.0 or higher. To use this provider, you must also obtain a security certificate from an independent certificate authority.
- Microsoft Enhanced Cryptographic Provider version 1.0 or higher. To use this provider, you must also obtain a security certificate from an independent certificate authority.
- Microsoft Strong Cryptographic Provider.
- Schlumberger Cryptographic Service Provider.

Contact your administrator to determine whether you have these products available to your GroupWise system.

You can add security to the items you send by using digital signatures or encryption.

The Sign Digitally option enables you to add a digital signature to your email message. When you add a digital signature to your message, recipients of the message who have an S/MIME-enabled email system can verify that the item actually originated from you.

The Encrypt for Recipients option allows you to digitally encrypt the message. This assures you that only recipients who have an S/MIME-enabled email system will be able to read the contents of the message.

You use your security certificate (explained later) to digitally sign your messages. You use other users' public security certificates to verify digitally signed items that you receive from them.

Security Certificates

A security certificate is a file that uniquely identifies a specific individual or organization. You must obtain a security certificate before you can send security items.

If you are using a Microsoft security provider, you can use your web browser to obtain a security certificate from an independent certificate authority. If you are using Entrust as your security provider, you must use an Entrust certificate. You manage your certificates by choosing Tools, Options, Certificates.

We provide a more in-depth discussion of security certificates in Chapter 11. Refer to that chapter for the default security options you can set for your GroupWise client.

NOTE

Novell provides a list of certificate authorities you can use with GroupWise at www.novell.com/groupwise/certified.html.

Marking Items Private

Sometimes you may want to store information in your mailbox that is private and you don't want your closest Proxy associates to see. You can add an extra measure of control on any item in your mailbox—email messages, appointments, tasks, notes, or any other message—by marking the item "Private." Marking an item Private does not change the way GroupWise handles the message, but it does place a lock on the item.

You should mark items Private when you have granted others access to your mailbox. Unless you grant them the right to read items marked Private, any item you mark as Private will be invisible to them. To mark an item Private when composing the message, choose Actions, Mark Private, or you can simply press F8. To mark a received item Private, press F8 when the item is highlighted.

NOTE

If the item being marked Private is a calendar item, a padlock icon appears next to the item. If it is any other kind of item, no indication is given that the item is private, except for a check mark next to the Mark Private option under the Actions menu.

To remove the Private setting, highlight the item and choose Actions, Mark Private. This action removes the check mark.

My Subject

If you have ever received an email with an inaccurate or unrelated subject to the message, you'll be glad to know that GroupWise 7 provides you with the ability to change a subject to something you specify.

When you open a newly received message, click the Personalize tab, enter a new subject line on the My Subject line, and click Close.

This feature is especially handy when you have a rule that executes based on the content in the subject line. Also note that when you are searching or filtering for messages, the original and personalized subject are both searched.

NOTE

Personalized subjects are visible only to the user who customizes the item. Any reply emails use the original subject.

Creating Discussions (Posted Messages)

In GroupWise terminology, a *discussion* is an advanced message type that enables related messages to appear under one umbrella, called a *discussion area*. These messages are posted in the discussion area's shared folder. You can view the history of the discussion participants' thought processes and the flow of their posted messages in a discussion area by using the Discussion Thread option under the View menu.

NOTE

The terms *discussion, discussion area,* and *posted message* are synonymous.

Discussion areas and posted messages are created, stored, and accessed through shared folders.

TIP

It is a good idea to include the word *discussion* in the name of the shared folder that will hold discussions to differentiate it from other shared folders.

To create a new discussion, follow these steps:

1. Highlight a shared folder in the Folders area.

2. Choose File, New. Select Discussion/Note from the list of message types. As a shortcut, you can click the down arrow next to the Create New Mail button on the Toolbar and choose Posted Message.

3. Enter a subject line and message body, attach any files you want, and click Post to place the new discussion in the shared folder.

TIP

The posted discussion and all replies have a "thumbtack and piece of paper" symbol next to them. This is the icon for a discussion message.

To read and reply to a discussion message, follow these steps:

1. Highlight a shared folder in the Folders area.

2. Choose View, Display Settings, Discussion Thread. The discussions in this folder appear, along with the replies in a nested fashion, as shown in Figure 8.11.

FIGURE 8.11
The Discussion view enables you to see the history of a discussion in nested fashion.

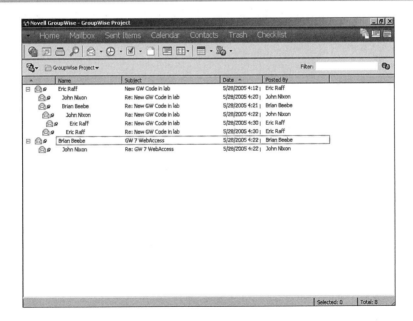

3. Double-click the discussion or reply you want to read.

4. To create a reply, click Reply. If you would like to post a reply in the discussion area, choose either the Reply to Selected Subject option or the Reply to Original Discussion Topic option in the Reply dialog box. Your reply will appear under the appropriate message. If you want to reply to any part of a discussion and not include your reply in the shared folder, select Reply Privately (outside discussion). Then send your reply as a regular mail message to the sender only or to all participants in the discussion.

NOTE

If someone is currently creating a reply to a discussion message, no one else can read the new reply message until the reply has been posted.

Discussions are useful for quickly sharing information with a large group of people and for achieving smooth workflow. Discussions also provide a public, recorded history of communications at your organization.

When you have a shared folder full of discussions and replies, you need a quick-and-easy way to navigate through that information. The first task is to view the messages as discussions. You do this by clicking the shared folder that holds the discussions and choosing View, Display Settings, Discussion Threads.

TIP

You can quickly switch into a discussion view by right-clicking in the Name or Subject columns and selecting View Discussion Thread.

To scan through the posted discussions and their replies easily, click the first message in the discussion (it is left-justified on the screen and has a plus sign next to it). Then choose View, Threads. You then see a menu choice as displayed in Figure 8.12.

The Next option highlights the next item in the discussion, and Previous highlights the previous one. The Expand and Collapse options expand and collapse the listing of discussions and their replies, respectively. This capability allows you to quickly navigate through discussion threads using the keyboard. You also can enable the QuickViewer (Ctrl+Q) for a quicker way of viewing items as you navigate through discussion threads.

FIGURE 8.12
The Threads menu option allows you to navigate through discussions.

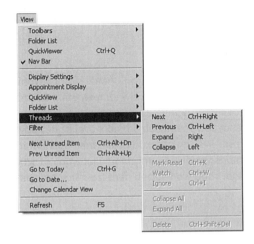

Mailbox Setup and Maintenance Features

The features in this section have more to do with the configuration and maintenance of your mailbox than they do with the message-by-message advanced features discussed in the first half of this chapter.

These features may require some assistance from your GroupWise administrator. Feel free to investigate the powerful options available, such as Junk Mail Handling.

Here's a list of the features covered in this section:

- Internet-enabled features (accessing other email accounts, IMAP, and NNTP)

- Junk Mail Handling (automatically moving unwanted messages to a Junk Mail folder)

- Managing mailbox size (keeping track of the size of your mailbox)

- Repairing your mailbox (maintaining and fixing problems with your mailbox)

Internet-Enabled Features

The GroupWise 7 client has the capability to access multiple email accounts in addition to the GroupWise mailbox on a GroupWise post office. Using the GroupWise client to access other mail accounts relieves you from using multiple email programs to access these additional accounts. These Internet accounts are accessed through a POP or IMAP connection. The GroupWise 7 client also supports access to newsgroups and can function as an NNTP reader. Procedures for setting up each of these access methods are discussed in the proceeding pages.

NOTE

See Appendix D, "POP Versus IMAP Accounts," for more information on what POP and IMAP accounts are and which one would work best for your needs.

Using the Internet mail account with the GroupWise client is as easy as using any other personal folder. You can read, forward, reply to, delete, and otherwise manage your Internet mail just like you can any other GroupWise message.

To get your new email messages from your Internet mail account, from the Accounts menu, choose Send/Retrieve, All Marked Accounts or Send/Retrieve, <Internet Account Name>. Your computer uses either a network or dial-up connection to establish a connection with the mail server, retrieves your new messages, and sends outgoing messages.

NOTE

From a storage perspective, after you access an Internet email account using GroupWise, the messages are stored in your GroupWise mailbox, having been "pulled" from the Internet mail server. The exception is an IMAP4 mailbox, in which case the messages are copied from the IMAP server to your GroupWise mailbox.

Enabling access to an Internet mail account using GroupWise requires you to know information about how to connect to each mail account. This information tells the GroupWise client where your Internet mailbox may be located and how to access it.

NOTE

When you set up an Internet mail account, you are provided with certain information, such as the mailbox type (POP3 or IMAP), server name, your login name for the server, your password on that server, and the email address for the account. You need all this information to set up access to the account using GroupWise. You can obtain this information from your Internet service provider (ISP) where your Internet mail account is located.

To access Internet mail accounts using GroupWise, you can technically be in online, cache, or remote mode. However, if you want to access external mail accounts (POP3 or IMAP) in online mode, the system administrator must have enabled this setting for your system. If you do not have an Accounts menu option, you are not enabled to access external accounts while in online mode. You then need to use cache or remote modes to set up additional accounts. Chapter 10, "Remote Access," discusses how to set up GroupWise for cache and remote modes.

Setting Up POP Access to Internet Mail Accounts

From the GroupWise client, if you create a POP account, you can store messages in a personal folder or your mailbox. If you create an IMAP or NNTP account, the mail or newsgroup items are stored in special IMAP or NNTP folders.

NOTE

To learn more about personal folders, refer to Chapter 5, "Message Management."

Follow these steps to set up a POP connection to an alternate mail account:

   1. From the GroupWise client, choose Accounts, Account Options.

NOTE

If GroupWise is running in online mode, the Accounts menu may not be displayed. Check with your system administrator if you use online mode and you need to add an external Internet account. You can also switch to cache or remote modes to access the Accounts menu.

   2. From the Accounts dialog box, choose Add.

   3. If prompted, enter your country, area code, and outside line access number. Click Close.

4. From the Create Account screen, shown in Figure 8.13, enter a name for the Internet mail account. Because this is just a label for what you want to call this service, you can enter anything you'd like.

FIGURE 8.13
You use this dialog box to specify the account name and account type.

5. Select the type of Internet mail account (POP3) and click Next.

NOTE

See Appendix D for more information on what POP and IMAP accounts are and which one would work best for your needs.

6. In the Create Internet Account screen, as shown in Figure 8.14, enter the following fields as provided by your ISP and click Next:

- **Incoming Mail Server**—This is the POP3 server where your mail is stored.

- **Login Name**—This is the ID provided to you to access the incoming mail server.

- **Outgoing Mail Server**—Usually, the same as the incoming mail server, this server is used when sending messages from this particular Internet account.

- **Email Address**—This is the email address for this Internet mail account.

- **From Name**—This is the name you would like displayed in the From field when you reply to messages that you receive in this Internet mail account.

FIGURE 8.14
This dialog box enables you to configure your Internet mailbox connection information.

7. In the next screen, you configure the method you'll use to access your Internet mail account, either connecting through the LAN or using your modem. Usually, this will be a LAN connection. Choose the appropriate method and click Next.

8. In the Create Internet Account screen, shown in Figure 8.15, you select the folder (by clicking the box next to the desired folder) and place it within your GroupWise folder structure to hold incoming mail for this Internet mail account. (You can also create a new folder by clicking the Create New Folder for Account option at the top of the dialog box and entering a folder name after you click Finish.) If you want to have this mail show up in the main Mailbox folder, you can select it. This way, all your new mail—whether from a GroupWise user or sent to your Internet account—will show up in your Mailbox folder.

9. Click Finish to complete the Internet mail account setup. Both your regular GroupWise account (if previously configured) and the new Internet mail account you just set up are listed in the Accounts box, as shown in Figure 8.16.

FIGURE 8.15
You can create a new folder to contain the POP Internet account messages.

FIGURE 8.16
Your Internet account is now listed and ready for GroupWise to access.

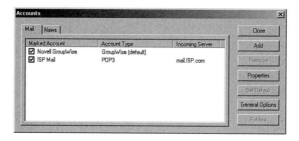

If you need to enter additional configuration settings for an account, you can go to the properties of the account. From here, you can set other configuration items on the account such as whether to use SSL or if you are required to log in before sending mail from the account.

The check box next to the new account indicates that this account will be synchronized by default. If you want to manually synchronize the new account, you should clear the check box. To issue a manual synchronization of the account, choose Accounts, Send Receive, and select this particular account from the list of available accounts.

Setting Up IMAP Access to Internet Mail Accounts

IMAP (also known as *IMAP4*) is another type of Internet mail account that provides the use of folders and other advantages over traditional POP3 mailboxes. GroupWise can be used as an IMAP mail client, similar to the way it can be used as a POP client.

If you have an IMAP mail account, you can use IMAP folders to store and organize the IMAP messages. One benefit to IMAP mailboxes is that messages are still available on the mail server after the IMAP mail client has retrieved them.

NOTE

See Appendix D for more information on what POP and IMAP accounts are and which one would work best for your needs.

To set up an IMAP folder, follow these steps:

1. Determine where you would like to place the IMAP folder in your folder structure.

2. Highlight the "parent" folder under which you want to place your IMAP folder. Right-click and choose New Folder. Select IMAP Folder as the folder type and click Next.

3. From the Create Account screen, enter a name for the IMAP folder in the Account Name field. One suggestion would be to use the name of your IMAP4 service provider. Click Next.

4. In the Create Internet Account screen, complete the following fields, as shown in Figure 8.17, and click Next:

    - **Incoming Mail Server**—The name of the IMAP mail server, as provided to you by your ISP

    - **Login Name**—Your login name to the IMAP server

    - **Outgoing Mail Server**—The name of the outgoing SMTP mail server, as provided to you by your ISP

    - **Email Address**—Your Internet mail address for this IMAP mail account

    - **From Name**—The name you want to use to send all IMAP messages from

FIGURE 8.17
You use this dialog box to create an IMAP Internet account.

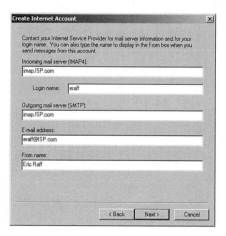

5. In the next screen, enter the connection method you want to use to connect to the IMAP mail server and click Next.

6. In the Create Folder screen, you can enter a description and position for the IMAP folder, as shown in Figure 8.18. When you are done, click Next.

FIGURE 8.18
You can place an IMAP folder where you decide in your Cabinet or folder structure, just like any other folder.

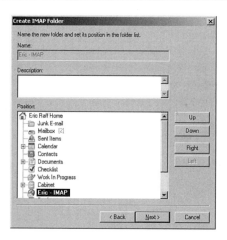

7. On the Display screen, you can configure the sort options, columns, and other customizable settings for this folder. These settings are described in Chapter 10. Click Finish after you have made your desired changes. Notice that the new IMAP folder has been created. To access your IMAP messages, simply click the IMAP folder. You are prompted for your IMAP server login information, as shown in Figure 8.19.

FIGURE 8.19
You need to log in to your IMAP service.

8. Enter your login name (it will probably appear automatically) and your password. You can click the Save Password box, if desired. Click OK. Your IMAP messages appear in the right pane of the GroupWise client.

Usually, the default settings for the IMAP folder will suffice. To perform additional configuration, right-click the IMAP folder and choose Properties. The following tabs are used to configure the folder, as shown in Figure 8.20:

- **General**—Includes the email address, from name, organization, and reply address.

- **Server**—Includes the ISP IMAP server name, login information to the IMAP mail server, and the SMTP mail server name. You can also define whether you want to use a secure connection to the Internet mail server.

- **Connection**—Specifies the method to connect to the IMAP mail server.

- **Advanced**—Includes the root folder path (the folder on the IMAP server that contains your Mailbox folders), other folder options, IMAP and SMTP port information, SSL options, and download options.

NOTE

For both POP and IMAP accounts, if you do not use an SSL connection, your username and password are likely to be sent over the network unencrypted, making it simple for an intruder to discover your POP or IMAP account's username and password.

■ **Signature**—Includes signature information placed at the end of messages sent from your IMAP mail account.

FIGURE 8.20
You can customize your IMAP folder using this dialog box.

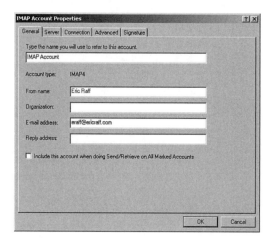

The IMAP mail protocol is a very popular mailbox standard, and GroupWise allows you to configure access to it as well as your corporate email.

NNTP Folders and Internet Newsgroups

Internet newsgroups (which use the NNTP protocol to send and receive news information) are a useful tool for sharing information related to a specified topic, such as car repair.

GroupWise 7 can access NNTP newsgroup information and store the messages under a separate folder. The newsgroups are updated with new information as it becomes available. The newsgroups appear under the NNTP folder you create.

To set up an NNTP newsgroup folder, follow these steps:

1. Determine where in your folder structure you want the NNTP folder to be placed.

NOTE

Separate folders under the main NNTP folder are automatically created for the different newsgroups you subscribe to.

2. Right-click the "parent" folder under which you want to set up the NNTP folder and choose New Folder. Select NNTP Folder and click Next.

3. In the Account Name field, enter a name for the NNTP folder, such as Newsgroups, and click Next.

4. In the Create News (NNTP) Account screen, shown in Figure 8.21, enter the following information and click Next:

   - **News (NNTP) Server**—This is the NNTP server name, as provided to you by your ISP.

   - **My Server Requires Authentication**—If your ISP's newsgroup server requires authentication, enter your ISP login name and password.

   - **Email Address**—This is your ISP email address.

   - **From Name**—This is the name your newsgroup postings will be from.

TIP

You may want to change your real email address when using NewsGroups so that web crawlers are not able to harvest your real email address. Figure 8.21 shows an example of this. A person would know to remove the -NOSPAM- from the email address if he or she wanted to send email to you. If this email address is harvested by some sort of newsgroup scanner, you would not be affected. Also, you should put the incorrect text after the @ symbol so that your organization's mail servers never even get the messages.

5. In the Create Internet Account screen, set up the method to connect to your ISP, just as you did for your Internet mail account, and click Next.

FIGURE 8.21
NNTP newsgroup account access is configured in this dialog box.

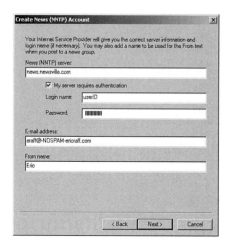

6. Enter a description and the position of the new NNTP folder (see Figure 8.22) and click Next. The name of the folder is the name you entered in the Account Name field in step 3.

FIGURE 8.22
The NNTP newsgroup account is represented by an NNTP folder.

7. Establish the folder's default settings, such as columns and the sort method, and click Finish. These settings are described in Chapter 11.

Now that you have set up the NNTP folder, you can begin to access newsgroups.

ACCESSING NEWSGROUPS AND USING THE NNTP FOLDER

To subscribe to newsgroups, right-click the NNTP folder and choose Subscribe to Folders. Your computer accesses the news server and pulls down a listing of all available newsgroups, as shown in Figure 8.23.

FIGURE 8.23
The NNTP server displays the available newsgroups.

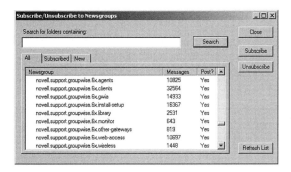

NOTE

Your computer may slow down and may even *appear* to stop responding while downloading the thousands of newsgroups (sometimes up to 50,000) on the news server. It should "come back to life" after a while, usually a few minutes. The count of newsgroups flashes at the bottom of the screen while downloading.

Select the newsgroup(s) you would like to subscribe to and click Subscribe. Ctrl+click to select multiple newsgroups. You can also search for newsgroups by entering search criteria in the Search for Folders Containing box and clicking the Search button.

TIP

You can view the newsgroups you are subscribed to by clicking the Subscribed tab. To unsubscribe to a newsgroup, select the Subscribed tab, highlight the desired newsgroup, and click Unsubscribe.

Click Close, and your newsgroup will appear as a subfolder under your NNTP folder.

SUBSCRIBING TO ADDITIONAL NEWSGROUPS

To obtain a new list of available newsgroups, right-click the NNTP folder and choose Subscribe to Folders. Your computer uses the connection method you set up earlier to establish a connection with the newsgroup server and then updates your NNTP folder with new newsgroups. You can then use the New tab to see any new newsgroups available. Use the steps described earlier to subscribe to a new newsgroup.

ACCESSING NEWSGROUP MESSAGES

When you click a newsgroup, the messages it contains are listed in the right pane of the GroupWise window, as shown in Figure 8.24.

FIGURE 8.24
Newsgroup messages appear within the subfolder under the main NNTP folder.

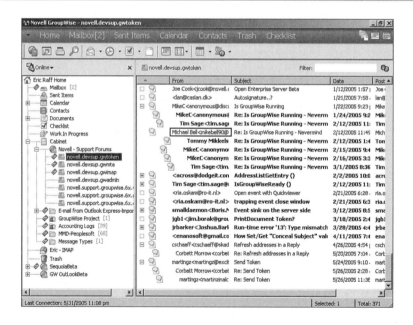

Newsgroup messages can be handled just like any other email. You can reply back to the sender, include the entire newsgroup as a recipient, or forward or delete the message, if desired. You can also create a new discussion topic in the newsgroup.

TIP

You can copy (that is, *link*) a newsgroup message to another folder by clicking the message and dragging it to the other folder.

The actions you need to perform on the newsgroup itself are available to you by right-clicking the newsgroup:

- **Send/Retrieve**—This command updates your mailbox with new messages, sending any replies or new discussions.

- **Reset**—This command enables you to download entire newsgroups, with fresh copies of all postings.

- **New Discussion**—This command allows you to enter a new discussion topic in the newsgroup.

- **Collapse All Threads**—This command collapses all messages; only the discussions are listed.

- **Mark All Read**—This command allows you to mark all postings as "Read." This capability can be helpful if you subscribe to a new newsgroup and do not want to see the unread icon for all the previous postings. Simply mark them Read, and then as new postings arrive, you will know which ones are new.

- **Search on Server**—This command enables you to search the news server for messages, by sender or subject.

These steps are adequate for accessing most newsgroups; additional configuration of the NNTP folder is covered next.

ADDITIONAL CONFIGURATION OF THE NNTP FOLDER

Usually, the default settings for the NNTP folder will suffice. To perform additional configuration of the NNTP folder, right-click the NNTP folder and choose Properties. You can use the following tabs to configure the folder, as shown in Figure 8.25:

- **General**—Includes the email address, from name, and reply address

- **Server**—Includes the ISP news server name and the login information to the news server if required

- **Connection**—Specifies the method to connect to the news server

- **Advanced**—Includes the NNTP port, SSL options, download options, and general settings

- **Signature**—Includes the signature information placed at the end of posted messages to newsgroups

FIGURE 8.25
Additional configuration of the NNTP folder is accomplished using this dialog box.

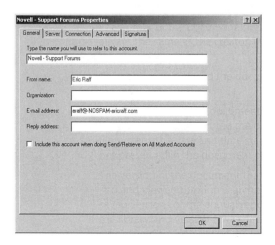

NNTP newsgroups are very good for accessing communities of information related to a specific interest or topic.

Importing Messages, Addresses, and Account Settings

GroupWise allows you to import items, addresses, and settings from other email programs installed on your computer.

To import these items, open the GroupWise Importer by choosing File, Import POP3/IMAP. You see the screen shown in Figure 8.26. From here, follow these steps:

1. The GroupWise client displays any possible mail programs that are installed on the computer from which it can import mail. Select the email program to import from and click Next.

2. On the next screen, select the email messages, account settings, or address book items to import, or choose a combination of these items. Click Next.

NOTE

Steps 3–10 assume you selected all three options (email messages, account settings, and address book items) in step 2.

FIGURE 8.26
This dialog box allows you to choose which email program you want to import from.

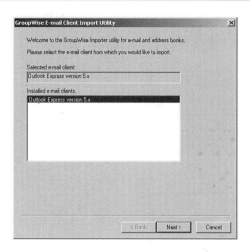

3. On the next screen, select the folders from the existing email program to import (see Figure 8.27). You can select all or some of the folders. Click Next.

FIGURE 8.27
You can select the folders to import messages from.

4. On the following screen, you specify the name and location of the GroupWise folder that will hold your imported email messages (see Figure 8.28). In the Name field, enter a name for the folder and use the buttons on the right (Up, Down, Right, Left) to place the folder in your GroupWise mailbox. Click Next.

FIGURE 8.28
This screen enables you to configure the folder that the messages will be imported into.

5. On the next screen, you name the new personal address book that will hold your imported addresses. Enter a name for the new address book and click Next.

6. On the next screen, you import the settings for the email program installed on your computer, which in this case is Outlook Express (see Figure 8.29). Click the check box next to the account name you want to import settings from. You can also rename this account by clicking the Rename button, entering a new account name in the resulting dialog box, and clicking OK. Click Next.

7. On the Choose Folders for New Accounts screen, shown in Figure 8.30, you determine which GroupWise folder will hold the messages sent to that email account. It is a good practice to make a new folder for the account. Click the Change Folder button and then click the check box next to an existing folder (if desired) or click the Create New Folder for Account button to enter the name and location of a new folder. Click Next.

FIGURE 8.29
You can select the account to import settings from in this screen.

8. You then see a summary page, similar to the one shown in Figure 8.31, of all your selections. If you would like to make changes, use the Back button to do so. When everything is satisfactory, click Next to begin the import. You see a new screen with status bars for the import as it happens. The amount of time this process will take depends on the number and size of the email messages and addresses you are importing.

FIGURE 8.30
On this screen, you can set up a new folder to hold the messages for the imported account.

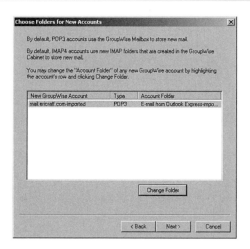

FIGURE 8.31
You see the summary page before beginning the import.

9. After you have finished the import, you see a results screen that displays the success or any errors of the import. Click Done to end the GroupWise Importer.

10. You now have the following items (assuming you selected all three import sources):

- Email messages imported into a folder you specified.

- A new personal address book containing the addresses you imported.

- A new account for GroupWise to get messages from based on the settings you imported. The process of accessing and using the new account is identical to accessing and using an account you create manually. We cover that in the next section.

Congratulations! You have imported your other email program's settings into GroupWise, and you are now ready to use GroupWise to access the outside email account.

Junk Mail Handling

Email spam is one of the most annoying and time-consuming distractions of the digital age. It seems that once your email address gets into public circulation, there is no end to the useless and mailbox-clogging messages you receive.

GroupWise 7 features a powerful *Junk Mail Handling* function that lets you automate the process of dealing with spam, such as solicitations and other inappropriate messages. When enabled, the junk mail feature can either block the message (you will never see it), or it can place the message into a folder called Junk Mail, where you can then review it to verify that it is indeed junk mail.

NOTE

Junk Mail Handling does not apply to internal email messages originating from users on your GroupWise system. It applies only to messages in which the sender's email address is in the format of *name@domain.com*, *name@domain.org*, *name@domain.net*, and so on.

You can use the Junk Mail Handling feature in one of three ways:

- You can block individual email addresses or entire Internet domains. You accomplish this by adding these addresses or domains to a Block List. Messages received from these addresses or Internet domains are blocked and never arrive at your mailbox.

- You can establish a Junk List and add individual email addresses or entire Internet domains to this list. Messages originating from these addresses or domains are delivered to the Junk Mail folder in your mailbox. You can specify that items in this folder be automatically deleted after a certain number of days.

- You can route all messages from individuals who are not in your personal address books to the Junk Mail folder. This is known as a *white list*, meaning that you will get mail delivered to your mailbox only from users in your personal address book. All other mail will go to the Junk Mail folder by default.

The Junk Mail folder is not enabled by default when you begin using GroupWise. It is created when you enable the Junk Mail Handling feature. If Junk Mail Handling options are enabled, this folder cannot be deleted.

TIP

When you enable the junk mail feature, you do not need to be running the GroupWise client for it to work or be active. The settings you define for Junk Mail Handling are stored and executed by the GroupWise post office agent that your GroupWise client connects to. This allows the GroupWise system to keep your mail filtered and managed even when you may not be running the GroupWise client.

Here's how to enable Junk Mail Handling and create the Junk Mail folder:

1. Choose Tools, Junk Mail Handling.

2. On the Settings tab, enable the Junk Mail Handling features you want to implement.

3. Click the Junk List tab and add email addresses or Internet domains.

4. Click the Block List tab and add the email addresses or Internet domains you want to block.

5. Click OK.

To delete items from the Junk Mail folder, right-click the folder and select Empty Junk Mail Folder.

TIP

When you receive an email message from a user or Internet domain that you want to add to either the Junk List or Block List, simply right-click the message, select Junk Mail, and then select either Trust Junk Sender or Block Sender.

The following sections describe each tab used to configure Junk Mail Handling in the GroupWise client and what each function does.

Settings Tab

The Settings tab is the place where you control whether the junk mail feature is enabled and what lists are active that the junk mail engine will reference. The following choices are available from the Settings tab and allow you to enable or disable the various junk mail handling features:

- **Enable Junk List**—Checking this option places mail items from users who are on the Junk List into the Junk Mail folder for your review.

- **Enable Junk Mail Using Personal Address Books**—Checking this option places all mail *not* in your personal address books (including Frequent Contacts) in the Junk Mail folder for your review. This setting allows you to get mail only from users defined in your address books and can be very effective in blocking unwanted spam. If enabling this setting, you will want to monitor your Junk Mail folder and add senders to your address books that you want to receive mail from. (When reading the message, right-click the From address and select Add to Frequent

Contacts to quickly add the sender's address to your Frequent Contacts address book.)

- **Automatically Delete Items**—This option allows the Junk Mail folder to automatically be cleaned up after a number of days you specify.
- **Enable Block List**—This option blocks (deletes) all mail from any user on the Block List tab. If a message is blocked, it is not placed in the Trash folder; it is literally blocked and never delivered to your account.

Junk List Tab

On the Junk List tab, you can place addresses and domains that you want to junk instead of block. (Junk means that the items will be placed in the Junk Mail folder.) Items on this list are active when you enable the Junk List option from the Settings tab. You can have up to 1,000 user entries or 500 domain entries on this list.

Note the Last Used and Count columns. They report how often you receive mail from specific domains or user addresses. This allows you to remove ineffective or rarely used addresses or domains, keeping your junk list updated and working optimally.

Block List Tab

On the Block List tab, you can place addresses and domains that you want to block completely. (Block means that the email is completely blocked and you never see it in your mailbox, Junk Mail folder, or Trash.)Items on this list are active when you enable the Block List option from the Settings tab. You can have up to 1,000 user entries or 500 domain entries on this list.

Note the Last Used and Count columns. They report how often you receive mail from specific domains or user addresses. This allows you to remove ineffective or rarely used addresses or domains, keeping your block list updated and working optimally.

Trust List Tab

A feature that works in tandem with Junk Mail Handling is the Trust List. You use the Trust List to perform the opposite task as the Block List. For example, suppose your main competitor is Lights Unlimited. Therefore, you decide to add the lightsunlimited.com domain to your Block List so that you never receive messages from anyone employed at Lights Unlimited. However, you happen to have a good friend from high school who takes a job at Lights

Unlimited. You can use the Trust List to allow email messages from your friend to bypass the block you placed on the lightsunlimited.com domain. You can have up to 1,000 user entries or 500 domain entries on this list.

Note the Last Used and Count columns. They report how often you receive mail from specific domains or user addresses that you specifically trust.

NOTE

If a list contains more than 1,000 user entries or 500 domain entries, the GroupWise system will automatically reduce the list to 1,000 entries. It does this by referencing the last-used value for each entry and removing the entries that have the oldest last-used dates on them.

Managing Your Mailbox Size

In most GroupWise environments, the system administrator sets size limits on users' GroupWise mailboxes. If you tend to keep every email you receive, if you simply don't keep up with the items coming into your mailbox, or if you simply send and receive a lot of large file attachments, sooner or later you will run into the mailbox size limit like a brick wall.

When this happens, you need to archive or delete items from your mailbox before you can send new GroupWise messages.

NOTE

If your reach your mailbox size limit, you are not prevented from receiving new mail, only from sending it until you clean up your mailbox.

To find out your mailbox size restriction and how much capacity you have remaining in your mailbox, choose Tools, Check Mailbox Size. The dialog box shown in Figure 8.32 appears. From online mode, if this section is grayed out, this indicates that size restrictions have not been configured.

TIP

You can also double-click the Mailbox Size text at the bottom of your GroupWise item list to bring up the Mailbox Storage Size Information screen.

FIGURE 8.32

The Mailbox Storage Size Information screen allows you to monitor the size of your mailbox and quickly remove items that are taking up valuable space.

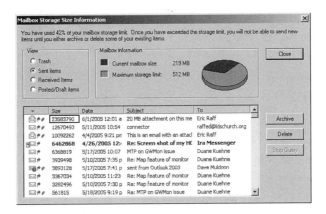

NOTE

The Check Mailbox Size option is available only in online mode if the administrator has applied disk space restrictions to your account. It is always available in cache or remote modes to help manage the size of your Cache/Remote mailbox.

The Mailbox Storage Size Information screen is very useful. It allows you to quickly scan the locations where large messages are most likely to be found— the Sent Items and Received Items folders. It also sorts them by size in descending order.

Notice in Figure 8.32 that a few very large messages are clogging the Sent Items folder. If you click one of the large messages and select Delete, the message will be deleted from the source folder *and* emptied from the Trash (in other words, it's gone!). The disk space totals should update dynamically, so you can easily keep track of how much space your cleanup is recovering.

Here are some additional tips for keeping your mailbox size under control:

- Frequently empty your Trash.
- Frequently clean out your Sent Items folder.
- Sort your mailbox items by size and delete the largest items.
- Don't send messages with very large file attachments.
- Use the GroupWise Archive feature (explained in Chapter 5) to save messages to your hard drive or manually save attachments to your local hard drive and delete the message from your mailbox.

- Monitor the Mailbox Size status bar located at the bottom-right area of the GroupWise main window. When it gets above 75%, start doing some housekeeping.

- If you send an email with a large attachment, be sure to delete that item from your Sent Items folder (not the recipient's mailbox, of course) and then empty your Trash folder.

- Use the settings for automatically deleting and/or archiving your messages and calendar information. These settings are described in Chapter 11.

You should make it a regular practice to clean out your sent items, your folders, and your Trash.

Repairing Your Mailbox

Although GroupWise is probably the most stable, fault-tolerant, and highly available messaging system on the market, the ability to create a copy of your mailbox in either cache or remote mode (Chapter 10) implies that occasional repairing of that local message store will need to take place.

NOTE

If you run GroupWise only in online mode, your system administrator will automatically take care of any repairs you might have to run on your mailbox.

If you get a displayed notice stating "GroupWise has encountered a problem with your mailbox and will repair it the next time you start GroupWise," you should shut down the GroupWise program and allow it to complete the automatic repair the next time you start it.

Most problems in GroupWise are transparent to you as a user. In other words, GroupWise can detect and repair a small database problem before it ever manifests into something larger. However, larger problems may occasionally occur.

In addition, it is a good practice to run a periodic repair on your mailbox even if no problems are occurring.

To perform the repair process, choose Tools, Repair Mailbox. You may be prompted to perform a backup first (contact your system administrator to determine whether this needs to occur).

NOTE

You must be in remote or cache mode or viewing the archive to see the Repair Mailbox menu option. Whatever mode you are in (remote, cache, or viewing the archive), Repair Mailbox will repair the instance of the databases that you are accessing when you issue the Repair Mailbox option. Contact your administrator if you are in any of these modes and you do not have the option to repair your mailbox. The administrator can then enable this feature by placing the proper files in the installed client directory.

You then see the dialog box shown in Figure 8.33.

FIGURE 8.33
The Repair Mailbox options allow you to set up a maintenance process on your remote, caching, or archive mailbox.

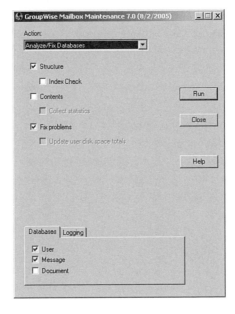

NOTE

A detailed description of all the Repair Mailbox options is beyond the scope of this book. You should contact your GroupWise administrator for further information as to the many options.

For most repairs, you can select the default Analyze/Fix Databases, with the Structure, Contents, and Fix Problems options selected. Also, keep the User and Message databases checked on the Databases tab. Then click Run.

An amazing amount of technical information is displayed; the repair (also known as *GroupWise Mailbox Maintenance*) may take awhile to run, depending on the size of your mailbox and the number of messages.

After the repair process is finished, you can peruse the log file as it is displayed or simply close it and continue using GroupWise.

Summary

In this chapter, you saw how the powerful advanced features of GroupWise can help you be more productive using rules, Proxy, and sending options. We also covered how Internet accounts and newsgroups can be accessed using GroupWise and how to monitor, manage, and repair your mailbox. Chapter 9, "Document Management," covers using GroupWise as a knowledge repository and document-management system.

CHAPTER 9

Document Management

The document management capabilities built into GroupWise make it a unique product in the email and groupware industry. The GroupWise document management service is a feature that lets you manage your documents within the GroupWise system. By integrating messaging and document management, GroupWise makes it easy to access documents and share them with others.

Document management is very different from file management. In file management, you store your files in directories and subdirectories on your hard drive (or on a network drive). In document management, all documents are stored in a central location on a network. Instead of storing your documents in directories and subdirectories, you store them in a database system.

You can use GroupWise document management features to perform the following tasks:

- Store document files in the GroupWise system
- Access common files shared by members of your organization, company, or department and share your files with other users
- Maintain multiple versions of documents
- Search for documents stored in the system

NOTE

GroupWise document management must be configured at the GroupWise system level before individual users can utilize the document management features. If you are unsure about whether document management is available at your organization, ask your system administrator.

Introducing Document Libraries

Document libraries are the heart of GroupWise document management. A library is a document storage location in a GroupWise system. The system administrator sets up each library. GroupWise users can then store documents in these libraries and can access shared documents placed there by other users. Documents placed in a GroupWise library retain their native formatting and document type; GroupWise simply stores them and allows you to manage them from within your GroupWise client.

A GroupWise library is similar to a real-world public library. If you need a particular book, you can quickly find out whether it is at the library by checking the card catalog system. You can locate a particular book by its author, title, or subject matter. Instead of books, GroupWise libraries store documents. You can find a document in a GroupWise library by running a search based on its title, author, or subject, as well as a number of other criteria, collectively known as *document properties*.

Accessing Libraries

The system administrator sets up each library and determines library access privileges. For example, the administrator may set up a library containing documents that everyone in the company needs to access, such as product marketing documents and expense report forms. The administrator might decide to grant only the View right so everyone can read the documents, but nobody except the administrator can change them. If your personal documents are stored in the library, the administrator needs to grant you different access rights for those documents. To manage your personal documents in a library, you need to be able to view, create, modify, and delete them.

If you have questions about what you can or cannot do within a library in your system, ask your administrator. By default, you should have access to at least one library with rights to store documents in that library.

Using Library Documents

After a document is placed into a library, it can be accessed only through GroupWise or through an application that uses GroupWise document management services (known as an *integrated application*). GroupWise can automatically recognize integrated applications when the GroupWise client is installed. You can determine which applications are integrated during the initial GroupWise setup. After GroupWise is installed, you can turn applications on and off for specific applications. (For a detailed explanation of working with integrated applications, refer to "About Integrating GroupWise with Your Application" in the GroupWise Online Help system.)

Many Windows-based applications support GroupWise document management, such as the latest versions of Microsoft Word, Microsoft Excel, WordPerfect, and Quattro Pro.

If you need to work on a document when you are not logged in to GroupWise, you must first "check out" the document from the library and place it in a directory or on a disk. When you are finished working on the document, you check it back into the library. We explain how to check documents in and out under the section titled "Checking Out Documents" later in this chapter.

Documents stored in the library can be accessed in two ways: through document references in your GroupWise mailboxes or through document searches. A document reference is an item in your mailbox with a document icon, similar to a mail message item with a mail icon. Both access methods are explained later in this chapter.

Setting a Default Library

A default library is the library where you store your documents by default. Although you might have access to many GroupWise libraries, you should specify one as default library. With GroupWise 7, you should already have a default library configured unless your administrator modified the standard configuration.

To set a default library, follow these steps:

1. Choose Tools, Options.
2. Double-click the Documents icon. The dialog box shown in Figure 9.1 appears.

FIGURE 9.1
Set your default library with the Documents Setup dialog box.

3. Highlight the library you want as your default library and click the Set Default button.

4. Click OK to save your settings and then click Close to exit Options.

NOTE

All libraries to which you have been granted the View right will appear in the list when you double-click the Documents icon. However, if you plan to store personal documents in your default library, you will need more than just the View right. Your system administrator can tell you which libraries are suitable for storing personal documents.

After you designate a default library, you can perform all the document management functions that are enabled by your rights assignments. Of course, before you can do anything with library documents, the documents must first be placed in the library. You place documents in a library either by importing them or by creating them in the library.

Importing Documents into a Library

Four methods exist for importing documents into a library: Quick Import, Custom Import, drag and drop, and the MAPI Send To feature.

NOTE

After a document is moved into a library, it can be accessed only through GroupWise or applications that integrate with GroupWise document management services. For example, if you create a document using Microsoft Word and save it in the library, you can still work on the document, but you must use the GroupWise document management dialog boxes to retrieve the document in Word. You can choose to copy documents into the library and maintain a copy outside the library, but you must then decide how both versions will be kept current.

Using Quick Import

Quick Import copies your documents into the default library with the default document property settings. (Document properties are explained under the section titled "Understanding Document Properties" later in this chapter.) Quick Import does not let you customize documents individually. Use a Quick Import when you need to place many files into the library all at once and you are not concerned about customizing the document properties for each document.

Follow these steps to perform a Quick Import:

1. Choose File, Import Documents. The dialog box shown in Figure 9.2 appears. Notice that the Quick Import option is selected by default.

2. Click either the Add Individual Files button or the Add Entire Directory button.

3. If you selected the Add Individual Files option, navigate to the desired directory, highlight the files you want to import, and click OK. Repeat this step to add files from other directories.

4. If you selected the Add Entire Directory button, navigate to the desired directory or directories, and place check marks in the boxes next to the directories that contain files you want to import.

5. Repeat steps 2–4 until all the files and directories are listed in the Select Files to Import dialog box.

6. Click Next when all files are listed in the Select Files to Import dialog box. The Create Document References dialog box appears, as shown in Figure 9.3.

FIGURE 9.2

Place your documents in your default library using the Select Files to Import dialog box.

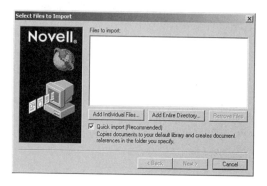

FIGURE 9.3

Specify where document references should reside with the Create Document References dialog box.

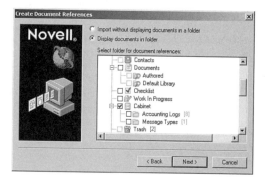

7. Choose the Import Without Displaying Documents in a Folder option to import the documents into the library without creating document references in your mailbox, or choose the Display Documents in a Folder option to create document references in a folder you specify.

8. If you chose to display the documents in a folder, click a check box in the Select Folder for Document References window to designate where the document references will appear. (If you don't select a folder, a document reference will not be created.)

9. Click Next.

10. Click Finish to perform the import or click Back to modify your selected options. An import progress dialog box will appear, showing you the status of the import and indicating whether any of the documents have failed to import correctly.

NOTE

Quick Import places *copies* of documents into the library and leaves the source files in your directory structure unchanged.

Using Custom Import

Custom Import gives you much more control over importing documents into the library. Custom Import lets you perform the following actions:

- Specify which library you will import the documents into
- Specify document properties on a per-document basis
- Move or copy documents into the library

To import documents using Custom Import, follow these steps:

1. Choose File, Import Documents.
2. Clear the Quick Import option by clearing the check box.
3. Click either the Add Individual Files button or the Add Entire Directory button.
4. If you selected the Add Individual Files option, navigate to the desired directory, highlight the files you want to import, and click OK. Repeat this step to add files from other directories. If you selected the Add Entire Directory button, navigate to the desired directory or directories and place check marks in the boxes next to the directories that contain files you want to import.
5. Repeat steps 2–4 until all the files and directories are listed in the Select Files to Import dialog box.
6. Click Next when all files are listed in the Select Files to Import dialog box.
7. Click Next. The Import Method dialog box appears.
8. Choose between the Copy Files into GroupWise and the Move Files into GroupWise options and click Next.

NOTE

The Move option removes the files from your directories and places them in the library. Be sure you don't accidentally move operating system or application files into the library.

9. (Optional) If you want a log file, select the Store All Status and Error Messages into a Log File option and specify a path and filename for the log file.

10. Click Next. The Select Library dialog box appears.

11. Select the library into which the files will be imported and click Next. The Create Document References dialog box appears.

12. Choose the Import Without Displaying Documents in a Folder option to import the documents into the library without creating document references in your mailbox. Alternatively, choose the Display Documents in a Folder Option to create document references in a folder you specify.

13. If you chose to display the documents in a folder, click a check box in the Select Folder for Document References window to designate where the document references appear. Click Next. The Set Document Property Options dialog box appears, as shown in Figure 9.4.

FIGURE 9.4
Specify custom parameters for your documents with the Set Document Property Options dialog box.

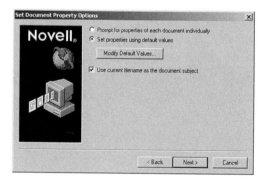

14. Choose the Prompt for Properties of Each Document Individually option if you want to set different document properties for each document you chose in steps 4 and 5. (This step could be time consuming if you are importing many documents.) Alternatively, choose the Set Properties

Using Default Values option to use the default properties for all documents.

15. (Optional) Click the Modify Default Values button to establish default document properties for the files being imported.

16. If you don't want the document filename to be the document subject line for each document, clear the Use Current Filename as the Document Subject check box. (If you clear the check box, you will be prompted to enter a subject for each document individually. Again, this step could be tedious if you are importing several documents.)

17. Click Next. The Import Documents dialog box appears.

18. Click Finish to start the import process or click Back to modify your selections.

After the import finishes, document references will appear in the folder you selected (if you chose the Create Reference option) and your documents will be available from the library. Remember, others cannot access these documents because you have not set up sharing properties. Also, remember that you must be running GroupWise to access the documents in the library.

Using Drag and Drop

An alternative method for performing a quick import is to use the drag-and-drop technique to import your documents into a GroupWise library.

Here's how to use the drag-and-drop technique:

1. Open Windows Explorer.

2. Navigate to the file or files you want to import and then highlight the files by Shift+clicking or Ctrl+clicking.

3. Drag the files into a folder displayed in the GroupWise client.

These documents will be stored in your default library, and document references will be created in the destination folder.

Using MAPI

You also can use the MAPI Send To feature of Windows Explorer to import documents into a GroupWise library.

To use the Send To feature, follow these steps:

1. Open Windows Explorer.

2. Navigate to the file or files you want to import and highlight the files by Shift+clicking or Ctrl+clicking.

3. Choose File, Send To, GroupWise Library.

The documents will be stored in your default library; however, document references will be placed in the Documents folder.

Creating New Documents

In addition to importing existing documents into a GroupWise library, you can create new documents in a library.

To create a new document, follow these steps:

1. From the main GroupWise screen, choose File, New.

2. Click Document. The New Document dialog box appears, as shown in Figure 9.5. When you create a new document, GroupWise prompts you to select a method for creating the document. You can select an application, a template, or a file. These options are explained in Table 9.1.

FIGURE 9.5
Create new documents in your default library with the New Document dialog box.

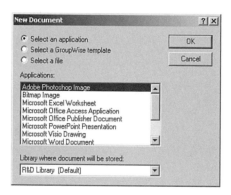

3. If you want to use a specific application to create the document, select the application and click OK. If you want to base the document on a template, select the template and click OK. If, instead, you want to base the document on a file, select the file and click OK. The New Document dialog box appears, prompting you to enter a subject for the document.

4. Enter a subject.

5. If you want to open the document, verify that the Open Document Now check box is selected and then click OK. GroupWise will open the application associated with the document type, the application, or the file extension, depending on the creation method you selected. For example, if the file extension is .doc, GroupWise will launch the Windows application that is associated with .doc files.

TIP

If you are opening an application that does not support GroupWise document management, you will get a warning stating that you are opening a nonintegrated application. Click OK to bypass the warning. If you don't want to see the warning again, click the Do Not Show This Message Again check box. You can use nonintegrated applications with GroupWise document management; just don't change the filename assigned by GroupWise when the document is open.

6. Create the document using the application.

7. Save the document using the assigned filename.

8. Close the application.

The document will be saved in the GroupWise library.

TABLE 9.1
Options for Creating a New Document

OPTION	FUNCTION
Select an Application	You can select an application to create a document based on that application. The Applications list box shows all the applications that are registered in the Windows Registry.
Select a GroupWise Template	A template is a file you use to create other documents, such as a word processing document preformatted with the company letterhead, or a spreadsheet file that is set up to calculate an expense report. You can select GroupWise templates to use a document in the library as the foundation of a new document. If you have documents that you often use as a basis for creating new documents, you can add them to the library and assign them the template document type. These templates will then appear in the templates list.

TABLE 9.1
Options for Creating a New Document (Continued)

OPTION	FUNCTION
Select a File	You can select a file anywhere on your system and use it as a foundation for a new document.

Creating Document References

When you create or import a document into the library, you have the option to create a document reference within a GroupWise folder. A document reference is similar to the icons you see in the mailbox when you receive a mail message. It is a pointer you use to access the document in the library.

TIP

If a document already exists in the library and you just want to create a document reference for it in your mailbox, choose File, New, Document Reference. You can also create a document reference by using the GroupWise Find feature to locate a document and drag the document to your mailbox or other folder.

A document reference can exist in the same folder as GroupWise mail messages, or you can create folders in your mailbox for your documents (just like you would create directories in a file system). By default, document references are placed in the Documents system folder.

Checking Out Documents

When you open a document from the library, the document is marked as In Use and cannot be opened and modified by other users. However, sometimes you might want to work on the document while you are not running GroupWise. For example, you may need to modify the document while at home or while on a business trip. In this situation, you would need to "check out" the document.

When you check out a document, the document is marked as In Use until you check it back in. Other users cannot modify the document; GroupWise users who have View rights, however, can view the document.

You have two options when checking out documents:

- Check Out Only
- Check Out and Copy

If you choose the Check Out Only option, the document is marked as Checked Out in the library and cannot be modified by others, but it is not copied to a directory for you to access it.

If you choose the Check Out and Copy option, the document is copied to the directory you specify.

TIP

To find out who has a document checked out of the library, right-click the document reference, choose Properties, and then select the Activity Log tab.

Here are the steps to follow to check out a document:

1. Highlight the document reference in your mailbox.
2. Click Actions, Check-Out (or right-click and select Check-Out). The dialog box shown in Figure 9.6 appears.

FIGURE 9.6
Use the Check-Out dialog box to copy a document to a local location for offline access.

3. Type a filename for the document in the Checked Out Filename field. (By default, GroupWise uses the document number as the checked-out filename. You can specify a different filename.)

4. Enter a path for the document in the Checked Out Location field.

5. Click the Check Out button.

6. Click the Close button.

After you have checked out a document, you can open it from the directory and change it while you are not running GroupWise. The changes you make do not appear in the document in the library until you check it back in or update it.

Checking In Documents

After you have finished modifying a document that you have checked out from a library, you must check the document back in so that your changes are reflected in the library. Checking in a document also unlocks the document so other users can modify it.

TIP

You can check in multiple documents at once by holding Ctrl and clicking multiple documents in the Documents to Be Checked In dialog box.

Here's how to check in a document:

1. Highlight the document reference in your mailbox.

2. Click Actions and then Check-In (or right-click and select Check-In). The dialog box shown in Figure 9.7 appears.

3. Choose the check-in method.

You have four options for checking in documents, as shown in Table 9.2. When you check in a document, you also have three options that relate to document versions, as shown in Table 9.3.

FIGURE 9.7
Use the Check-In dialog box to place an updated document back into the library.

TABLE 9.2
Check-in Method Options

OPTION	EXPLANATION
Check In and Move	Moves the document to the library and deletes it from the check-out location
Check In and Copy	Copies the document to the library and leaves a copy in the check-out location
Check In Only	Checks the document back in to the library but does not update the document in the library with any changes you made to the checked-out version
Update Without Checking In	Updates the document in the library with the changes you have made but does not unlock the document

TABLE 9.3
Check-in Version Options

OPTION	EXPLANATION
Checked-out Version	Keeps the same document version as the version you checked out

TABLE 9.3
Check-in Version Options (Continued)

OPTION	EXPLANATION
New Version	Lets you specify a new document version
New Document	Lets you create an entirely new document in the library and specify new document properties

Remember that if you are updating documents and are connected to the GroupWise system, you do not have to go through the check-out, check-in process. When you open a document in the library, it is marked as In Use until you close the document. Other users cannot open and modify the document while you have it open. You need to check out a document only when you will be working on it while not connected to GroupWise.

Copying Documents

Use the document copy feature to create a document identical to one in the library and make changes without altering the original.

When you copy a document, you need to specify the new document's properties, including which library it should be stored in. You can manually specify the properties, or you can use the properties of the source document.

To copy a document, follow these steps:

1. Highlight one or more document references in your mailbox.

2. Select Actions, Copy Document. The Copy Document dialog box appears, as shown in Figure 9.8.

FIGURE 9.8
Use the Copy Document dialog box to make a duplicate of an existing document in a library.

3. Choose the library where the document will be copied to from the drop-down list.

4. Specify the method for creating the properties for the new document(s).

5. Click OK.

New document references appear in your mailbox.

Deleting Documents

If you have Delete rights, you can delete documents from the library. You have three choices when deleting documents:

- **Remove Document from Folder**—This option deletes the document reference from your mailbox, but the actual document remains in the library.

- **Delete the Selected Version from Library**—This option deletes the document reference and the selected version of the document, but previous versions remain in the library.

- **Delete All Versions of the Document from Library**—This option removes the document reference from your mailbox and all versions of the document from the library.

GroupWise automatically deletes documents that have exceeded their defined document life, as specified in the document type definition. Each document type has an expiration date and expiration action (delete or archive). Your system administrator configures the expiration date and expiration action. The only control you, as a GroupWise user, have over how long a document is stored is in selecting a specific document type. If you have questions about how long specific document types are stored, contact your GroupWise administrator.

To delete a document, follow these steps:

1. Highlight the document reference in your mailbox.

2. Choose Edit, Delete (or right-click and select Delete).

3. Choose the deletion method you want, as described earlier in this section.

4. Click OK.

The document is deleted according to the method you selected. If you get an error message that indicates the deletion failed, you do not have Delete rights to the document or library.

Searching for Documents

One advantage of document management is that it makes finding documents easy. Instead of hunting through directories and trying to remember filenames, with GroupWise document management, you can search for documents using a number of different criteria, including a simple full-text search for specific words contained in the document.

NOTE

Documents must be indexed by the GroupWise system before they can be returned by a search. Because of this, if you import a document and then immediately search for it, you may not see the document in the search results. Check with your administrator to find out how often the indexing process runs for each library. Many times this process will be running continuously as set up by the administrator.

Understanding Document Properties

Each document in a GroupWise library has a set of attributes that uniquely identify the document, such as the author's name, the date the document was created, and the document type. These attributes are *document properties*. You use document properties to find documents that have been placed in a library.

You can set document properties when you import a document into the library or when you create the document. You can also edit the document properties through the document reference by right-clicking the document reference and selecting the Properties option. The document properties screen is shown in Figure 9.9.

TABLE 9.4
Document Properties

PROPERTY	DESCRIPTION
Library	The library that contains the document.
Document Number	A number assigned by GroupWise that is used by the document management service to identify the document.

FIGURE 9.9
Use the document properties screen to obtain details about a document in a
GroupWise library.

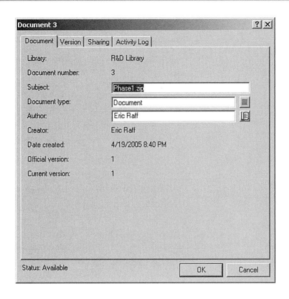

TABLE 9.4
Document Properties (Continued)

PROPERTY	DESCRIPTION
Subject	A text field that enables you to assign a descriptive subject for the document, such as "1996 Annual Report." When you import documents, you have the option to make the filename and path the document subject. Otherwise, you can specify the subject as you create the document, or you can edit the subject in the properties screen.
Document Type	A classification for the document that is used to categorize and establish the usage of the document. For example, some common document types include Agenda, Contract, Memo, Minutes, Proposal, and Report. These classifications, or types, facilitate searches for specific documents. An important field in Document Type is the expiration setting. The expiration setting determines when a document expires and what should be done with the document when it expires.

TABLE 9.4
Document Properties (Continued)

PROPERTY	DESCRIPTION
Author	The author of the document. The author is not always the same as the creator. The author can be any GroupWise user.
Creator	The person who placed the document in the library.
Date Created	The date and time the document was placed in the library. (If you imported the document from a file system, the date and time stamp on the file is not preserved in the document properties.)
Official Version	The version of the document that will be identified and viewed through searches. For example, if seven versions of the annual report were stored in the library, and version 6 was designated as the official version, it would be the version found in searches by GroupWise users who have View rights to the library. (Version 7 could be a draft in progress that is not yet ready for official release.) Any version of a document can be identified as the official version. If you do not specify an official version, the current version is the official version. Usually, the creator of the document designates the official version, but the right to set the official version can be granted to others.
Current Version	GroupWise document management services allow up to 100 versions of a document. The current version is the latest version of the document.
Description	A text field that enables you to describe the current version of the document. By default, the description for the first version of a document is "Original."
Status	The document status possibilities include "Available" (the document is available to be opened or checked out of the library), "In Use" (another user currently has the document opened or checked out), and "Checked-Out" (another user has checked out the document).

TABLE 9.4
Document Properties (Continued)

PROPERTY	DESCRIPTION
Sharing	This field shows the GroupWise users with whom you have shared the documents. You control the sharing properties for the documents you add to the library. By default, a document is not shared and cannot be accessed by other users. Sharing documents is discussed later in this chapter. (The rights you specify for shared documents apply to all versions of the document.)
Activity Log	The Activity Log property shows you a chronological log of the actions that have been performed on the document, such as who created the document, who has opened the document, who has viewed the document, and who has edited the document.

As shown in Figure 9.9, there are four categories of document properties: Document, Version, Sharing, and Activity Log. The most common document properties and their descriptions are listed in Table 9.4.

NOTE

You must have the Edit right to the library to change a document's properties. You likely have this right for your documents, but you may not have this right for public documents, depending on the library configuration set by your administrator.

Setting Default Document Properties

You can set default properties that will be used for all documents you import or create. To set default document properties, follow these steps:

1. Choose Tools, Options.
2. Double-click the Documents icon.
3. Highlight the library you are using and click the Properties button.
4. On the Property Configuration tab, shown in Figure 9.10, select the document property fields that you want available for your documents by default.

FIGURE 9.10
Set default document properties with the Setup Properties dialog box.

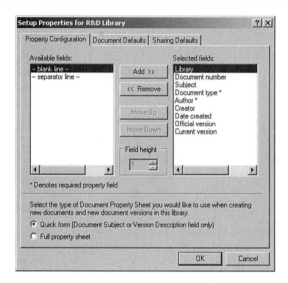

5. On the Document Defaults tab, you can specify a default document sub-ject, document type, and author.

6. On the Sharing Defaults tab, you can set default sharing options. This capability is useful if you want all the documents you add to the library to be shared with others by default.

TIP

If you are collaborating with others in a workgroup, you can use this sharing fea-ture to specify all the other GroupWise users who should have access to your documents.

7. Click OK when you're finished setting default document properties.

The values you set become the default properties for any documents you create or import in the library.

Using Find

In Chapter 5, "Message Management," we discussed how to use the Find fea-ture. This chapter discusses how to perform a full text search to find items, including documents that contain specific words or phrases. The Advanced Find options are very useful for searching document libraries.

NOTE

When you use the Find feature, GroupWise searches for your document in the default library first. If no documents are found, you should verify that a library is selected under the Look In section.

To find a document using Standard Find options, follow these steps:

1. Choose Tools, Find (or use press Ctrl+F).
2. Select the Find tab.
3. Specify a full text search or a subject line search (click the arrow next to Full Text to select the subject).
4. Type the word or words you want to find in the text box.
5. (Optional) Specify either From/Author or To/CC.
6. (Optional) Specify the item type you want to search for, such as email or document.
7. (Optional) Specify the item source, such as received or posted.
8. (Optional) Specify a date range to search.
9. Specify the folders to search by clicking the boxes next to these folders.
10. Click OK to perform the search.

TIP

You can expand the mailbox to select individual folders or click the All Libraries icon to select individual libraries.

GroupWise performs the search and returns a list of documents or messages that meet your specified search criteria.

Here's how to find a document using Advanced Find options:

1. Choose Tools, Find.
2. Select the Find tab.
3. Click the Advanced Find button.

4. Specify the Find criteria using the Advanced Find dialog box. Figure 9.11 shows how to find all entries where the author is Eric Raff, the library is the R&D Library, and the subject contains the word *GroupWise*.

FIGURE 9.11
Use Advanced Find to specify detailed search options.

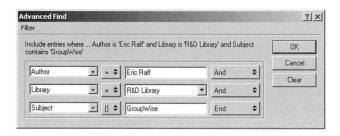

5. Click OK to accept the advanced search criteria.

6. Specify any additional search options and click OK to begin the search.

GroupWise presents you with a list of the documents that meet the search criteria.

Sharing Documents

When you place documents in a library, you control who has access to those documents through the Sharing tab of the document properties screen. You also control what rights others have to the document.

Here's how to share a document with other users:

1. Right-click the document reference in your mailbox and choose Properties.

2. Click the Sharing tab. The dialog box shown in Figure 9.12 appears. The default sharing property is Not Shared. Not Shared means that no other GroupWise user has access to the document. Notice that GroupWise inserts General User Access and Creator Access in the Share list. By default, general users (all users with access to the library) do not have any rights to the document, and the author/creator has full rights to the document.

FIGURE 9.12
Use the Sharing tab to grant other users access to your documents in the library.

3. Click the Shared With option.

4. Type the username in the Name field and click Add User. Alternatively, you can click the Address Selector button and double-click the users' names in the address list. The names appear in the Share List window.

5. Assign the proper rights to the desired users (see details in the following set of steps).

By default, the new users have the View right, which means that the users can locate the document in searches and can view the document, but they cannot modify it.

NOTE

The rights you specify are for all versions of a document. If you want to specify different rights for each version of a document, click the Version Level Security button.

To specify additional rights, follow these steps:

1. Highlight the user in the Share List window.

2. Click the check boxes for Edit, Delete, Share, or Modify security to grant those rights. Table 9.5 lists the user rights options for a document.

TABLE 9.5
User Rights Options for a Document

RIGHT	DESCRIPTION
Edit	Users can make changes to the document.
Delete	Users can delete the document. Use this right with care.
Share	Users can add the document to shared folders, thereby sharing the document with other GroupWise users.
Modify Security	Users can modify the rights for the document. If you grant this right, the users can modify the other rights and could grant themselves the Edit and Delete rights.

Use the General User Access entry to grant the same rights to all users who have access to the library. For example, if for some reason you want everyone to be able to delete the file, highlight General User Access and grant the Delete right.

NOTE

A user must have the Edit and View rights before he or she can have the Modify Security right.

When you grant users the Edit or Delete right, GroupWise automatically gives them View rights to the document. Without the View right, a user cannot see the document in the results of a Find operation, in shared folders, and so on.

When you grant other users rights to the document, the users do not automatically receive a document reference in their mailboxes. They can access the document only by using Find.

Typically, you grant rights to a document, and those rights apply to all versions of that document. However, you can use the Version Security option to specify rights only to a specific version of a document.

Set security on a specific version of a document by following these steps:

1. Right-click a document and select Properties.

2. Click the Sharing tab.

3. If necessary, add a user as instructed previously.

4. Highlight the user in the Share List window.

5. Click the Version Level Security button.

6. Enable the specific rights for this version by placing a check in the appropriate check box, as shown in Figure 9.13.

FIGURE 9.13
The Sharing feature lets you specify security at the document version level.

7. Click OK to close the Version Level Security dialog box.

8. Click OK to close the document properties screen.

The users to whom you granted rights will now be able to perform additional operations on the document.

Using the Find Results Folders with Document Management

The GroupWise Find Results Folder feature is very powerful when combined with the GroupWise document management capabilities. You can create folders that allow you to display only documents that have specific properties.

A common use of these folders is to display the document references of all the documents you have stored in the library or to create folders that contain the document references of specific document types, such as contracts.

To create a Find Results folder that displays all your documents, follow these steps:

1. Right-click your Cabinet or a folder and select New Folder.

2. Select the Find Results Folder type.

3. Select the Custom Find Results Folder option and click Next.

4. Give the folder a name (such as My Documents).

5. (Optional) Give the folder a description.

6. Click Next.

7. In the Create Find Results Folder dialog box, select only Document as the item type.

8. Enter your name in the From/Author field.

9. In the right pane, specify which libraries should be searched. If you leave your home selected, you will most likely see duplicate references in the folder because any document references in your mailbox will also be displayed.

10. Set any other options you desire, such as a date range.

11. Click Next.

12. (Optional) Change the View By, Sort By, and Sort Order settings so the items are displayed according to your personal preference.

13. (Optional) Select your desired item source.

14. Select only Document as the item type. By default, all options are checked, so you should deselect all the other item types.

15. (Optional) Edit the columns that should display when the folder is accessed.

16. Click Finish.

This folder will now display all the library documents you have authored.

TIP

Find Results folders have an icon showing a folder with a magnifying class on them to distinguish them from normal folders. When you click on a Find Results folder, it dynamically performs a find using the specified criteria and displays the results. Consequently, any new items matching the criteria specified in the folder properties will be displayed.

Performing Mass Document Operations

GroupWise document management services let you perform operations on many documents at once by using the Mass Document Operations option. With this option, you can perform these operations on several documents at once:

- Change document properties
- Move
- Delete
- Change sharing
- Copy

NOTE

A system administrator can grant a GroupWise user "manage" rights. If you have received manage rights to a library, you have additional capabilities available to you when performing mass document operations. For information on the actions you can perform with the manage rights, refer to the GroupWise Help feature.

For example, if you need to move or copy a large number of documents from one GroupWise library to another, you should use the Mass Document Operations option.

To use the Mass Document Operations option, follow these steps:

1. (Optional) In your GroupWise mailbox, highlight the documents on which you want to perform the operation.
2. Choose Tools, Mass Document Operations. The dialog box in Figure 9.14 appears.
3. Select the desired operation: Change Properties, Move, Delete, Change Sharing, or Copy.
4. Choose your selection method.
5. Click Next.

Follow the prompts to perform the operation. (The prompts will vary depending on the type of operation you are performing.)

FIGURE 9.14
Use the Mass Document Operations dialog box to manipulate many library documents at once.

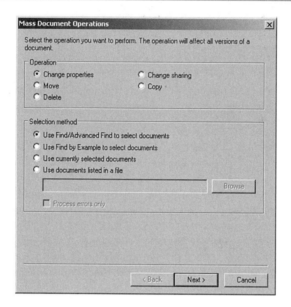

Echoing Documents to Your Remote Mailbox

If you use the remote features of GroupWise (discussed in the next chapter), you can "echo" documents from your default library to a library created in your remote mailbox, which is located on your hard drive.

This feature lets you work on documents that are stored in the library locally while you are not connected to your master GroupWise mailbox. This feature maintains two copies of your documents: one in the library and one in your GroupWise remote mailbox stored on your local hard drive.

When you reconnect, you can then update the documents you have modified.

Here's how to enable document echoing:

1. While in online mode, choose Tools, Options.
2. Double-click the Documents icon.
3. Select the General tab.

4. Choose the Echo Documents to GroupWise Remote option.

5. Click OK.

Documents will be echoed to your remote mailbox any time you close or check in a document in your master mailbox. A document reference is created for the echoed document in your remote mailbox.

NOTE

You cannot set your mailbox to echo documents while you are in remote or cache modes. You must be in online mode to enable document echoing.

Summary

This chapter explained the basics of GroupWise document management and GroupWise libraries, including accessing GroupWise libraries, importing documents, working with documents in a GroupWise library, setting security options on documents, and deleting documents.

In the next chapter, we explain how to use GroupWise remote and cache modes to remain connected while you are away from the office.

CHAPTER 10

Remote Access

With today's mobile workforce, access to email and scheduling information is more critical than ever. If you can access your GroupWise system regardless of where you are, you can communicate with your customers and coworkers as if you were sitting in your office.

One way to access your GroupWise system when you are away from the office is to use the GroupWise client running in remote or cache mode. This chapter addresses how to configure the GroupWise client for remote access. We explain the steps necessary to access information when you're out of the office—how to request your messages and how to connect to the system and download your messages. We also explain the different techniques to use when you are connected to a network and when you are working offline using a remote mailbox.

NOTE

In addition to the traditional remote mode, GroupWise 7 has a hybrid mode known as *cache mode* that functions similar to the standard online mode but has some remote mode characteristics. When you use cache mode, you won't notice much difference between the standard online mode and the cache mode, except perhaps a slight delay in sending and receiving messages.

If you run GroupWise in cache mode, check with your GroupWise administrator to see whether your GroupWise system is set up to access your mailbox from outside your corporate network in cache mode. If so, you don't need to make any configuration changes to the GroupWise client. You can simply continue working in cache mode wherever you have a network connection—whether that be while you are at work, on the road, or at home. All you should need is an Internet connection. Cache mode is discussed under the section titled "Understanding Cache Mode" later in this chapter.

Using GroupWise remote mode is just one way to access your GroupWise information when you aren't directly connected to your corporation's network. Also, if your GroupWise system is configured to allow web browser access to GroupWise, you can use GroupWise WebAccess to access your GroupWise account from anywhere on the Internet. GroupWise WebAccess is explained in the aptly titled Chapter 13, "GroupWise WebAccess."

Connecting to Your Mailbox Using Remote Mode

You have three options to connect to your GroupWise mailbox using remote mode:

- **Modem**—You can use a dial-up connection to the GroupWise Async Gateway, which forwards your incoming and outgoing messages.

- **Network**—You can use a drive letter and path to your post office on a network, possibly achieved through a dial-in, network-connection software package such as NetWare Connect. This mode is not discussed in this book because it is rarely used any more. It mainly exists because of legacy connection methods that were more commonly used in previous years.

- **TCP/IP**—You can use the TCP/IP address of the GroupWise Mail server that synchronizes your master mailbox with your remote mailbox.

Traditionally, the most common method of connecting remotely to a GroupWise mailbox has been to use a dial-up connection through a modem. However, with home-based broadband network access becoming more commonplace, TCP/IP connections are becoming increasingly popular because of the increased speed and reliability over traditional dial-up connections.

NOTE

Before configuring GroupWise in remote mode, you must make sure you are running GroupWise from your local hard drive. In some installations, the GroupWise client might run from a network location. If you are unsure about the location of the GroupWise program, contact your system administrator.

Configuring the GroupWise Client

You can begin the configuration of remote mode in two ways: while attached to your corporate network or when disconnected from the corporate network. We suggest that you configure remote mode when you are connected to your corporate network, if possible, because the procedure is automated. You will likely be able to use this method if you have a laptop computer that you use in a docking station when you are in the office and outside the docking station while away from the office.

Configuring GroupWise Remote When Attached to the Network

To begin installing GroupWise in remote mode (assuming you are connected to the corporate network), follow these steps:

1. Choose Tools, Hit the Road.

2. Enter your GroupWise password. If you don't have a password on your master mailbox, you will get a warning dialog box explaining that a password must be set. Click OK, and GroupWise lets you set a password by presenting the Security Options dialog box. After you set your password, click Next. The Hit the Road Wizard starts.

3. Select This Machine and click Next. (Selecting Another Machine will place your mailbox information on a floppy diskette[s] where you can then update another computer. This option is mainly left over from older GroupWise versions and is rarely used today with high-speed TCP/IP connections available.)

4. Enter a local path for GroupWise to use for remote mode (for example, `c:\gwremote`). If the directory you specify does not exist, GroupWise will create it for you. Click Next.

5. Click Yes if you're prompted to create the folder.

6. In the GroupWise Async Gateway box, select the gateway your computer will use for remote mode. (If no numbers are displayed, click Next, and you will be able to enter the number later.)

7. In the Update Your Remote Mailbox screen, shown in Figure 10.1, select the items you want to be available when you are working remotely.

8. Click Finish.

FIGURE 10.1
Select which types of GroupWise items to have available while you're working offline in remote mode.

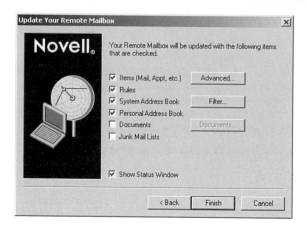

9. If you get a prompt asking whether you want to use your master mailbox password to access your remote mailbox, choose Yes or No, depending on your preference. If you answer Yes, you will be prompted to enter your password when you launch GroupWise in remote mode. If you answer No, you will *not* be prompted for your GroupWise password when you launch the client in remote mode. We recommend you answer Yes to prevent an unauthorized user from gaining access to your mailbox if they have access to your computer.

10. After you answer the password prompt, the GroupWise client will access your post office and download your mailbox information to the Remote directory on your computer. You will see the dialog box shown in Figure 10.2. Depending on the size of your account and your connection speed, this process can be lengthy. You may want to choose Hit the Road at an interval when you will be away from your desk for a period of time.

You are now ready to use GroupWise in remote mode. At this point, however, you are still in online mode. To begin using GroupWise in remote mode, choose File, Mode, Remote.

FIGURE 10.2
The Updating Mailbox dialog box shows you the progress of the remote Mailbox update process.

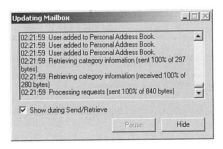

Configuring GroupWise Remote When Disconnected from the Network

If you need to set up GroupWise to work in remote mode and you are not connected to your corporate network, you can manually set up the GroupWise client for this mode. These instructions make two assumptions:

- That you have already installed the GroupWise client locally on your computer

- That you or your system administrator has set a password on your master mailbox and you know that password

If either of these assumptions is not valid, contact your system administrator before configuring GroupWise in remote mode.

NOTE

To accomplish these steps, you need to know the name of your GroupWise domain and post office, along with the information required in steps 2 and 4. You can get this information from your system administrator or help desk.

To begin the configuration process, follow these steps:

1. Double-click the GroupWise icon or choose Start, Programs, Novell GroupWise, GroupWise. The GroupWise Startup screen appears. (The GroupWise Startup screen is explained in Appendix A, "GroupWise Startup Options.")

2. Click the Remote Mailbox Path option.

3. Enter a local path for GroupWise Remote, such as **c:\GWRemote**.

4. If you are prompted to create the directory, select Yes.

5. Click OK. GroupWise starts and prompts you to create an account.

6. Click OK. The Create Account dialog box appears, as shown in Figure 10.3.

FIGURE 10.3
Use the Create Account dialog box to set up remote mode while you're offline.

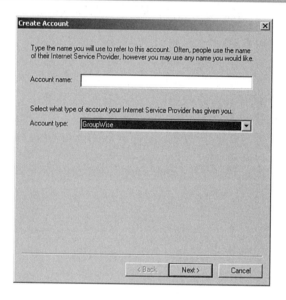

7. Enter the name you'll use for the account. (GroupWise is a common name to use for the account.)

8. Select GroupWise in the Account Type field.

9. Click Next. The Create GroupWise Account dialog box appears, as shown in Figure 10.4.

10. Enter your GroupWise user ID in the User ID field.

11. Enter the name of your GroupWise domain in the Domain field.

12. Enter the name of your GroupWise post office in the Post Office field.

FIGURE 10.4

Enter your GroupWise system information in the Create GroupWise Account dialog box.

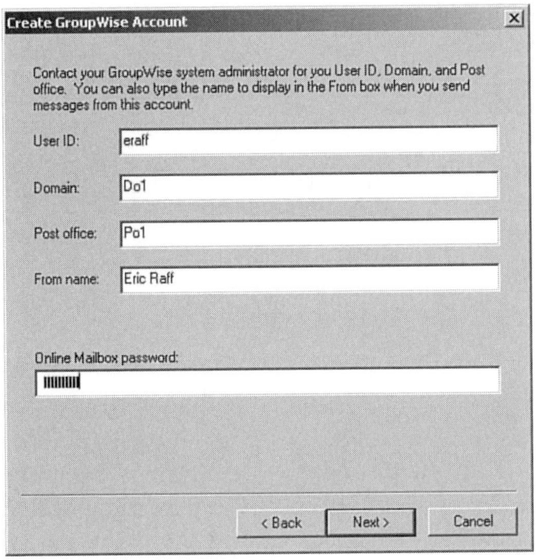

NOTE

The Domain and Post Office fields *must* be entered correctly; otherwise, your new remote connection will not connect properly to initiate the synchronization process. Check with your GroupWise administrator or help desk if you need to know what your domain and post office are.

13. Enter your full name in the From Name field. (This is the name that will appear on mail messages you send from GroupWise Remote.)

14. Enter your GroupWise password in the Online Mailbox Password field.

15. Click Next. The Create GroupWise Account dialog box appears.

16. Select the appropriate location in the Connecting From field. (Default Location is fine if no other locations are configured.)

17. Click the Connect To button. The Create Connection dialog box appears, as shown in Figure 10.5.

FIGURE 10.5
Use the Create Connection dialog box to specify the type of connection you will use
with GroupWise Remote.

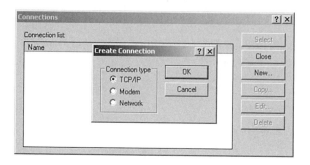

18. From this dialog box, you define how the GroupWise Client will connect
to your master mailbox. The most common method used today is the
TCP/IP method, followed by the Modem connection. As mentioned previously, the Network connection is rarely used and will not be discussed.
When using a TCP/IP connection, the GroupWise client will share your
existing TCP/IP connection such as that created when you dial an
Internet service provider (ISP) or are connected to a TCP/IP network
through your computer's network card. Select TCP/IP; then click OK.
The TCP/IP Connection dialog box appears, as shown in Figure 10.6.

FIGURE 10.6
The Connection dialog box allows you to define what type of connection you want
to use.

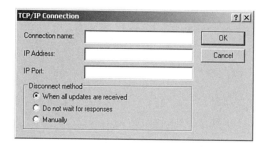

19. Enter a recognizable name in the Connection Name field, such as
GroupWise TCP Remote Connection.

NOTE

Steps 20 and 21 require information that you must obtain from your system administrator or help desk.

20. In the IP Address field, enter the IP address or name as directed by your system administrator or help desk personnel.

21. In the IP Port field, enter the port (a four-digit number) as directed by your system administrator or help desk personnel.

22. In the Disconnect Method section, leave the default selection When All Updates Are Received.

23. Click OK to accept changes and close the TCP/IP Connection dialog box.

24. In the Connection dialog box, highlight the connection you just created and click Select.

25. The last dialog box allows you to specify what connection the GroupWise client will use to share the TCP/IP Connection. Select LAN to have GroupWise use the existing TCP/IP connection that must be present before you synchronize GroupWise in remote mode. This could be a TCP/IP connection through your network card (wired/wireless) or through a modem to an ISP. If your computer is set up to dial an ISP, you can have GroupWise dial this connection automatically by selecting Connect Using My Modem and Phone Line and then selecting the Dial-Up connection already defined on your computer. Figure 10.7 displays an example of using a TCP/IP connection and having GroupWise dial an ISP connection already defined on the computer.

26. Click OK in the Create GroupWise Account dialog box. You are asked whether you want to use your online mailbox password to access your remote mailbox. Select Yes if you want to protect your remote mailbox with your password; otherwise, select No.

GroupWise is now configured to run in remote mode with a modem connection.

Setting Up Modem Connections

Setting up modem connections requires having some information prepared before this configuration can be complete. The information needed is outlined in steps 7 through 9 in this section.

GroupWise remote connections via a modem are used if you are in a physical location where a TCP/IP connection is not available. Modem-based remote connections allow you to dial directly into your company's GroupWise system using a dial-up connection over a modem.

FIGURE 10.7

Setting up a TCP/IP connection through a dial-up Internet service provider (ISP).

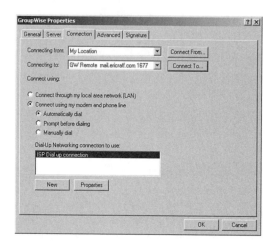

To set up a modem connection, follow these steps:

1. Choose Accounts, Account Options.
2. Highlight the GroupWise Account and select Properties.
3. Select the Connection tab.
4. Click the Connect To button.
5. Click New to create a new connection and select Modem from the Create Connection screen. The Modem Connection dialog box appears, as shown in Figure 10.8.
6. Enter a recognizable name in the Connection Name field, such as **GW Remote Modem Connection**.

NOTE

Steps 7 through 9 require information that you must obtain from your system administrator or help desk.

7. In the Phone Number area, enter the area code and phone number of the GroupWise Async Gateway.

FIGURE 10.8

The Modem Connection dialog box allows you to configure a modem connection with the required parameters to connect to a GroupWise Async gateway.

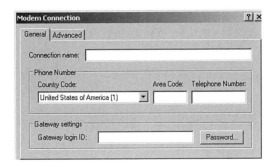

8. In the Gateway Settings area, enter the gateway login ID in the appropriate field.

9. Click the Password button, enter the gateway password, and click OK. Then reenter the gateway password to confirm it and click OK again.

10. Click OK in the Modem Connection dialog box.

11. In the Connection dialog box, highlight the connection you just created and click Select.

12. Click OK from the Connection tab in the GroupWise Properties window.

13. Click Close to close the account window.

GroupWise is now configured to dial up to a GroupWise system directly and synchronize your mailbox.

Modifying Your GroupWise Remote Options

After GroupWise is configured on your remote computer, a new icon labeled Accounts (Remote) is available in the Tools, Options menu. This icon is used to set default parameters for GroupWise Remote operations. When you double-click this icon, you see the Accounts dialog box, shown in Figure 10.9. (You can also access the accounts settings by choosing Accounts, Account Options.)

FIGURE 10.9

Use the Accounts (Remote) options to establish GroupWise Remote parameters.

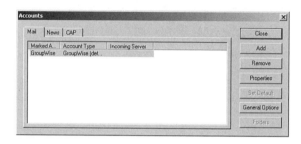

From the Accounts dialog box, you can select an account and click the Properties button to modify the connection properties for GroupWise Remote. You can also click General Options to force GroupWise to synchronize with the master mailbox on given intervals.

TIP

The Account options are also available from cache mode. The options vary when in this mode. The primary difference is that in remote mode you can be very granular with what you request to synchronize, whereas in cache mode, the GroupWise client will attempt to synchronize all item types.

The important options you can configure in the properties screen are explained in Table 10.1.

TABLE 10.1

GroupWise Remote Connection Properties

PROPERTY	EXPLANATION
Time Zone (located on Server tab)	GroupWise needs to know the time zone the where you reside so it can automatically adjust appointment times. This setting is important if you live in a time zone different from the time zone where your master GroupWise system is located. GroupWise automatically adjusts the appointments you create depending on the time zone information entered here.
Delete Options (located on the Advanced tab)	The Delete Options let you configure the synchronization of deleted messages between your master and remote mailbox. The options at the top of the dialog box let you specify

TABLE 10.1
GroupWise Remote Connection Properties

PROPERTY	EXPLANATION
	what happens to messages in your master mailbox when you delete messages from your remote mailbox (and vice versa). The Always Delete option automatically deletes messages from your master mailbox (a deletion request will be sent to the server the next time the client connects). The Never Delete option indicates that messages from your master mailbox are not to be deleted. The Prompt Me option asks what to do with the master mailbox each time you delete a message from your remote mailbox.
Item Downloads (located on the Advanced tab)	This setting specifies which items to download when you connect.
Item Downloads (located on the Advanced tab, mailAdvanced button)	This setting lets you set date ranges for items you want to download from your master box. This capability is helpful if you want to synchronize only specific dates or specific folders containing mail. The Advanced button gives you complete control over exactly what is synchronized when you are working in remote mode.

NOTE

The selections you make in the Tools, Options, Accounts (Remote) menus are system defaults. You can override the default options during a specific connection if you want. You do this by choosing Accounts, Send/Receive, GroupWise Options.

Using GroupWise in Remote Mode

Very few functional differences exist between using GroupWise in remote mode and using GroupWise while logged in to the network (online mode). The same set of program files are used, the screens all look the same, and you access all your information the same way.

When you use GroupWise in online mode, you are working directly with your master mailbox, which is stored on the network. When you leave the office and need to use GroupWise, the program will use a remote version of your mailbox, which is stored on the computer you are using remotely. The messages and Calendar items you create in remote mode are stored in the remote mailbox until you connect to the GroupWise system and synchronize the two mailboxes.

One way to utilize GroupWise's remote mode is to utilize the Hit the Road process at the end of each day. This way, you can take a copy of your master mailbox out of the office (on a portable computer). You can then use the GroupWise client to read, delete, and reply to messages in the remote copy (all without ever connecting to the Internet or to the GroupWise system via a modem). The next time the client is connected to the master mailbox (when you get back to the office), the GroupWise client will prompt you that items are pending in the remote mailbox. If you select Yes, your remote data and changes will be synchronized to the master mailbox, causing items to be removed, new messages and message replies to be sent to users, and so on. The Hit the road process is further described in the section called "Understanding Hit the Road."

Introducing the Remote Menu

One of the most noticeable differences between GroupWise running in the standard network mode and GroupWise remote mode is a new menu item called Accounts. The following selections are available from the Accounts menu:

- **Send/Retrieve, <Remote Account Name>**—Here, you can configure and initiate the remote connection. (The remote account name is the name you specified previously for your GroupWise remote account.)

- **Send/Retrieve, GroupWise Options**—Here, you can specify which items you want to download during the connection.

- **Pending Requests**—You use this selection to view and manage requests waiting to be uploaded and responded to by the master system. Usually, you don't need to do anything in this screen.

- **Connection Log**—You use this selection to view the connection details in the log file. You can also see this information if you click the Show Log button when you make a connection to the master system.

- **Show Status Window**—This selection displays the connection status window.

- **Auto Send/Retrieve**—This toggle setting turns off the automatic send/retrieve mode, which is configured under Account Options, General Options. This mode is also known as *synchronized mode*. When this option is enabled, GroupWise automatically uploads and downloads at a specified time interval as long as a connection can be established to the GroupWise system.

The Accounts menu also appears when you are running in cache mode, but it generally does not appear when you're running in online mode.

NOTE

You can see the Accounts option while running in online mode if your GroupWise administrator has enabled your account to store POP, IMAP, and News accounts in your online mailbox. Enabling these accounts is generally discouraged, however. Check with your GroupWise administrator to see whether your system has been configured to allow the storing of external accounts in the master mailbox.

Sending Messages

For the most part, there is not much difference between using GroupWise remotely and using it on the network: You use the Address Book (and Address Selector) and send messages, create Calendar entries, and reply to and forward messages the same way. The only difference is that you need to connect to the master system to actually send messages. If you are running in cache mode, the GroupWise client will automatically try to synchronize immediately when you send a message. This is one major difference between remote and cache modes. When in remote mode, you must manually synchronize the mailbox to push up sent items. In cache mode, when you send mail, the GroupWise client automatically synchronizes with the online mailbox.

TIP

As you compose items and send them, the number of unsent items appears in red parentheses next to the Sent Items folder. This feature provides a visual indicator that you need to synchronize your mailbox to cause the sent items to actually be synchronized, making them truly sent. It can also signify that there are connectivity problems; if this number never disappears, you know that your client is not successfully synchronizing. Also, note that if you send a large file, synchronizing this file with the online mailbox may take several minutes. Be patient when sending large emails.

Busy Search

Busy Search is slightly different if you are in remote mode. When you are creating an appointment while you are out of the office, you might not want to wait until the appointment request has been received (and either accepted or declined) by the people you need at the meeting. If you need faster information about whether the invitees are available for an appointment, set up Busy Search in the normal way. (See Chapter 7, "Group Calendaring and Task Management," for a complete discussion of Busy Search on the network.)

After you have configured the appointment information for the Busy Search, choose to connect now or wait until the next time you connect to send the Busy Search request to the GroupWise system, as shown in Figure 10.10. Either way, you will receive the results of your Busy Search, and you can continue creating your appointment request.

FIGURE 10.10
The Busy Search option lets you generate an immediate request for free/busy information from GroupWise users when scheduling an appointment.

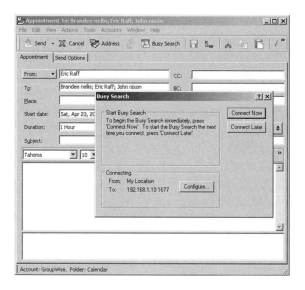

TIP

You should save your incomplete appointment in the Work In Progress folder while you are waiting for the outcome of the Busy Search. When the results arrive, open the draft appointment, complete the information, and choose Send.

Don't forget to connect again to actually send the message to the system. If you are running in synchronized mode (that is, Auto Send/Retrieve is turned on), the Busy Search happens during the automatic synchronization process.

Connecting to the Master System

GroupWise remote mode is a *request-based system*, which means that you work offline reading messages, creating new appointments, and making other changes to your remote mailbox. After you have made all your changes and are ready to connect to the main system, you will generate a list of requests for items.

One request will be to send out all your outgoing messages. Another request will be to retrieve new messages sent to you since the last time you connected to the main GroupWise system. You can make other requests (for example, to get a new copy of the Address Book). When you connect using any of the methods listed previously, your requests are transferred to the main GroupWise system.

The GroupWise system generates responses to your requests and then transfers them via your connection to the remote computer. Some of your requests will be handled in the same session in which you sent them (to get your new messages, for example), and others will be transferred the next time you connect.

After the request list has been completed, the connection is terminated, and the responses are added to your remote mailbox.

To request items, follow these steps:

1. Choose Accounts, Send/Retrieve, GroupWise Options. The dialog box shown in Figure 10.11 appears.

2. If you would like to refine your request for items to a specific set of items or a specific time range, click the Advanced button to display the dialog box shown in Figure 10.12. Choose the options you want from the following tabs:

   - **Retrieve**—Lets you configure the date range from which GroupWise will retrieve messages. The default is five days prior to the current day. If you have not connected in several days, you may need to increase this range. You can also choose the Retrieve All Changes Since I Last Connected option.

   - **Items**—Lets you select what message categories you want to update (Mail and Phone, Appointments, and so on) and set up a filter to retrieve specific messages matching certain criteria (for example, messages that contain "Miller Project" in the subject).

- **Size Limits**—Lets you retrieve messages that fall into a specific size range. (For example, you may choose to retrieve only messages with attachments that are less than 30KB in size.) You can also retrieve just the subject line and then get the message information later. This feature can be very useful to minimize connection time and phone charges.

FIGURE 10.11
Use the Send/Retrieve dialog box to update your remote mailbox with information from your master mailbox.

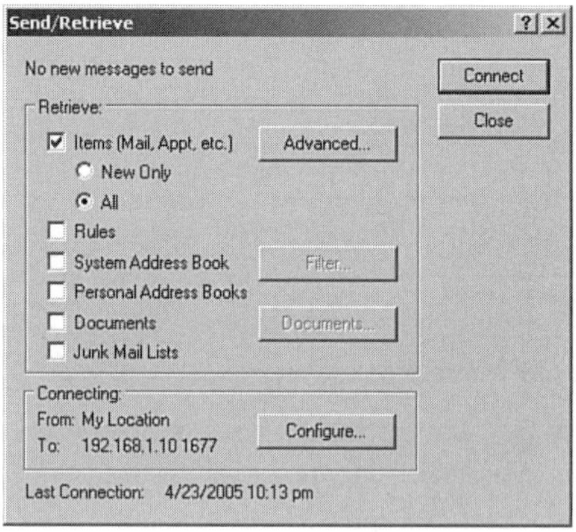

TIP

If you are reading a message that has been truncated due to size limitations, you can select Accounts, Retrieve Selected Item, and the entire message will be downloaded during your next remote connection. If several messages in your mailbox have been truncated due to file size limits, Ctrl+click to select each message in the main GroupWise screen and then choose Accounts, Retrieve Selected Items. The complete messages will be downloaded during your next connection.

TIP

If you open a message item and a file attachment appears grayed out, you can right-click the attachment and select Retrieve Now to have the GroupWise client query the master mailbox for the specific file.

- **Folders**—Lets you select the folders you want updated. You can use this feature in conjunction with the Rules feature to move only those messages you want retrieved to a certain Remote folder so that you can simply download messages from this folder. The Folders feature makes the remote connection more efficient. Simply click the box next to the folder to select it for updating.

FIGURE 10.12
Use the Retrieve Options dialog box to refine your remote mailbox update request.

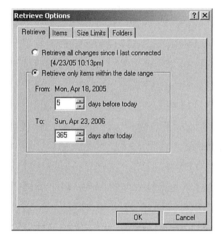

3. Click OK to return to the Send/Retrieve dialog box.

4. Make other selections from the Send/Retrieve dialog box, as desired:

- **Rules**—Updates all rules between the remote and master mailboxes.

- **System Address Book**—Updates your remote mailbox with the most current Address Book. Click Filter to select which address book you want (your Post Office or Domain address book).

- **Personal Address Book**—Synchronizes your master and remote personal address books.

- **Documents**—Lets you select the documents you want to retrieve if you have GroupWise document management services enabled on your system. You can select documents from their folders, and the documents will be transferred to your mailbox. See Chapter 9,

"Document Management," for more information about document management.

- **Junk Mail Lists**—Lets you download to your remote mailbox the list of junk mail addresses you have configured for your master mailbox.

5. Verify that the connection you want to use appears at the bottom of the dialog box. If you need to change the connection, click the Configure button and set up the desired connection. See the sections earlier in this chapter on setting up TCP/IP and modem connections for more information.

Choose Connect to complete the request and connect to the master system. To see the details of the connection, click the Show Log button. The Updating Mailbox window appears, showing the real-time connection and update information as the client synchronizes. Figure 10.13 displays the session information, which can be helpful in troubleshooting. This information is saved to a log file and can be accessed from the Connection Log option under the Accounts menu.

FIGURE 10.13
The Updating Mailbox dialog box shows the connection activity and is useful when you are troubleshooting remote connection difficulties.

Understanding Hit the Road

One of the easiest features of GroupWise is also probably the most useful feature for remote users. Hit the Road is a one-step way to update your remote mailbox before you leave the office.

The Hit the Road feature is used while you are connected to the network and directly accessing your master mailbox. As your final preparation for leaving the office, you use the Hit the Road feature to do a last-minute synchronization of your remote mailbox. This prevents a long connection during your first GroupWise remote connection after leaving the office.

TIP

If you use Hit the Road while connected to the network, a network connection is created automatically. You don't have to manually enter the network connection information discussed earlier.

The instructions in this section assume that you have already configured your system to use GroupWise in remote mode.

To use Hit the Road, follow these steps:

1. While logged in to GroupWise on the network, finish all messaging transactions (replies, new messages, and so on).

2. Choose Tools, Hit the Road.

3. When prompted, enter the password for your mailbox in the dialog box.

4. Select which items you want Hit the Road to update to your remote mailbox this time. You can configure the items each time you use Hit the Road.

NOTE

If you want to customize your item choices, click the Advanced button and make the appropriate selections.

5. You can choose which address book you need to use by clicking the Filter button next to the System Address Book item. Select any of the items in the list to limit your address book as you like.

6. If GroupWise document management is set up on your system, you can also select the documents you need by clicking the box next to Documents. You can then select the documents you need by clicking the Documents button and making your selections.

7. Click Finish. This action initiates a network connection to your post office, and the items you selected are downloaded into your remote mailbox.

You are now ready to "hit the road."

NOTE

You will see two or three extra windows open and close automatically while the synchronization takes place. If you want more information about what is happening, click the Show Log button of the Network Connection dialog box.

TIP

There is no "Hit the Road" option when you are running in cache mode. The reason is that, by nature of running in cache mode, you should always be within five minutes of having your cache mailbox in sync with your online mailbox. You can simply undock or disconnect your computer, and you are ready to "hit the road" for lack of a better expression.

Understanding Smart Docking

Suppose you are using a notebook computer and have been away on a business trip. When you come back into the office and log in to GroupWise using online mode, any changes you made while on the road since your last connection can be automatically updated to your master mailbox on the network. This feature is known as *Smart Docking*.

When you start GroupWise the first time in online mode after being off the network, GroupWise automatically synchronizes the changes in your remote mailbox with your master mailbox. Because the connection type—modem or network login—is sensed automatically, no configuration is necessary. Figure 10.14 shows an example of the prompt you will receive if you have pending requests from the remote mailbox that still need processed when you connect in online mode.

With the Smart Docking feature of GroupWise, you don't need to worry about how you are connected to GroupWise; the program will keep your master mailbox synchronized with changes made in your remote mailbox. Of course, to get the updates from your master mailbox to your remote mailbox, you need to use the Hit the Road feature, as discussed in the preceding section.

FIGURE 10.14

The Smart Docking prompt allows you to process remote requests that are detected when you run GroupWise in online mode.

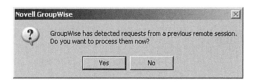

Understanding Cache Mode

A new GroupWise operating mode, known as *cache mode,* was introduced with GroupWise 6.0. (This mode was not available in GroupWise versions prior to 6.0.) Cache mode is a cross between the standard online mode (live connection to your master mailbox) and the remote mode discussed in this chapter.

Cache mode is similar to online mode because it is commonly used while you are actually connected to the network. The difference between online and cache modes is that when you are using online mode, you are maintaining a live connection to your GroupWise master mailbox. This mode uses GroupWise system resources even when you are not performing tasks in GroupWise. In some cases, online mode can stress the GroupWise delivery mechanism by creating unnecessary network and GroupWise traffic.

If you are running in cache mode, the messages you send to other users are sent immediately if the client can successfully connect to your online mailbox. Messages sent to you from other users are queued at your GroupWise post office, and the cache client will check for new mail every five minutes by default.

Settings in cache mode are controlled through the Accounts, Account Options. These options are different from the remote options, but they allow you to configure how the cache mailbox behaves in regards to synchronization. Cache mode is designed to connect any time a connection is needed, and it will attempt to connect automatically. For this reason, when you create an appointment and need to Busy Search users to check their availability, it will behave in the same manner as it would if you were using online mode. The client simply connects and performs the Busy Search in real time.

NOTE

Your GroupWise system administrator can force your GroupWise client to run in cache mode to more effectively manage system resources.

NOTE

Chapter 11, "Customizing GroupWise," discusses a few additional features that you can use in cache and remote modes. They are the cleanup and backup options that you can use to help manage the size of your cache mailbox and to automatically back up your GroupWise cache or remote data at regular intervals.

Summary

The GroupWise Remote features described in this chapter allow you to work with your GroupWise information when you are away from the office and need to access your mailbox through an Internet connection, a WAN link, or a telephone line.

The next chapter explains how to customize GroupWise to match your personal preferences and work style.

CHAPTER 11

Customizing GroupWise

GroupWise enables you to customize your environment to reflect your personal work style and preferences. In this chapter, we explain the options for customizing your GroupWise environment.

Often, you can select options to override the defaults you set. For example, you may decide to set your default message priority level to Normal. When you want to send a high-priority message, you can change the priority level to High for that particular message (without changing the default). The next message you create will again use the default, Normal-priority level, unless you decide to override the default again. In this chapter, we explain how to set GroupWise default options, how to customize the Toolbar and the Home view, and how to customize your folders.

GroupWise 7 also has the powerful capability of using certificates to encrypt and digitally sign messages. We discuss how to set up this option in this chapter as well.

Setting Default Options

When you choose Tools, Options from the main GroupWise menu, you see the dialog box shown in Figure 11.1. You use this dialog box to set your GroupWise default options (in other words, your preferences).

FIGURE 11.1
These option categories enable you to set the defaults for GroupWise.

You can set defaults for the GroupWise environment (that is, the overall program interface) for sending messages, document management, security, certificates, and the calendar. If you are running GroupWise in remote mode (discussed in Chapter 10, "Remote Access"), you will also have a Remote option.

NOTE

The default settings for document management (the settings that correspond to the Documents icon in the Options dialog box) are explained in Chapter 9, "Document Management."

Environment Options

The Environment preferences group enables you to modify characteristics of the overall GroupWise program interface. When you double-click the Environment icon, you see a dialog box with seven (eight in remote and cache modes) tabs: General, Views, File Location, Cleanup, Default Actions, Signature, Backup Options (remote and cache modes only), and Appearance, as shown in Figure 11.2.

NOTE

In online mode, the Environment options tabs are all on the same row. Remote or cache mode places them on two different rows because of the extra Backup Options tab.

FIGURE 11.2
Environment options pertain to the overall default settings for GroupWise.

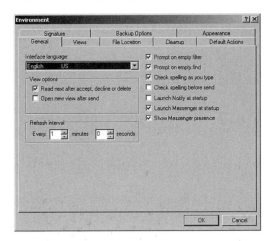

General

Under the General tab of the Environment options, you can set the following preferences:

- **Interface Language**—This is the language you want to use in the client interface (menus, views, and so on). If the language you desire does not appear, contact your system administrator. Additional languages can be defined as the GroupWise client is installed.

- **View Options**—These options enable you to read the next message after you accept, decline, or delete a message and to open a new, blank message after you send a message.

- **Refresh Interval**—This option determines how often GroupWise checks for new messages. (The minimum is 1 minute [the default], and the maximum is 60 minutes and 59 seconds.)

- **Prompt on Empty Filter**—This option causes a message to appear if a filter you created does not allow any messages to appear.

- **Prompt on Empty Find**—This option causes a message to appear if a Find session doesn't generate any results.

- **Check Spelling as You Type**—This new GroupWise 7 feature enables the GroupWise client to spell check as you type. Misspelled words are underlined in red. Right-clicking on a misspelled word provides a list of possible correct spellings to the word.

- **Check Spelling Before Send**—This option checks the spelling of each message (subject line and message body) when the Send or Post button is selected.

- **Launch Notify at Startup**—This option loads the Notify program, which will alert you to new messages and/or alarms set for appointments, when you start GroupWise.

- **Launch Messenger at Startup**—This option loads the GroupWise Messenger program, which allows you to chat with other contacts. You will not see this option if the GroupWise Messenger is not installed on your computer. Check with your system administrator to see whether your organization uses the GroupWise Instant Messenger program.

- **Show Messenger Presence**—This option shows the presence of other Messenger contacts in the Reply and Address Book interface. This makes it easy to see whether a co-worker is online from within the GroupWise client. You will not see this option if the GroupWise Messenger client is not installed. Check with your system administrator to see whether your organization uses the GroupWise Instant Messenger program.

After you have set the General tab's options, you can select the Views tab's preferences.

Views

On the Views tab, shown in Figure 11.3, you can set the following preferences:

- **Item Type**—Select the category (Mail, Phone, Reminder Note, Appointment, Task, and Calendar) and the message type (Group or Posted) for which you want to set the default.

- **Views**—Choose from a list of available views for the selected item type.

- **Set Default View**—Highlight the view you want as the default for the item type you specify. (When you choose File, New, this is the view that will appear for the message type you choose.)

- **Default Compose View**—Here, you can set your default compose format as either HTML or Plain Text. HTML provides many more options for message formatting. You can also set the default font and font size for the Compose and Read views.

- **Default Read View**—When reading messages, you can define whether the default view for the message is Plain Text or HTML. For plain text messages, you can also define the default font size and type to use when reading the message. For HTML messages, the sender defines the font type and format.

FIGURE 11.3
The Views tab's options configure the default views for sending and receiving messages.

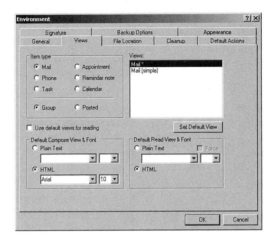

The Calendar default view is the view that appears when you select the Calendar View option from the Window menu.

The Use Default Views for Reading option enables you to read messages using your default views instead of the views the messages were sent with. For example, if someone sends you a Small Mail view message, you would normally see the message using the Small Mail view. However, if you marked the Use Default Views for Reading check box, you will see the message in whichever view you chose as the default.

File Location

Following are the preferences you can set on the File Location tab, which is shown in Figure 11.4:

- **Archive Directory**—The location of the parent directory of the actual archive directory that holds your archive message files. The system administrator may want you to place your archive files in a certain location.

- **Custom Views**—The location for Custom View files. (Custom views are specialized GroupWise views created with a view designer utility.) The GroupWise administrator will usually set this setting if needed for all users.

- **Save, Check Out**—The default location for messages and attachments that you save, and the default location to place the documents that you check out of a GroupWise library. (See Chapter 9 for more information on using GroupWise libraries.)

- **Caching Mailbox Directory (Online Mode Only)**—The path to your cached mailbox on your local computer. This option is available only in online mode (see Chapter 10).

After you have set up these file locations, you can configure the Cleanup tab's options.

FIGURE 11.4
These fields allow you to specify default file locations for some elements of GroupWise.

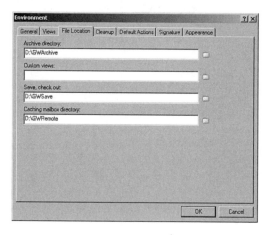

Cleanup

Following are the preferences you can select on the Cleanup tab, which is shown in Figure 11.5:

- **Mail and Phone**—Specifies how old a phone or mail message will be when it is automatically archived or deleted. (The minimum is 1 day, and the default is Manual Delete and Archive.)

- **Appointment, Task, and Reminder Note**—Specifies how much past calendar information you want to keep. (The minimum is 1 day, and the default is Manual Delete and Archive.)

- **Empty Trash**—Specifies how long any deleted item will stay in the Trash folder. (The minimum is 1 day, and the default is 7 days.) After messages have been emptied from the Trash folder, they are no longer retrievable.

FIGURE 11.5

You can determine default actions to be taken based on the age of your messages.

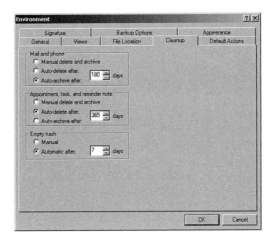

The options in the Cleanup tab are performed when you start GroupWise. For example, if you have set Cleanup options so that messages are archived after 180 days, the archiving occurs when you start GroupWise on the 180th day after a message was received. The automatic Cleanup options can cause a slight delay when you start GroupWise. If these options are grayed out, the GroupWise administrator has locked them down to system-defined settings, preventing you from modifying them.

NOTE

The GroupWise administrator can also implement additional cleanup policies that are active regardless of what you may have set on your own account. Check with your system administrator to see what cleanup policies may be in place in your environment.

Default Actions

The Default Actions tab, shown in Figure 11.6, enables you to configure what happens when you access different items in GroupWise. GroupWise 7 provides several new features here:

- **Sent Items**—These options specify what happens when you double-click a message you have sent. Open Item opens the message, whereas Show Properties displays the properties of the item.

- **Web Browser**—These options specify what happens when you click a web page address within a message. Use Existing Window redirects your open web browser to the address, whereas Open New Window launches a new web browser pointed to the address.

- **File Attachments**—These options specify what happens when you click a file attached to a message. View in a New Window opens a new message window displaying the contents of the file, whereas Open Attachment launches the application associated with the attached file. Warn If Larger Than Window allows you to receive a prompt on attachments that are larger than the defined size here. This option may be helpful if you do not want to view large attachments such as movie clips in the GroupWise client.

- **Start In**—This option defines which tab the GroupWise client starts in when launched. Choices here are Mailbox Folder or Home Folder.

- **Message Attachments**—These options specify what happens when you click a message attached to an email. You can choose to view the attachment in either a new window by itself or within the same window of the message you are reading. Do not confuse this with the File Attachments option mentioned earlier. This setting deals with attached messages, not attached files.

- **Show or Hide QuickViewer On**—These options allow you to configure what happens when you access QuickViewer (show or hide on all or selected folders or display a dialog box for a prompt). This allows you to have the QuickViewer active on certain folders, but not others.

- **Allow Offline Send/Retrieve**—This option sets what happens if the GroupWise client is working in offline mode. You can set the offline setting in cache or remote modes from the File menu. This setting allows you to tell the client that you do not have a connection to synchronize your mailbox and whether you can synchronize during this state.

- **HTML External Images**—This option is new to GroupWise 7 and can be very helpful from a security standpoint. It controls what the GroupWise client does if you open an email that has embedded links to images that are not located in the mail message itself. Setting this to Always Show Warning will give you a prompt if you open a message that attempts to load an image from an external website. You can also allow messages from any users in your Frequent Contacts folder to automatically be displayed; this way, you can prevent a pop-up on messages received from people you regularly communicate with.

- **Plain Text Reply Format**—This option is also new to GroupWise 7. It controls the format of replied messages that are in plain text and the way the original message is displayed. It also can control whether your reply text is at the top or bottom of your message. Experiment with these settings until you find just the right look and feel for your plain-text replies.

- **HTML Reply Format**—This option, new to GroupWise 7, controls the format of replied messages in HTML format. Setting it to HTML Enhanced will indent the original message and apply a light tan color around it. You can also define where your reply text is located and whether you want to include the headers of the original message. Experiment with these options until you find just the right look and feel for your HTML replies.

FIGURE 11.6
You can determine the default activities when accessing messages, web addresses, and other items within the Default Actions tab.

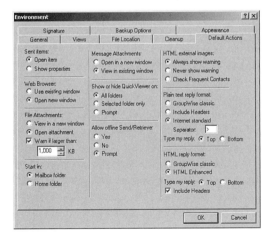

After you have set up the default actions, you can configure your signature.

Signature

You can enhance your GroupWise messages with Internet-style, custom signatures. Signatures are added to the end of any message you send. GroupWise 7 supports multiple signatures, allowing you to select the appropriate signature as you send a message. You can create signatures in HTML format, allowing you almost unlimited flexibility with your signatures. For example, you can create a business signature with your business contact information and company logo that you apply to business-related messages. You can also create other signatures that you could apply to personal, fun, or family-type messages. Because your signatures can be HTML based, you can add animated graphics, images, tables, bullets, font types, colors, and so on.

GroupWise also enables you to send your own personal information (name, phone numbers, and so on) as it appears in the Address Book or from a user-defined file using the vCard format. This allows recipients of a message to simply double-click on your attached vCard file to import your contact information into their contact list no matter what mail system they may be running.

NOTE

The vCard format is a standard contact format that allows you to share your contact information with users in other mail systems. Contact your system administrator for information about creating your own custom vCard file.

You also can specify additional signature information for each mail account (POP or IMAP) you are accessing with GroupWise. (This topic is covered in more detail in Chapter 8, "Advanced Features.")

To configure signatures or vCard sending options, click the Signature tab in the Environment dialog box, as shown in Figure 11.7.

Following are the options available in the Signature tab:

- **Signature**—When you select this check box, you can type a signature in the Signature box as you want it to appear at the end of your messages. Selecting this option also allows you to create multiple signatures; to do so, click the New button. HTML formatting options are available to enhance your signature.

- **Signature Name**—This field defines what signature is being displayed. When you create multiple signatures, you can select each signature from this drop-down list.

- **Electronic Business Card (vCard)**—This check box enables the sharing of your personal information in the vCard (VCF) format. vCard is a format for contact information that is recognized by many Internet-based and other types of email systems. Sending a message with a vCard adds a VCF file as an attachment. The recipient then opens the attachment and specifies which address book to add the contact into. For example, if you send a vCard attachment to a GroupWise recipient, the contact information is added to that person's personal address book or Frequent Contact list. If you want to use a custom vCard, enter the path to your custom vCard file.

FIGURE 11.7
The Signature tab allows you to configure signatures that can be applied to outgoing messages.

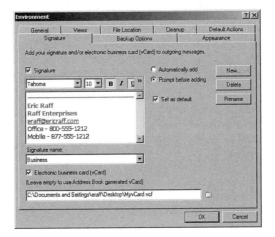

NOTE

If you leave the path to the vCard file empty, the information that you send when you include a vCard signature (that is, attachment) is pulled from the GroupWise system address book, which the administrator enters and creates.

- **Automatically Add**—This option automatically adds the default signature and/or vCard at the end of every message when you click Send.

- **Prompt Before Adding**—This option, the default, asks whether you would like to add a signature and/or vCard information when you choose Send. Being prompted allows you to select an alternate signature from the default signature.

- **Set as Default**—This option sets the currently displayed signature as the default signature.

- **New**—This option allows you to create a new signature. New signatures require a name to uniquely identify them.

- **Delete**—This option deletes the currently displayed signature.

- **Rename**—This option allows you to rename the currently displayed signature.

TIP

You can copy text into the Clipboard from any application and place it in the Signature box. Any text you enter will be preceded by two hard returns. This is helpful to know whether you want your signature to appear with exactly one line between it and the last line of text in your message. In this case, don't end that last line with a hard return.

Backup Options (Remote or Cache Mode Only)

On the Backup Options tab, you can specify a directory in order to back up your remote or cache GroupWise mailbox to a file location. Click Backup Remote Mailbox, enter the directory path, make a selection in the Backup Remote Mailbox Every # Days option, and click OK.

GroupWise backs up your remote mailbox to the location you specify. Remember, this option is available only in remote and cache modes. If you need to access this backup to restore mail, you can simply choose File, Open Backup, and you will see items that are located in the backup but not located in your remote or cache mailbox. This makes finding and restoring items very simple because you will see only the items in the backup location that may be missing from your main remote or cache mailbox.

Appearance

The Appearance option allows you to define the basic appearance of the GroupWise 7 client. Refer to Chapter 1, "Introduction to GroupWise 7," for a detailed description of what each appearance element represents. Figure 11.8 shows the available appearance options.

Following are the options available in the Appearance tab:

- **Choose a Scheme**—You can choose what client scheme you prefer. You may select to use the Default view, GroupWise 6.5 Look, the SimplifiedLook, or create your own custom look that may contain elements from both GroupWise 6.5 and GroupWise 7 if you like. These settings are stored on the GroupWise server and apply to any workstation that you use to log in to GroupWise.

FIGURE 11.8
The appearance options allow you to customize the look and feel of the GroupWise client.

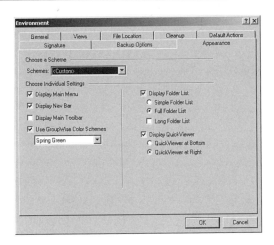

- **Display Main Menu**—The main menu is the menu bar that contains File, Edit, View, Actions, Tools, Window, and Help. You can also toggle this menu on and off by clicking the rightmost icon on the Navigation bar.

- **Display Nav Bar**—The Nav bar is the tabbed list of places you can quickly navigate to. It is a new toolbar introduced in GroupWise 7.

- **Display Main Toolbar**—The Main Toolbar is the Toolbar that contains the Address Book, Properties, Print Calendar, Search, and Compose buttons, among others.

- **Use GroupWise Color Schemes**—GroupWise 7 supports six new color schemes, allowing you to customize the overall color scheme that is used. Available color schemes are Blue, Olive Green, Silver, Sky Blue (default), Spring Green, and Sterling Silver. You can also quickly change the color scheme by right-clicking the Navigation bar and selecting Customize Nav Bar. At the bottom, you will find these same color schemes listed under the Color Scheme drop-down menu.

- **Display Folder List**—This option enables the folder list. You can choose between the Simple Folder List, which displays the cabinet folder and any subfolders, or the Full Folder List, which contains all folders. You can select the Long Folder List when you have the QuickViewer displayed at the bottom. This allows the folder list to extend from the top to the bottom of the GroupWise client, so it is not cut off by the QuickViewer.

- **Display QuickViewer**—The QuickViewer is a window that can be located either at the bottom or the right side of the GroupWise client. It displays contents and attachments from messages as you select the messages or attachments. This feature allows you to see the contents of items without double-clicking on them to open them, so it can be a real time-saver.

Send Options

When you double-click the Send icon, you see six tabs at the top of the Send Options dialog box: Send Options, Mail, Appointment, Task, Reminder Note, and Security (see Figure 11.9). Each tab contains customizable settings that affect the defaults for the messages you send.

FIGURE 11.9
On the main Send Options page, you can set defaults for all the messages you send.

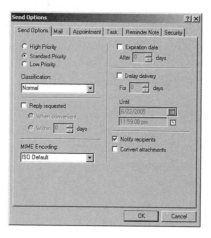

The Send Options tab affects all messages (email, appointments, reminder notes, and tasks), and its options are as follows:

- **Priority**—These options determine the default priority for each message type. High Priority means the message appears with a red icon in the recipient's mailbox, and GroupWise may deliver the message more quickly. Standard Priority means the message appears with a regular black-and-white icon in the mailbox. Low Priority means the message appears with a bluish icon in the mailbox.

- **Classification**—These options place a security header at the top of the message body, such as "Security: For Your Eyes Only."

- **Reply Requested**—This option enables you to inform the recipient that you would like a reply to the message. When you set the Reply Requested option, GroupWise inserts text in the message body, stating that a reply is requested and how soon the reply is desired. The message icon in the mailbox is represented by two-way arrows, indicating that a reply is requested. The When Convenient check box inserts "Reply Requested: When Convenient" in the message body, whereas Within X Days inserts "Reply Requested: By MM/DD/YY" in the message body.

- **MIME Encoding**—This is the encoding method for the email and attachments sent to Internet recipients. If you use languages other than English, you may want to set this to UTF-8.

- **Expiration Date**—This option enables you to specify when the message will be automatically deleted from the recipient's mailbox if the message is not opened.

- **Delay Delivery**—This option enables you to create and send a message now that will be delivered in a specified number of days or on a certain date and time in the future.

- **Notify Recipients**—This option specifies whether recipients receive a Notify message when the message arrives in their mailboxes. Understanding this feature is important because the ability to receive notifications about new messages is based on the sender having this option set. By default, it is enabled.

- **Convert Attachments**—This option specifies whether to convert attachments that are received through a gateway from another mail system. If the attachments are not converted, you will need the application with which the attachment was created to open it. This option is rarely used anymore in GroupWise because most gateways convert attachments automatically.

After you have configured these general send options, you can set up default status tracking per message type (mail, appointment, task, or note).

Status Tracking and Return Notification

The Mail tab, shown in Figure 11.10, and the Appointment, Task, and Reminder Note tabs enable you to configure the amount of status information and return notification available for each message you send. Following are the options available on these tabs:

- **Create a Sent Item to Track Information**—This option specifies whether to create an entry in the Sent Items folder to track sent messages.

  Delivered shows you if and when the message was delivered to the recipient's mailbox.

  Delivered and Opened shows you when the message was delivered and when the message was opened.

  All Information shows you all the aforementioned information, plus information about when the message was deleted, accepted, declined, forwarded, and so on.

  Auto-Delete Sent Item automatically removes the message from your Sent Items folder after all recipients have deleted the item and emptied it from their Trash folders.

- **Return Notification**—This option specifies an action that will automatically happen when the recipient opens, accepts, deletes, or completes a message or calendar item.

  Mail Receipt means you'll receive an email message in your mailbox informing you of the event.

  Notify means you'll receive an onscreen notification message informing you of the event. (The Notify program must be running for this setting to work.)

  Notify and Mail means you receive both of these message types.

- **Internet Mail**—If you check this box, you can enable GroupWise to send an email when the receiving email system has successfully delivered the message. The receiving system needs to support this feature, known as *Extended SMTP (E-SMTP)* and *Delivery Status Notification (DSN)*.

The Appointment, Task, and Reminder Note tabs in the Send Options dialog box have the same configuration options as the Mail tab.

Security

GroupWise includes support for programs that encrypt and digitally sign messages. What is important to remember about message security is that the recipient must be able to understand and decrypt the messages you send.

FIGURE 11.10
The Mail tab allows you to set up default options for status information and return notification for email messages.

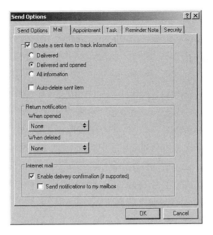

You need to set up your certificates using the Certificates option, described in Chapter 8. The default security options in this tab, shown in Figure 11.11, enable advanced security for all the messages you send and are as follows:

- **Conceal Subject**—This option prevents the message's subject line from appearing in the recipient's message list. The subject line appears only when the recipient opens the item. You should use this feature as an additional security measure when prying eyes may obtain information simply by seeing the subject line in the mailbox.

- **Require Password to Complete Routed Item**—For messages that are sent sequentially using a routing slip (covered in Chapter 3, "Messaging Fundamentals"), each user will be required to enter his or her GroupWise password to mark it "Completed."

- **Select a Security Service Provider**—GroupWise 7 supports several different security providers, with the Microsoft Enhanced Cryptographic Provider being the default. The other security providers allow you to use additional security devices to secure your mail. Check with your system administrator about what security provider you should use in your organization.

■ **Secure Item Options**—Using S/MIME, this option enables you to encrypt the contents of a message and/or digitally sign the message using a certificate. The message can then be sent to any recipient internally within your organization or over the Internet. Setting these options allows you to encrypt or sign every message sent. Otherwise, you can encrypt or sign specific messages by clicking on the Sign or Encrypt icons in the Send Toolbar when you are composing a message.

NOTE

The other security options on the Security tab of the Send Options dialog box enable you to configure the encryption and digital signatures of your messages. These options are available only if you have previously installed an encryption program that is GroupWise enabled.

FIGURE 11.11
The options in the Security tab establish the default encryption for messages.

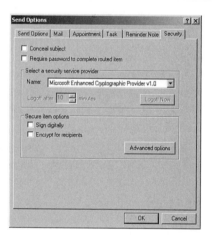

Many organizations provide certificates to use with GroupWise. Any certificate that supports the Microsoft Cryptography 1.0 API can be used with GroupWise; this includes Novell's Certificate Server. The Help, Help Topics, Index, S/MIME topic contains more information about S/MIME.

TIP

As discussed in Chapter 8, you can set message send options on a message-by-message basis. To set send options for an individual message, open the new message window, click the Send Options tab, click the Security button, and select the appropriate options.

If you set up security options for encryption and/or digital signatures, you will be prompted for your certificate password for *each* message you send. A portion of your certificate will also be sent with each message for decryption and signature verification.

Your geographic location determines the level of encryption allowed. For example, 128-bit encryption is only allowed in the United States. The Help, Help Topics, Index, S/MIME topic contains more information about encryption levels.

If you receive a message that has been encrypted or digitally signed, you will be prompted to accept a portion of the certificate. Clicking the Advanced Options button on the Security tab opens the Advanced Security Options dialog box, shown in Figure 11.12, which enables you to set the following options:

- **Encrypted Item**—Establishes your preferred encryption algorithm for messages. (The default is 40 bits.)
- **Signed Item**—Sends your message in clear text (default) and/or includes your certificate.
- **Certificate Revocation**—Checks incoming signed and encrypted messages for certificates that have been revoked, and sets the warning level. (This option is disabled by default.)
- **S/MIME Compliance Check**—Sets the version of S/MIME that you want as the standard for your messages. (Version 3 is the default.)

Regardless of whether you access these security options through Send Options or Security, or set them up for each message as you send it, the encryption and digital signatures add a powerful layer of security to the GroupWise messages you send and receive.

FIGURE 11.12

You use this dialog box to set up the advanced security options, including encryption.

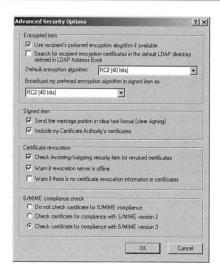

Security Options

When you double-click the Security icon, you see the Security Options dialog box. These options affect your entire mailbox. You can also set up the encryption and digital signature default options using the Send Options tab. Remember, this tab is a duplicate of the Security tab under Send Options.

Password

One of the most important security options is located on the Password tab, which is shown in Figure 11.13. You use this password to enter your mailbox when you start GroupWise and with the Web access gateway, routed item completion, and remote mode configuration.

To set a password on your mailbox, follow these steps:

1. Double-click the Security icon and click the Password tab once.

2. If you are changing a password, enter your old password in the Old Password field.

3. Type a password in the New Password field and in the Confirm New Password field. Click OK to set the password. The next time you start GroupWise, you must type in your password.

4. The Clear Password button is visible in remote or cache modes or if your GroupWise system is not configured for LDAP authentication. It is generally not a good idea to clear your GroupWise password. Clicking this button will clear your remote/cache or online password based on the mode you are in.

NOTE

Figure 11.13 shows that the administrator has enabled LDAP authentication. LDAP authentication allows you to use your network password (eDirectory password) to log in to GroupWise. If the change password interface is grayed out, the administrator has set your GroupWise system so that you cannot change your LDAP (or network) password through the GroupWise client. Your administrator should then provide an alternate method that you can use to change your network or GroupWise password in this case.

FIGURE 11.13
This dialog box controls the password for your mailbox.

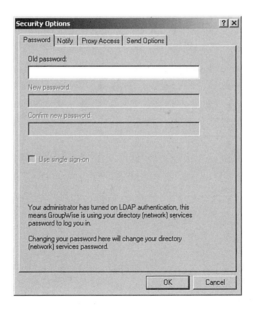

After you have set up your password, you can move ahead to configuring the Notify options.

Notify

The Notify tab enables you to use the Notify program to alert you when you receive a message or even when someone else receives a message. You can also be alerted by alarms set in your own calendar as well as in other people's calendars. As with the Proxy feature, the other person must grant you the right to subscribe to notifications or alarms within his or her GroupWise account. (See "Using the Proxy Feature" in Chapter 8 for instructions on granting access to your mailbox.) The Notify tab's options are shown in Figure 11.14.

FIGURE 11.14

You can use Notify to be alerted to other users' email messages and appointments.

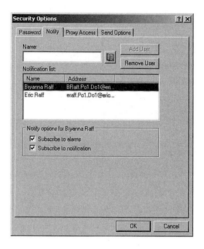

To receive notification when someone else receives a message (or to be alerted for another person's alarms), follow these steps:

1. On the Notify tab of the Security Options menu, click the Address Book icon to the right of the Name field. Select a user from the list and click OK. Alternatively, you can type the name of the user in the Name field and click Add User.

2. With that person's name highlighted in the Notification List, check the Subscribe to Alarms or Subscribe to Notification box. Notice that your name is already on the list because, by default, you are subscribed to your own alarms and notifications.

3. Click OK to apply your change. Your Notify program will now alert you for messages and/or alarms for both yourself and the other users you selected. Remember that in order to receive notifications when other

users get mail, these other users must grant you the rights to subscribe to their notifications and alarms.

In the next section, you establish the rights other people have to your mailbox through Proxy.

Proxy Access

The Proxy Access tab establishes the rights that other users have to your mailbox when they use Proxy. This process is explained in detail in Chapter 8.

Send Options

The Send Options tab of the Security Options dialog box is described in the "Security" section earlier in this chapter.

Certificates

Certificates are used to encrypt, decrypt, digitally sign, and verify messages both internally in your GroupWise system and over the Internet. The Certificates option enables you to set and manage certificates (yours and recipients') for use in GroupWise.

You use your public certificate to sign messages and to send to others to allow them to verify your signature on the message. Certificates have two elements: a public key and a private key. From the perspective of encrypting and sending a message, after you have imported another user's public certificate, you can encrypt and send messages to that user using the public key element from the certificate. When the other person receives the encrypted message, that user can use the private key element in his or her certificate to decrypt the message.

From the perspective of receiving an encrypted message, you must have already sent your certificate to the sender. That person can use his or her public key element of your certificate to encrypt the message, and you can use the private key element of your certificate to decrypt the message.

NOTE

A further discussion of how to obtain a certificate file and the details of public and private keys are beyond the scope of this book. For information on how to obtain a certificate, check with your system administrator if you need to encrypt or sign messages.

My Certificates

The My Certificates dialog box, shown in Figure 11.15, enables you to obtain a certificate, import an existing certificate, or view and manage the properties of your certificate. This dialog box shows a list of your certificates.

FIGURE 11.15
This dialog box allows you to configure your certificates to use in encryption.

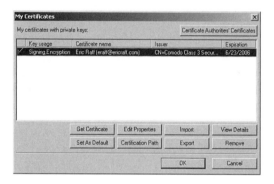

The My Certificates dialog box offers the following features:

- **Get Certificate**—Clicking this button starts your web browser and points to either a location defined by your system administrator or the Novell GroupWise Certificate page (www.novell.com/products/groupwise/certified.html), where you can get information on supported certificates.

- **Edit Properties**—This button enables you to edit the properties of your certificate.

- **Import**—Clicking this button enables you to browse to the file location of your certificate. Certificate files end with a `.p12` or `.pfx` extension. You also need to enter your certificate password. You need to select the Allow Export of Private Key in the Future option to export the private key portion of your certificate to a file for backup or other purposes.

  After you click OK in the Import My Certificate screen, you are asked to set the security level in the Private Key Container dialog box. Low grants others permission to use your certificate without notification, Medium (the default) requests your permission when the certificate is going to be used, and High requests your permission with your password.

- **View Details**—This button enables you to see the detailed information about your certificate.

- **Set As Default**—If you have multiple certificates, this button enables you to designate the default certificate for encrypting and signing messages.

- **Certification Path**—This button shows the list of Certificate Authorities (CAs) that provided you with the certificate.

- **Export**—This button enables you to export the selected certificate to a file.

- **Remove**—This button enables you to remove the selected certificate from use in GroupWise.

These options are needed for most certificate configurations.

NOTE

You must set a default certificate before you can sign a message. Figure 11.15 shows a green check mark next to the certificate. This check mark indicates that the certificate has been set as the default.

Certificate Authorities' Certificates

Clicking the Certificate Authorities' Certificates button in the upper-right corner brings up a dialog box that displays Intermediate and Root certificates. These are preconfigured lists of Certificate Authorities used worldwide to enable encryption and digital signatures. When you use certificates, they are issued by an authoritative source. This list shows the many trusted authorities that can issue certificates your computer will trust automatically.

Date Time Options

The Date & Time icon in the Options dialog box opens the Date Time Options dialog box, shown in Figure 11.16. This dialog box contains three option categories: Calendar, Busy Search, and Format.

Calendar

The Calendar options, shown in Figure 11.16, are as follows:

- **Month Display Option**—First of Week enables you to specify which day you want to display as the first day of the week in your Month Calendar view. Highlight Day visually distinguishes the selected days (such as weekends) on the Month Calendar view for quick viewing of the weekdays, for example. Show Week Number displays the number of the week on the left side of the Month Calendar view.

- **Appointment Options**—Include Myself on New Appointments automatically adds your name as a recipient of any new meeting you create. Display Appointment Length (Duration) displays the length of time the meeting will take in hours and minutes. Display Appointment Length (End Date and Time) displays the date and time of the meeting. Default Appointment Length specifies the default duration of the appointment messages you send.

- **Work Schedule (*Time Zone*)**—Start Time specifies the normal time your workday starts. End Time specifies the time your workday normally ends. The Work Days section specifies your scheduled workdays.

FIGURE 11.16
The Date Time Options dialog box allows you to set defaults for calendar components of GroupWise, such as your work schedule.

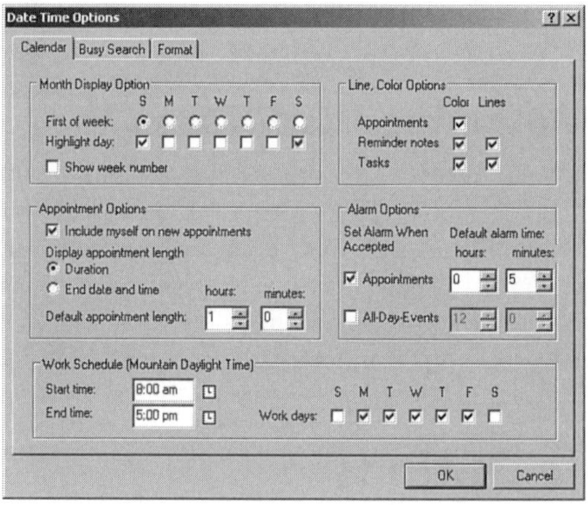

NOTE

The Work Schedule option displays a different setting when people use Busy Search to invite you to meetings. It also highlights the workdays and times in the Week Calendar view.

- **Line, Color Options**—These settings let you customize the appearance of appointments, reminder notes, and tasks in your calendar with lines and colors.

- **Alarm Options**—You use these options to configure whether alarms are set on appointments and all-day events. You can also set the default alarm interval, which defines how many minutes before an appointment or all-day event you will receive an alarm in GroupWise Notify.

After you have configured the main calendar options, you can set up defaults for using Busy Search.

Busy Search

The Busy Search tab options, shown in Figure 11.17, are as follows:

- **Appointment Length**—Specifies the default length for appointments you create with the Busy Search feature
- **Range and Time to Search**—Enables you to specify the default number of days you want to search along with the default times that will be searched
- **Days to Search**—Enables you to choose the default days you want included in the Busy Search

FIGURE 11.17
The Busy Search tab allows you to configure the default options for the Busy Search feature.

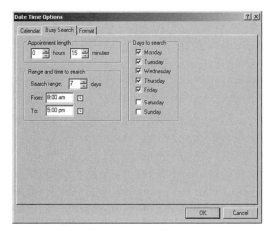

The Busy Search defaults will be used each time you perform a Busy Search when scheduling appointments.

Format

The Format tab options enable you to select your preferences for the display of dates and times. These options, shown in Figure 11.18, are as follows:

- **System Formats**—Enables you to set the default system time format as well as access the Windows Regional Settings dialog box

- **General GroupWise Format**—Enables you to specify a date and time display format that will be used as the default throughout the GroupWise screens

- **Specific GroupWise Formats**—Enables you to specify different formats for the GroupWise main window, properties, and file information

FIGURE 11.18
The Format tab allows you to establish the default date and time formats for use by GroupWise.

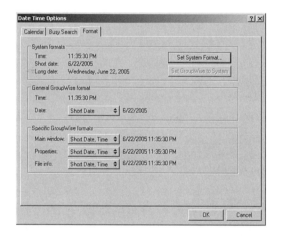

You set up the default behavior of GroupWise by using the option categories described in this section under Tools, Options.

Customizing the Home View

GroupWise 7 supports a new Home view. You can customize it so that it contains just the information you need. Figure 11.19 shows an example of a customized Home view that displays unread items, a summary calendar, and items that need to be followed up. This view allows you to easily see email that you need to read, items you need to follow up for the day, as well as your appointments from today through the next few days. You define the number of days; the default is 15.

FIGURE 11.19
The Home tab allows you to see all your relevant GroupWise information from one location.

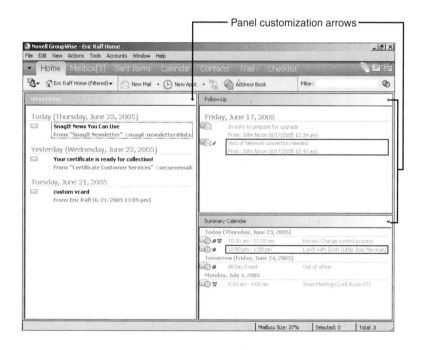

When you're working with the Home view, it is important to understand a new GroupWise 7 concept called *panels*. You can think of panels as areas that display any content that can be viewed through GroupWise. You could see all unread email in a panel, or all appointments, tasks, and notes for one day in a panel. Panels are extremely powerful and provide great flexibility. If you have ever wished that you could see data in a different view or have different types of data all displayed through one interface, panels are the answer. The great thing about panels is that you can place as many as practical in the Home view. This makes the Home view function the one place where you can pull all sorts of information together into one main window.

The first time you access the Home view, you see an introductory page that explains what the panel is and how you can customize it. From this page, you can go directly to the Home view or choose never to show this help screen again.

The Home view uses panels to display various content within GroupWise. This customizable feature allows you to place any content that the GroupWise client can display into it. You can drag and drop the various panels to different locations, allowing you to arrange the content in the order that best suits your needs. To drag a panel, simply click on the panel header and drag it to the desired location. You can also resize panels by holding the mouse over the border until your mouse cursor turns to a double line. Click and drag the panel size to the desired width or height; then release the mouse button.

The simplest way to add panels to the Home view is to click on the down arrow in the upper-right corner of any panel. Figure 11.19 highlights the arrows that you can use to customize the Home view. When you click one of these arrows, you have the following options:

- **Maximize**—This option maximizes the current panel to full screen. When a panel is maximized and you are able to click on its down arrow again, you can access a restore option, which places the panel back to its normal size. This option allows you to quickly enlarge a selected panel and then restore it to the original size again.

- **Edit**—This option takes you into an edit mode for the selected panel. From this interface, you can modify any of the aspects of a particular panel. For example, you can modify how content is displayed in a panel and how the information is presented inside the panel. The edit interface is very powerful, allowing you to place *any* GroupWise content inside a panel.

- **Close**—This option removes a panel from the Home view. It does not delete the panel but simply removes it. You can add the panel back later if you want.

- **Add Panel**—This option enables you to add an existing panel to the Home view. You can then drag the panel to the location you desire. From the Add panel interface, you can also create new panels that have descriptive names for what they will contain. This feature allows you to have a collection of panels that pull display information out of GroupWise in the Home view.

- **One Column**—This option shows all panels stacked vertically. You can place as many panels into this One Column view as desired.

- **Two Column**—This option shows two columns each, allowing you to place any number of panels in the column. This view is recommended because it allows you to divide the screen in more ways.

To manage all your various panels from one interface, you can use the Customize Panels interface. You access this utility by right-clicking the Home tab and selecting Properties. Next, select the Display tab. From here, you can click on the Customize Panels button. Figure 11.20 displays the Customize Panels interface.

FIGURE 11.20

The Customize Panels interface allows you to manage all your panels from one interface.

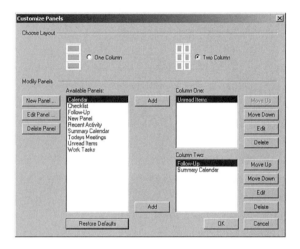

The Customize Panels interface provides a central interface into your Home panel. From here, you can delete, modify, or create panels; modify the layout of the Home view; and adjust the arrangement of the panels. The Available Panels column lists all the defined panels you can add to the Home view. GroupWise 7 includes several predefined panels that help pull common information together for you.

Creating custom panels is one of the most powerful features of the GroupWise 7 client. When you create a panel, you can pull information and filter it inside the panel so that you can see exactly what you need within a panel. Figure 11.21 displays the new Create Panel interface.

FIGURE 11.21
The new Create Panel interface.

The components of the new Create Panel interface are as follows:

- **Name the New Panel**—Here, you provide a descriptive name of what content the panel will display.

- **Choose Folder or Address Book**—In this section, you define what content will be presented in the new panel. You can select any existing GroupWise folder or address book.

- **Choose Display Settings**—This drop-down list enables you to define how the contents inside the panel will be displayed. You can choose Details, Calendar, Checklist, or Discussion thread.

- **More Display Settings**—This button displays additional display options that you can define for the panel. This interface provides all display options that are available and is a powerful feature, allowing you great flexibility as to how the content is displayed.

- **Choose Filter**—This button displays the GroupWise Filter dialog box. They are the same filter options that you can define in other places for GroupWise. You could use the filter options to see only the desired content in a panel.

Customizing the Nav Bar

By default, the Navigation Bar (Nav bar) contains the following tabs: Home, Mailbox, Calendar, Sent Items, and Contacts. At the right of the Nav bar, there are also icons to display the folder list, QuickViewer, and main menu. You can customize the Nav bar by adding additional folders. To customize it, right-click anywhere on it and select Customize Nav Bar. Figure 11.22 displays the Nav bar customization screen.

FIGURE 11.22
The Nav Bar customization screen.

Checking any folder on this screen places that folder on the Nav bar. From this interface, you can also change the color scheme of the GroupWise client.

TIP

You can add a folder to the Nav bar and then set it to be viewed as a panel. You then have created the equivalent of a new Home view that can contain various panels. You manage the panels just as you would the panels in the Home view.

You can also change the font size and color scheme of the Nav bar. Right-clicking the Nav bar gives you the options to change the text color and font size. The Reset Nav Bar option resets the Nav bar font and color to the default scheme settings. Resetting the Nav bar does not remove any additional folders that you may have added.

Customizing the Toolbar

You can customize the Toolbar to include the functions and features you use frequently, and you can arrange them in the order that makes the most sense to you.

Toolbars can appear in many different GroupWise screens. You have the option of seeing a Toolbar for each message view and for the main GroupWise screen, and you can set different options for each.

To customize any Toolbar, right-click the Toolbar and select Customize Toolbar. The Toolbar Properties screen appears, as shown in Figure 11.23.

FIGURE 11.23
Customizing GroupWise toolbars.

The Show tab enables you to select what should be displayed on the Toolbar—only the picture or both the picture and text. If you prefer larger icons, select the Picture and Text option that is larger in size. You can also specify one or multiple rows. In addition, you can select whether to display the Display Mode drop-down list and Item and Folder context toolbars in the Toolbar. By default, these items are not displayed.

The Customize tab, shown in Figure 11.24, enables you to specify which GroupWise features appear on the Toolbar.

FIGURE 11.24

The Customize tab allows you to place the buttons you use most often on the Toolbar for quick, one-click access.

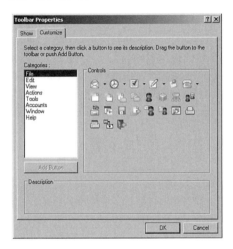

Follow these steps to add a menu option to the Toolbar:

1. Click the category the feature belongs to (for example, the Tools category contains options for the Address Book and Hit the Road tools).

2. Double-click the button you want on the Toolbar. The button then appears on the Toolbar.

3. Click and drag the button to your desired location on the Toolbar.

In the Toolbar Properties screen, you can arrange the existing Toolbar buttons by clicking and dragging them to the desired locations. To remove a button from the Toolbar, click the button and drag it off the Toolbar.

Customizing Your Folders

In Chapter 5, "Message Management," you saw how to use folders to help organize your messages. By adjusting the properties of the folders in your mailbox, you can arrange to see folder contents when a folder is opened, see who has access to the messages in the folder (if anyone), and specify which columns are displayed. Each folder can be customized individually. For example, the mailbox can be set up to display only the Subject and From fields, and the Sent Items folder can be set up to display Subject, Opened Status, and Date fields.

Property Sets

Even though you can set up a parent/child folder structure, folder properties are set for each folder individually. These folder properties are grouped into the following sets:

- **General**—Holds general information about the folder, such as the owner and a description
- **Display**—Configures folder settings to determine how messages are displayed in the folder and what columns are used
- **Sharing**—Determines access to the messages in the folder

NOTE

The people who share a particular parent folder do not necessarily share the sub-folders under the folder. Shared access to folders is set for the individual folder.

The properties available for folders differ, depending on the type of folder you are configuring. All folders contain the General and Display tabs. The Trash folder contains a Cleanup Property tab.

TIP

When you right-click the Cabinet, you can select Sort Subfolders to quickly alpha-betize the first-level subfolders. To sort a set of nested folders, select Sort Subfolders from the parent folder.

User-created folders contain a unique tab called Sharing. The Sharing tab enables you to share the folders with other GroupWise users.

To display or change the properties of a folder, simply right-click the folder and choose Properties.

GENERAL

The General folder properties, shown in Figure 11.25, are as follows:

- **Type**—Describes the type of folder: Personal, Calendar, Mailbox, and so on
- **Owner**—Specifies the creator of the folder
- **Contains**—Provides a summary of the folder's contents
- **Description**—Gives a general description of the folder

After you have configured the general options for a folder, you can customize the display settings.

FIGURE 11.25
The General tab contains the name, owner, and other information about the folder.

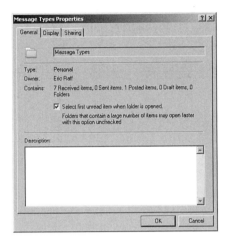

DISPLAY

Figure 11.26 shows the Display tab of a personal folder. This interface configures the default display options for the selected folder. Every time the folder is accessed, the settings you make in the Display tab of the folder properties will be active.

Here's a list of the settings you'll find in the Display tab:

- **Setting Name**—You can choose from this drop-down list of preconfigured folder settings.

- **Description**—This field contains a description of this group of folder settings.

- **View By**—This option allows you to set the display to the Message Details, Message Thread, or Calendar format for the items in this folder. The Summary and Columns options to the right are new in GroupWise 7. The Columns view is the traditional view of items. The Summary view shows each item type on two lines—one with the sender, one with the subject and date. This setup may be desired if you have the QuickViewer on the right because you can have more space to see the From and Subject lines of an item.

- **Sort By**—This option determines a piece of information about the messages by which all messages in this folder will be sorted (for example, Date, From, and so on).

- **Show Group Labels**—New to GroupWise 7 is the ability to group messages or items together based on the date. This option places all mail on each day under a group label of the day.

- **Hide Non-Checklist Items**—This option is active if you have the View By option set to Checklist. You can have checklist items and non-checklist items in the same folder. Enabling this setting hides the non-checklist items in the folder.

- **Override QuickViewer Visibility**—This option allows you to override your general QuickViewer settings. For example if you generally use the QuickViewer, but you want to disable it on a particular folder, you can check the option to override QuickViewer visibility. Alternatively, if you generally do not have the QuickViewer enabled, you can check both options to override and show the QuickViewer. This would allow you to use the QuickViewer on just the selected folders that you want.

FIGURE 11.26
The Display tab allows you to customize the viewing and sorting options for the folder.

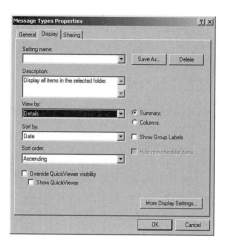

Clicking the More Display Settings button opens a new window that allows you to define additional display options. They include item source, item type, and a date range. The date range is a handy feature that lets you see only messages between a date range. It uses the current date to determine how many days in the past and future to display content.

After you have set up the display options, you can establish shared folders.

SHARING

Sharing options for folders determine who has access to the messages inside of them. Chapter 5 discusses how to use shared folders in detail.

These settings allow you to customize your folders.

Adding Columns to Folders

When viewing the contents of a folder, you can add or remove columns. This enhances your ability to see additional information about an item. The best way to manage which columns are displayed is to right-click in any column and select the desired columns. GroupWise 7 supports the addition of many different columns. The options from the QuickMenu are only a few of them. To see all the available columns, click the More Columns option. Figure 11.27 displays the interface used to add additional columns.

FIGURE 11.27
The Select Columns interface allows you to add additional columns to a folder.

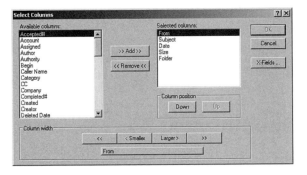

Here's a list of the available options in the Select Columns interface:

- **Available Columns**—This option lists all available columns that GroupWise 7 supports. If you are not sure what a particular column may represent, go ahead and add it to the Selected Columns side to see if you can see any valuable information from it. Remember that to remove a column, you can drag and drop it from of the column heading section. Your mouse will turn from a hand icon into a trash can icon when doing this.

- **Selected Columns**—This option lists the columns that are presently being displayed. Use the Add or Remove buttons to add or remove columns to the selected columns list.

- **Column Width**—This is a crude interface for adjusting the column width. It is much simpler to simply place the mouse at the column edge, where it will change to a large plus icon, and then click and drag the column widths to the desired size.

- **Column Position**—Here, you can adjust the position or order that the columns are displayed in. You can also drag and drop columns to the desired order to change their positions.

- **X-Fields**—This new option for GroupWise 7 allows you to create columns that display the X-Fields that are placed in received Internet messages. X-Fields can contain a wide variety of information from the mail client that sent a message to the spam score of a message. Clicking on the X-Fields button allows you to create a new X-Field that you can then add to your list of visible columns. To see what X-Fields you may want to add, you can open a received message that was sent through the Internet. Then click on the Message Source tab. From here, you can see the X-Fields. They begin with *X-*. Some common X-Field names are X-Mailer, X-Spam-Score, X-Spam-Flag, and X-Priority. Check with your system administrator to see whether your organization adds X-Fields to inbound Internet email that may interest you.

NOTE

You can sort on only one column at a time.

Show Appointment As

The Show Appointment As option enables you to specify an appointment with different "busy properties." For example, when you create a new appointment, you can set it up as a "tentative" appointment that can be scheduled over, or you can set up a period of time (an appointment) as time "out of the office." People who perform a Busy Search will see the different types of appointments and have more information about your schedule than just "busy."

Free, Tentative, Busy, and Out Of Office are the four options you can choose to assign to an existing appointment in the calendar. To set this option, highlight the appointment, choose Show Appointment As from the Actions menu, and select one of the four choices, as shown in Figure 11.28.

TIP

Right-clicking an appointment brings up a QuickMenu with the Show
Appointment As option available.

FIGURE 11.28
You can show your appointments as Free, Tentative, Busy, or Out Of Office with this
option.

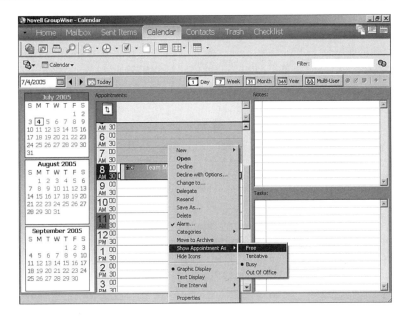

Headers

You can change the look and feel of the headers in GroupWise (the area
between the Toolbars and the messages and calendar information).

By placing your mouse pointer in a header area and right-clicking, you can
choose from options to change the header color, text color, and font size.
This makes GroupWise much more readable and provides more contrast with
different colors.

If you make a change to the header that you don't want anymore, you
can choose Reset to Defaults on the QuickMenu, which you access by right-
clicking.

Other Customization Tips and Tricks

The following sections describe a few other quick and easy things you can do to customize the way the GroupWise 7 client behaves. We hope you will find these suggestions helpful.

Change Attachment Window View

You can modify the way attachments are viewed in the Attachment window. To set the Attachment view option, open a message and then right-click in the Attachment window. Select the View option and then choose to view the attachments as large or small icons in List or Detail view. When you choose a view, the GroupWise client will remember the setting as you work with attachments in other messages.

View the Mailbox as a Checklist

You can view your mailbox in the checklist format. This allows you to drag items to the top of your item list, where they can be easily accessed or act as a reminder for you to follow up on the item. To enable this, right-click your mailbox and select Properties. Under the View By drop-down list on the Display tab, select Checklist. Click OK and save the change. At the top of your mailbox, you will now see a line item that says to "Drag items here to add them to the checklist." You can now drag email up to this area, and an arrow will appear representing where the checklist item will be placed. Figure 11.29 displays the Mailbox folder being viewed as a checklist.

Control From, To, CC, and BC Layout

You can control how the From, To, CC, and BC fields are displayed when reading mail or through the QuickViewer. By right-clicking inside the header bar when reading messages, you can choose from the options Show Multiple Recipients, Separate TO/CC/BC, or Align Colons. Figure 11.30 displays this QuickMenu. If you uncheck the option Separate To/CC/BC, the To, CC, and BC fields will all be displayed on the same horizontal line, which decreases the size of the header information.

FIGURE 11.29
Viewing your mailbox as a checklist.

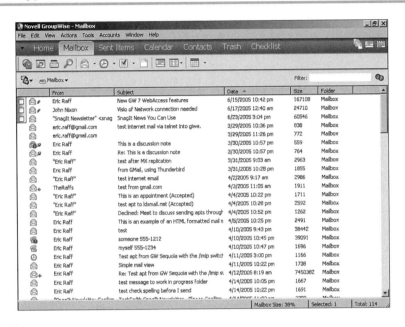

FIGURE 11.30
Customizing options for the QuickViewer and item read headers.

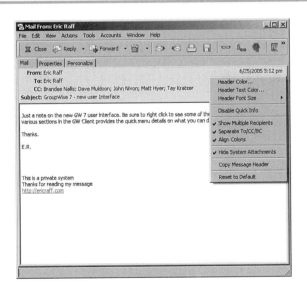

Customize Calendar Background Colors

You can change the background colors in the calendar. To do this, open the calendar and then right-click anywhere in the appointments, tasks, notes, or all-day events sections. Select the Background Color option. From here, you can change the background color for all-day events, appointments, reminder notes, and tasks. You can also disable any background colors so all calendar items are displayed on a white background. Another setting in the Background Color Settings is the option to remove the lines separating items in the Notes and Tasks windows.

Creating Find Results Folders

You can create folders that perform dynamic searches for any item type you want. This capability is helpful if you want to be able to click on a folder and have it dynamically locate all messages from or to a certain person, or that have a particular word in the email, or that exist in a particular category. To create Find Results folders, simply right-click on any of your existing folders or on the Cabinet, and select the New Folder option. From here, you can specify a Find Results folder, and either choose from a list of predefined Find Results folders or create your own custom Find Results folder. Give the folder a name, and then define what you want to query when you select the folder.

Using Rules to Categorize Messages

Using the GroupWise 7 client, you can create a rule that automatically categorizes messages that meet certain criteria. This capability may be helpful if you want to apply a category to all specific messages you receive on a certain topic or from a certain user. To do this, create a new rule (Tools, Rules), and in the Action option, you can select Categorize. You can then select from any of your defined categories, and any matches to the rule will automatically be categorized for you. You can also create new categories from this interface making. Remember that the GroupWise rule processing engine is not dependent on the GroupWise client running and is handled by the GroupWise server.

Summary

In this chapter, we discussed the capabilities for customizing your GroupWise program—from setting your GroupWise defaults to customizing the look, feel, and content of the Home view, Toolbars, headers, and folders.

This chapter included specific examples, and we covered many of the possible customization capabilities in GroupWise to allow you to configure the program to your unique tastes.

In Chapter 12, "GroupWise on a PDA," we describe how to access GroupWise on a personal digital assistant (PDA).

CHAPTER 12

GroupWise on a PDA

The use of personal digital assistant (PDA) devices today is widespread. PDAs offer great benefits because these simple and compact devices provide access to your data. PDAs also support most of the message types that GroupWise supports, so naturally, you want to keep your PDA in sync with your GroupWise data. This chapter covers two aspects of using a PDA with GroupWise. The first method outlines how to keep the data in sync between your GroupWise mailbox and the PDA. To synchronize with GroupWise, your PDA must either be a Palm OS or Pocket PC/Windows Mobile–based PDA.

The second method explains how you can access your GroupWise mailbox from a PDA using a mini web browser on the PDA and a connection to the Internet or your corporate network. In this case, your PDA could be a telephone, Palm OS, Pocket PC/Windows Mobile, or any other such device that allows you to connect to the Internet.

It is important that you understand the difference between *accessing* and *synchronizing* when talking about PDAs. GroupWise allows you *access*, meaning that if your PDA can open a web browser and you see web pages, it can access your GroupWise information.

Synchronizing is a software-based means to copy the information in your GroupWise mailbox to your PDA, where you can access it regardless of whether you are connected to the Internet. You accomplish this by using the GroupWise PDA Connect program or third-party software tools.

Synchronizing GroupWise with a PDA Device

Novell provides a PDA synchronization engine called PDA Connect. This program sits between your GroupWise mailbox and the PDA Synchronization software, such as Microsoft's ActiveSync or Palm's HotSync Manager. This allows you to use the PDA's native synchronization program in conjunction with the PDA Connect program. Several third-party programs also provide enhanced synchronization methods such as over-the-air (OTA) synchronization. Check with your GroupWise administrator to see what handheld sync utility your organization uses.

The following sections discuss how to use the GroupWise PDA Connect program with a Pocket PC PDA. If you use a Palm OS PDA, the concepts are similar except that you need to use Palm's HotSync Manager instead of Microsoft's ActiveSync program.

Prerequisites

Before installing the GroupWise PDA Connect program, you need to meet the following prerequisites:

- Ensure that Microsoft ActiveSync is installed for the Pocket PC 2000, 2002, or 2003 or Palm's HotSync Manager is installed for the Palm OS 4.x or 5.x.

- Ensure that the GroupWise 6.5.3 or newer or GroupWise 7.x client is installed on the workstation. You can check your GroupWise version by choosing Help, About GroupWise.

- Ensure that you are not synchronizing any mail item types in Microsoft Outlook (such as email, calendar, tasks, or notes) with ActiveSync, PocketMirror, or Palm Desktop. You can set ActiveSync to sync files to your handheld. (You do not even need to have the Microsoft Outlook program installed for the GroupWise PDA Connect program to work.)

Installing GroupWise PDA Connect

Before synchronizing GroupWise with your PDA device, you must first obtain the GroupWise PDA Connect program. This program ships with the GroupWise 7 client and is also available from Novell's website. First, check with your GroupWise administrator to see whether your organization has a standard deployment method for this utility or where to obtain this utility.

Alternatively, you can download the GroupWise PDA Connect program from http://download.novell.com. Search for "GroupWise PDA Connect" to locate and download this free utility.

NOTE

The PDA Connect program is updated periodically. You can find the latest version on Novell's download page.

After you have downloaded and extracted the program, you can run setup.exe to begin the installation. Follow these steps to complete the installation:

1. Agree to the license agreement and select the desired destination folder.

2. Select the needed translator components for your device. You can select between Palm OS Devices and Pocket PC Devices. If the dependent ActiveSync or HotSync Manager is not installed, you will be warned that the installation cannot continue.

3. Select whether you plan to synchronize your PDA with your GroupWise account from a single PC or multiple PCs. If you select a single PC, the synchronization process will be faster each time you sync. If you select multiple PCs, a full synchronization must occur during each sync session. Single PC is usually the recommended option to select.

4. Review the summary screen and click Next to begin the file copy process. When this process is complete, click Finish to close the installation for the GroupWise PDA Connect program.

Now that you have installed the GroupWise PDA Connect program, you can configure it to synchronize your GroupWise information with your handheld device.

Launching and Configuring GroupWise PDA Connect

Installing the PDA Connect program places an icon labeled GroupWise PDA Connect on your Windows desktop. The first time you launch the GroupWise PDA Connect program, you need to configure it. Figure 12.1 displays the GroupWise PDA Connect program interface.

FIGURE 12.1
The GroupWise PDA Connect interface.

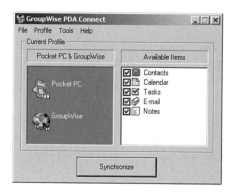

Under the General tab, you can set the following preferences:

- **Current Profile**—The PDA Connect program uses profiles to store all the information detailing how to synchronize your PDA with GroupWise. You can create multiple profiles as discussed later in this chapter. The current profile is listed in this window.

- **Available Items**—This section lists which components will be synchronized with the PDA.

- **Synchronize**—Clicking the Synchronize button initiates a sync of the selected items in the Available Items list.

The main menu contains the File, Profile, Tools, and Help menu options. From the File menu, you have the following options:

- **Force Full Synchronization**—This menu option expands to reflect each item type that you can synchronize. In a full synchronization, all information about the selected item type(s) is synchronized. This is in contrast to the default synchronization, which includes a specific date range of information to sync. (The default is seven days.) A full synchronization will take longer to complete because all items are being compared and synchronized.

- **Confirm Record Deletions**—This toggle option allows you to confirm record deletions that may occur. This option, which is enabled by default, allows you to make sure that items are not deleted without your confirming them first. It is recommended that you leave this option on until you are comfortable with what may be deleted. You can then disable this option to save time.

■ **Synchronize**—This option initiates a sync of the selected items from the Available Items list on the main screen.

The Tools menu provides access to the log files. You can configure log settings and schedule automatic synchronization to occur at defined intervals.

The Help menu contains in-depth information about each component in the PDA Connect program.

Working with Profiles

Profiles contain all the settings relevant to the way information is synchronized between the PDA and GroupWise. You manage profiles through the Profile menu option on the main menu. From the Profile menu, you can create a new profile, edit profiles, manage the current profile settings, rename the current profile, remove the current profile (if multiple profiles are defined), or select which profiles will be active. So what exactly does a profile contain? The best way to answer this question is to edit a profile and go through each of the available options. Figure 12.2 shows a profile called Pocket PC and GroupWise settings.

FIGURE 12.2
Settings of a Pocket PC and GroupWise profile.

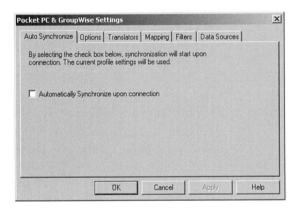

AUTO SYNCHRONIZE

A profile's Auto Synchronize tab allows you to specify that synchronization will take place as soon as the PDA Connect program is run. After you have defined and configured your settings, you will probably want to enable this setting.

OPTIONS

The Options tab defines the type of synchronization and the way conflict resolution is handled. Figure 12.3 shows the Options interface.

FIGURE 12.3
The Options tab of a profile.

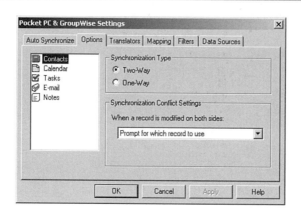

You can choose from the following options:

- **Synchronization Type**—You can select between Two-Way and One-Way synchronization for each item type (contacts, calendar, tasks, email, and notes). Two-Way sync will sync updated items in GroupWise and on the PDA in both directions. One-Way sync will take only items on either the GroupWise or PDA and sync them in one direction. When you select One-Way sync, you can define what side (GroupWise or PDA) records will sync from. Remember that you can define the synchronization type for each item type, allowing you to sync contacts in Two-Way mode but email in One-Way mode.

- **Synchronization Conflict Settings**—If an item type is set to Two-Way sync, you can define what happens when a particular record has been modified on both sides. You can choose to be prompted or to have the GroupWise or PDA side override the other side. Select your desired action from the drop-down list.

- **One-Way Synchronization Settings**—If One-Way sync is selected for an item type, this interface is displayed. From here, you can define what side is authoritative and whether changes on the other side will be ignored or overwritten.

NOTE

A full synchronization will override your one-way settings. This also applies to the full synchronization that takes place the first time you sync your device. You should not use filters when using one-way sync because duplicate records may occur. Filters are discussed later in this chapter.

TRANSLATORS

The Translators tab allows you to configure each translator setting. A translator is the software component that translates the data between the Pocket PC or Palm OS device and the GroupWise PDA Connect program. Figure 12.4 shows a Pocket PC and GroupWise translator.

FIGURE 12.4
The Translators tab from within a Pocket PC profile.

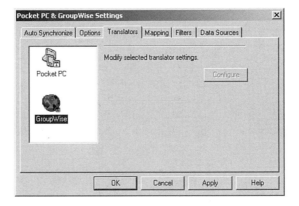

If you highlight the Pocket PC translator and click Configure, you can leave deleted email on your PDA device. If you select this option, be aware of the additional space required on your PDA to store all your email. There are no translator settings to configure for GroupWise, so the Configure button appears dimmed.

MAPPING

The Mapping tab allows you to control which fields in GroupWise map to the PDA fields and vice versa. This powerful feature ensures that as new fields are added to GroupWise or the PDA, you can map them appropriately. Mappings exist for each item type that can be synchronized. To manage the mappings, select the desired item type and then click the Mapping button. Figure 12.5 displays the contacts' mappings.

FIGURE 12.5
Available mappings for contacts.

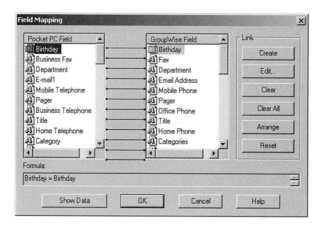

You can manage all the mappings if desired, including creating and editing mappings. Clicking the Show Data button at the bottom displays the data in each field. This makes it easy to see the types of data contained in each field. For detailed information on managing mappings, click the Help button.

FILTERS

The Filter tab allows you to define filters for each item type. Filters allow you to sync only the data that you want for each item type. For example, if you care only about phone and email addresses for contacts, you can create a filter that synchronizes only this information for you. Filtering can speed up the sync process as well as save memory on the PDA. The types of filters you can use depend on the item type you have selected. Figure 12.6 displays the Filter interface.

A common filter that you may want to modify is the age limit of email to synchronize. To access this filter, select the Email item type and click on the Translator-Defined Attributes link to the right. You can then set filters on your Inbox, Sent Items, and Drafts (Work In Progress) folders. For more information about the use of filters, click the Help button.

DATA SOURCES

The Data Sources tab allows you to set the GroupWise source folder that corresponds to each item type in GroupWise. For example, if you want to synchronize a personal folder into your mailbox on the PDA, you could define the source for the GroupWise mail to your personal folder. Figure 12.7 displays the Data Sources interface. For more information on modifying the data sources, click the Help button.

FIGURE 12.6
You can filter information from synchronizing to or from the PDA.

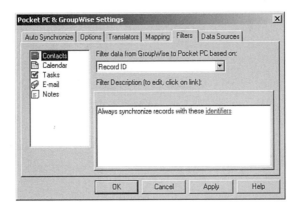

FIGURE 12.7
You can modify the source of data for the various components that will synchronize with a PDA.

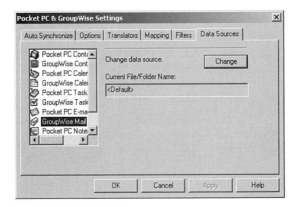

You can now begin synchronizing data with your PDA device. Remember that to sync your PDA, the GroupWise client and your sync software (ActiveSync or HotSync Manager) must be running.

Next, we show you how to access your mailbox from a PDA or wireless device.

Accessing GroupWise on a Wireless Device

The proliferation of wireless handheld devices has brought the power of the Internet to the palm of your hand. GroupWise has taken advantage of this handheld mobility by providing a WebAccess interface that enables you to manage your GroupWise mailbox. Therefore, you can perform many of the most common GroupWise tasks from the convenience and portability of your handheld device.

The following sections provide an overview describing how to access your GroupWise mailbox and perform basic messaging tasks using your PDA and the special PDA version of WebAccess.

System Requirements

Before you can use your handheld device to access GroupWise, you must meet the following requirements:

- You must have a PDA, wireless phone, or other handheld device that supports the Wireless Access Protocol (WAP). The device must have a microbrowser that uses Handheld Device Markup Language (HDML) 3.0 (or higher) or Wireless Markup Language (WML) 1.1 (or higher). The device must have wireless access to the Internet (or it must be able to access the Internet through a host PC to which the device can be connected). If you have a Palm OS device, your device must either support Web Clipping Applications (PQAs) or standard browsing. All versions of the Windows CE or Microsoft Pocket PC OS are supported. Basically, almost all new handheld/PDA/SmartPhones will be able to access GroupWise from their built-in browsers.

- You must have an account on the GroupWise system with a password set on your mailbox.

Accessing Your GroupWise Mailbox

To access your GroupWise mailbox with your handheld device, follow these steps:

1. Validate that you have a wireless connection and run the web browser on your device.

2. Enter the address (URL) to the PDA WebAccess page. Your system administrator must provide this address to you. The GroupWise login screen appears, as shown in Figure 12.8.

FIGURE 12.8
The login screen requests your login ID and GroupWise password.

3. Enter your GroupWise user ID and your mailbox password and then tap Login. The main GroupWise screen appears, as shown in Figure 12.9.

On the main GroupWise screen, you can access the major GroupWise features. The features corresponding to each of the icons shown in Figure 12.9 are described in the following sections.

TIP

Every screen that you access from this main screen has a link at the top labeled Main Menu. This link always returns you to the main GroupWise screen shown in Figure 12.9.

331

FIGURE 12.9
This PDA WebAccess screen provides access to the most common GroupWise functions.

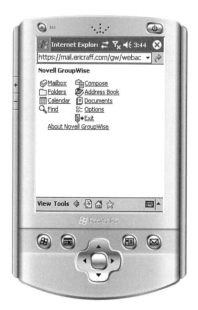

Mailbox

Tap the Mailbox link to open your GroupWise mailbox, as shown in Figure 12.10.

You can open any message simply by tapping the Subject line. You can perform other operations by tapping in the check box and then tapping on the button at the top of the screen.

NOTE

If you use the Change Folder option to access a folder other than your Mailbox folder and later return to the main menu, the last folder you accessed will be listed on the main screen, instead of the main Mailbox folder. If you use the Back button on your browser, the main Mailbox folder will still be displayed.

FIGURE 12.10
The PDA WebAccess mailbox enables you to manage your GroupWise messages.

Folders

The Folders link takes you to a view of your GroupWise system folders and also your Cabinet, as shown in Figure 12.11.

You can expand and collapse the Folders view by tapping the plus or minus icon or the up or down arrow (depending on your WebAccess configuration). To access the items in a folder, simply tap that folder.

When you are viewing the contents of a folder, you can return to the folder display by tapping the Change Folder link at the top of the screen.

Calendar

The Calendar link takes you to the Calendar view for the current day and displays the day's appointments, notes, and tasks, as shown in Figure 12.12.

Click the Goto Date link to access the appointments, notes, and tasks for a different date.

FIGURE 12.11
Tap the Folders link to view your GroupWise system and Cabinet folders.

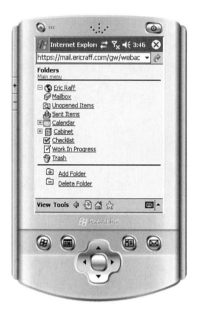

Find

The Find option is a very useful tool for the wireless WebAccess client. It allows you to quickly locate information contained in your GroupWise mailbox based on text in the Subject line, names in the From line, the item type, the item source (received, posted, or sent), or the folder or folders in which the item might be located.

Compose

The Compose button enables you to create GroupWise messages. When you tap Compose, you see the screen shown in Figure 12.13.

By default, you create a mail message when you tap Compose. Tap a different item type button to compose a different GroupWise message type.

You can tap the Address Book to locate the message recipients. Tap any of the text fields to input the subject and message using your handheld device's preferred text-entry method.

Tap the Send button to send the message.

FIGURE 12.12
The Calendar view shows the current day's appointments, notes, and tasks.

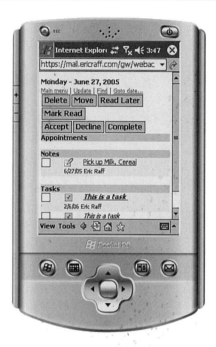

Address Book

The Address Book option brings up a search screen that allows you to search for individuals in the GroupWise system or personal address books, as shown in Figure 12.14. Enter a first name and/or a last name (the asterisk is acceptable as a wildcard character). Then select the Search option or scroll down and specify how many names to display in the results.

You can tap the down arrow in the Address Books field and select any of your personal address books you have configured. When a personal address book (such as Frequent Contacts) is active, you can tap the Add Entry icon at the bottom of the screen to add contacts to the personal address book.

FIGURE 12.13
The Compose link allows you to create GroupWise appointments, tasks, notes, and phone messages.

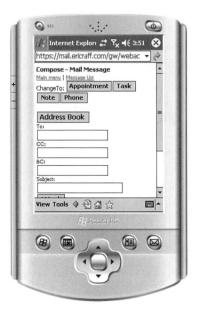

Documents

The Documents option on the main menu brings up the Document Search function, which enables you to search for documents in all available document libraries, as shown in Figure 12.15.

You can search in all document fields by selecting the Anywhere option, or you can search by subject or author. You display all available document libraries by scrolling down the screen. Place a check mark in the box next to any library that might contain the document you want to locate.

FIGURE 12.14
The Address Book option enables you to search the GroupWise system or personal address books.

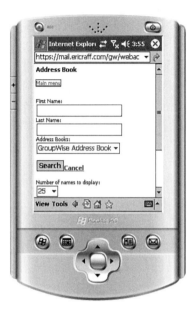

NOTE

Your PDA must have document manipulation software to view or edit documents.

Options

The Options link allows you to set a new GroupWise password on your mailbox. To do so, you enter your old password, enter a new password, and then confirm your new password.

Exit

The Exit button on the main GroupWise screen terminates your GroupWise session and returns you to the main GroupWise WebAccess login screen.

FIGURE 12.15
Use the Document Search option to find documents in GroupWise document libraries.

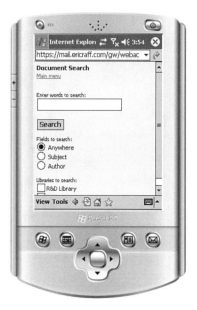

Summary

In this chapter, we discussed how to synchronize and access your GroupWise information from a PDA or handheld device. You can synchronize your PDA with GroupWise, allowing you to access your contacts, tasks, notes, mail, and appointments offline, or you can access your mailbox from a handheld device through WebAccess and the special handheld interface.

CHAPTER 13

GroupWise WebAccess

The WebAccess version of the GroupWise client enables you to access your GroupWise mailbox from your web browser, no matter where you happen to be in the world. With WebAccess, you can check your messages or send new GroupWise messages, process incoming messages, check your calendar, schedule appointments, send tasks, and more. You can use WebAccess to do almost all the GroupWise tasks you would do from the regular GroupWise client.

NOTE

The GroupWise system must be properly configured before you can access your mailbox from your web browser. Ask your system administrator whether your GroupWise system supports WebAccess.

In this chapter, we don't cover the concepts behind the topics discussed here (for example, when you should use a task in the calendar instead of an appointment); you can refer to earlier chapters for additional background information. Instead, we focus on how to perform these tasks in the WebAccess client.

Some functions are available in the Windows client program, but you can't access them using GroupWise WebAccess. They include discussion thread views, filters, POP3/IMAP/NNTP access, multiple calendar print options, address book sharing, and the capability to resend items.

GroupWise 7 WebAccess has six major new features:

- New look and feel to better match the GroupWise Windows client experience
- Drag-and-drop functionality
- Right-click context-sensitive drop-down menus

- Name completion when composing items
- Support for creating posted item types
- Folder management including shared folders

You will find that the GroupWise WebAccess client is a powerful, quick, and easy-to-use interface into your GroupWise information.

Running WebAccess

To run the WebAccess GroupWise client, simply launch your web browser and go to the web address (also known as a URL) established for your organization's GroupWise WebAccess. Ask your administrator or help desk for the web address you should use. When you access your WebAccess address, you encounter the login screen shown in Figure 13.1.

FIGURE 13.1
The WebAccess login page prompts you for your mailbox ID and password.

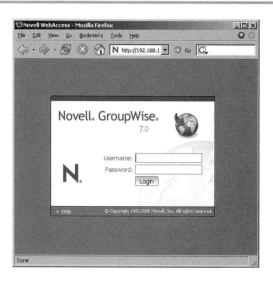

Enter your GroupWise user ID and your mailbox password (which is required) and click the Login button. The WebAccess main screen, shown in Figure 13.2, appears automatically. You can access all the messaging features of GroupWise from the main screen.

FIGURE 13.2

The WebAccess main screen gives you one-click access to most functions you will need.

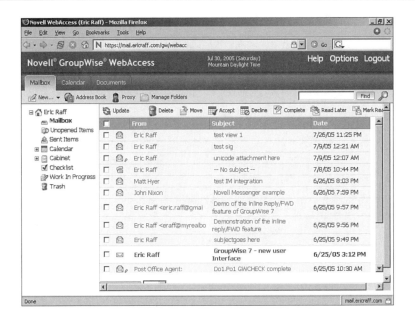

The basic layout of the WebAccess client interface consists of tabs across the top that will take you directly to your mailbox, calendar, or documents. Below these tabs are general actions that you can perform, including creating new item types, accessing the address book, gaining proxy access to users, or managing your folders. This interface provides a clean, intuitive environment to work with the content in your mailbox.

The GroupWise WebAccess client functions like a regular web page. To read a mail message, simply click on the From or Subject line of a message in your mailbox. A typical mail message is shown in Figure 13.3.

Notice that the typical mail message actions are available on the Toolbar, located just above the message. Attachments are shown listed with the message, and you can either view, open, or save the files to another location.

Because using the GroupWise WebAccess client is intuitive if you've used the regular GroupWise client (and have read this book), we won't document all the messaging features here. We'll just show you how to send an email message to help you get oriented.

FIGURE 13.3
A typical email message with a file attachment.

TIP

WebAccess now supports context-sensitive right-click operations. Try out this feature! Simply right-click on a message to see an available list of options that you can do with the item you right-clicked. This is a context-sensitive menu, so it may change depending on what you have right-clicked. You can use this menu to quickly check out the properties of an item just like you would in the Windows client or to quickly reply to a message, and so on. You can also right-click on your folders in the folder list to see your available options.

Sending Messages

Sending messages from the WebAccess client is as simple as reading them. The New button on the Toolbar allows you to compose any new item type including new mail, appointments, tasks, notes, phone messages, as well as any posted item types. A new WebAccess mail message screen is shown in Figure 13.4. Enter each field just as you would normally and click Send when you're done.

FIGURE 13.4
You can send messages easily with WebAccess.

TIP

Auto-name completion is now a feature of the WebAccess client. This feature works off the names in your Frequent Contacts address book. You simply begin typing a name into the To, CC, or BC field of an item, and WebAccess auto-completes the name for you. This makes addressing messages through WebAccess as quick and easy as when using the Windows client.

Across the top of the new item window, a Toolbar and three additional tabs are accessible. The Toolbar enables you to save the message so you can complete it later, spell check the message, change the item type of the message, and so on. The tabs allow you to attach files, set send options, or apply a signature to the message.

To attach a file, click the Attachments tab and use the Browse button to find the files to attach. Click Attach to add the files to the attachment list. If you want to remove an attachment, select it and then click the Remove button. After you have added all attachments to the message, click Send to send the message with all displayed attachments.

The Send Options tab allows you to set the classification, priority, reply options, and return notification on the message.

TIP

To find names in the Address Book while you are composing a new message, click the Address Book button on the Toolbar to search for contacts in the system or personal address books.

Managing Messages

From the WebAccess main screen, you can click the check box next to any message (or multiple messages) and use the following buttons to manage it:

- **Delete**—Deletes the message from the mailbox
- **Move**—Moves the message to a folder
- **Accept**—Accepts the appointment, task, or reminder note
- **Decline**—Declines the appointment, task, or reminder note
- **Complete**—Completes the task
- **Read Later**—Marks the message as unopened
- **Mark Read**—Marks the message as already read

With these buttons, you can manage your messages using the WebAccess client.

You can also drag and drop selected messages into any folder visible on the left, where your folder list is displayed. Be sure to expand a folder list so you can see the child folder before dragging items into it.

Managing the Address Book

The WebAccess Address Book interface provides access to the system address book, any personal address books in your account, as well as any LDAP address books that your administrator may have defined. It functions slightly differently than the Windows client in that you search for users rather than see all users by default. This speeds up access to the Address Book for large organizations. To open the Address Book, click the Address Book icon on the Toolbar. Figure 13.5 displays the default Address Book interface.

FIGURE 13.5
The GroupWise WebAccess Address Book.

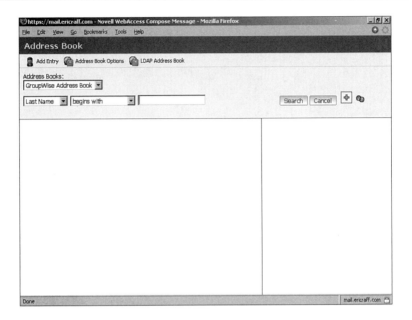

You can search for users, resources, or groups through the Address Book interface. If you don't define any search criteria, clicking the Search button lists the first 15 users, resources, and groups in the drop-down list at the top of your screen. In large GroupWise systems, this means you would have to click the Display Next button to see the next page of matches.

You will usually be better served by searching for specific users, resources, or groups to narrow down the matches. Additionally, the more characters you use in the Search field, the more the search is narrowed. The default interface allows you to quickly search for a user based on Name, Last Name, First Name, or Department information.

To the right of the Address Book interface, you will see two graphics that provide additional search options. They are the Entry Filter options, and they act as toggle buttons to display or hide additional search options. These options allow you to perform a more comprehensive and specific search. Figure 13.6 displays the two entry filters activated, allowing a search for a Person (user) with a last name that begins with Nellis AND a Department name that begins with ICS. You could also use this feature to search for resources or group entry types.

FIGURE 13.6
Searching for users in the GroupWise Address book.

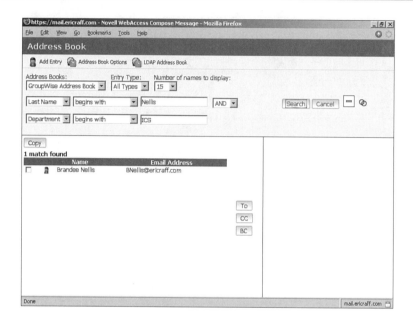

TIP

You can increase the number of displayed names from 15 up to 200 by clicking the interlocking circles icon to the right of the Search button. You will then see the option for the Number of names to display.

If you are not sure how to spell a user's name, you can simply enter the first character or characters of his or her first and last name and use the Begins With option. For example, if you were looking for a user named Ric Smyth, you could enter **Sm** in the Last Name AND **Ri** in the First Name field. Figure 13.7 shows an example of this type of search query and the listed results.

TIP

You can click each name that is returned from a search to see all the information about the user. This is a quick way to get the user's phone or department information. This is also the way you edit personal contacts.

FIGURE 13.7
Searching for a name when you are not sure of the proper spelling.

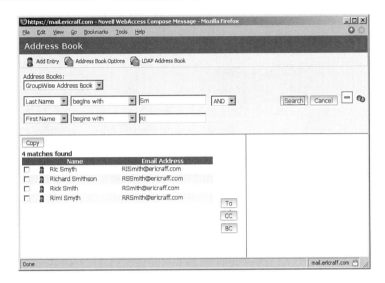

When you locate the name or names you want to send mail to, select them by checking the check box for each user. Then click the To, CC, or BC button to place the name on the right, where you can see who the message will be sent to. After you have listed all users that the message will be sent to, click the Mail button to bring up the compose window with your list of recipients. You can also click the Save Group button to save the list of users as a personal group in any of your address books.

The WebAccess client allows you to create, delete, and modify entries in any of your personal or shared address books, just as the desktop client does.

Managing the Address Book Entries

You can manage the information on your personal address books through the Address Book interface. Remember that personal address books can contain users, resources, groups, or organizations (companies). To update information about any of these item types, you must first search for the desired item type (user, group, resource, or organization). After you have located the desired item(s), you can move or copy it to a different address book, delete it, or modify it. To move, copy, or delete an address book item, select the item(s) and then click the desired button. To modify an existing item, click on the name of the item, and a new window will open displaying all the information about that particular item. From this window, you can modify any of the displayed fields. Figure 13.8 shows the interface used to modify a personal contact.

FIGURE 13.8
Modifying the properties of a personal contact.

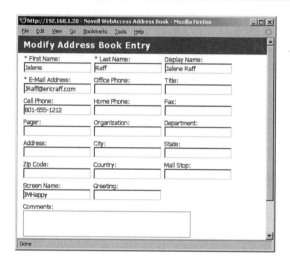

To add a contact, resource, or group to any of your personal address books, you use the Add Entry button on the Toolbar. The Add Entry interface allows you to quickly and easily add a person, resource, or organization to a personal address book.

Managing the Address Books

When you click the Address Book Options button, you see the screen shown in Figure 13.9. You use this screen to manage the Address Book itself (not the entries).

Select the Personal Address Books entry from the list and then choose from the following options:

- **Create Address Book**—Use this button to create additional personal address books.

- **Delete**—Use this link to delete the corresponding personal address book.

- **Save As**—Use this link to copy the selected personal address book to a new address book.

FIGURE 13.9
This screen allows you to manage the Address Book.

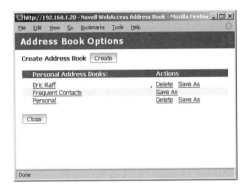

To modify an address book, click on the name of the address book. You can then rename the address book or update the description.

These options enable you to manage (modify and perform other tasks) an entire personal address book at a time.

Using the Calendar

You can manage your calendar using the WebAccess client; this works in much the same way as the regular client. The process of accessing and creating appointments, reminder notes, and tasks is easy using the WebAccess client.

Clicking the Calendar tab across the top of the WebAccess interface displays your calendar entries, as shown in Figure 13.10.

The current day with your appointments, notes, and tasks is displayed. You can navigate to the desired date by clicking the left and right arrows next to the current date or by using the Month view to the left. The Month view also allows you to jump forward or back by the month or year.

You can also display the calendar in a Day, Week, or Month view using the appropriate button on the Toolbar.

If you need to create a new appointment, task, or note, click the New button and select the appropriate item type.

FIGURE 13.10
The WebAccess GroupWise Calendar enables you to manage your appointments, notes, and tasks.

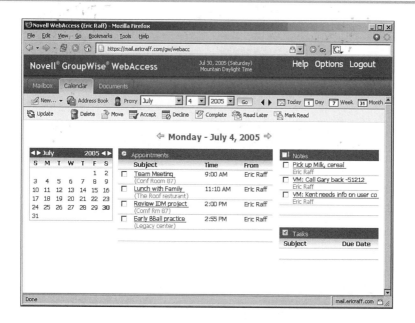

TIP

To see the details about a specific calendar event, place your mouse over the event, and a "bubble" window appears with the details listed. You can also single-click an entry, which opens a new browser window with all the details listed.

Accessing Other Mailboxes (Proxy)

One of the more powerful features of the GroupWise WebAccess client is the capability to access other mailboxes—the Proxy feature.

NOTE

Remember, each user controls the security on his or her own mailbox. You have to be granted permission to access another mailbox. This can be done with the WebAccess client, as described later in this chapter, or with the Windows client, as described in Chapter 8, "Advanced Features."

To start a Proxy session, click the Proxy button on the WebAccess toolbar. You then see the screen shown in Figure 13.11.

FIGURE 13.11
You can access other mailboxes using the GroupWise WebAccess Proxy screen.

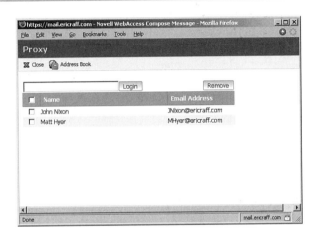

Any user or resource for which you have already accessed (proxied into his or her account) is listed. You can click the name of the user from the list to access his or her mailbox. If you need to act as a proxy for a user for the first time, you can enter the Mailbox name (if known) or use the Address Book button to browse the system address book to find the mailbox name. Then click Login. You then see the main WebAccess screen, but the information will be from the other user's mailbox (not your own). You then can perform the actions that the user has granted you (read, write, and so on).

You can identify that you accessed another user's mailbox in two ways. First, the name displayed has a green and gray people icon next to it. Second, the browser title bar contains the name of the user for whom you are acting as proxy. This way, even if you minimize the browser window, you should be able to see the name of the user on the minimized description.

Chapter 8 discusses the Proxy feature in more detail. To end the Proxy session, click the Logout button in the upper right or close the screen. Logging out closes the screen for you, and you return to your mailbox.

Using GroupWise WebAccess Find

The GroupWise 7 WebAccess client contains the powerful Find utility to allow quick location of messages that meet certain criteria. Similar to the Windows Find options, there is a quick find and a more advanced find option. Figure 13.12 points out the find locations on the main WebAccess page.

FIGURE 13.12
The GroupWise WebAccess Find sections.

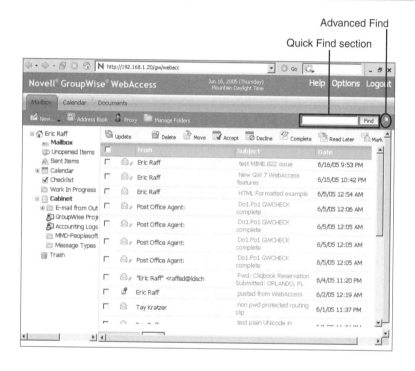

To perform a quick find, simply type your search text into the window at the upper right and click the Find button. A real-time search is done against your entire mailbox to locate any messages that have this text located in the From, To, or Subject lines.

If you want to use a more defined find—for example, to look for a specific subject or search specific folders—you should use the Magnifying glass icon to bring up a dedicated find window. Figure 13.13 displays this window. Here, we searched all mail received from John Nixon and searched in the Mailbox folder only.

FIGURE 13.13

The GroupWise WebAccess Find utility is an excellent tool for searching and locating messages with specific content.

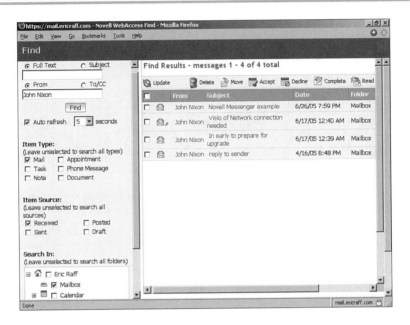

TIP

You can issue a find when you are acting as proxy for another user just like you would when in your own mailbox. This way, you can search for items in the account for which you are acting as proxy.

To use the Find feature, simply click your selections, enter the text you want to search for (if desired), select the folders to search (leave them all unselected for a full mailbox search), and click the Find button. The results are displayed on the right side of the screen. Performing the search may take a few seconds. The window automatically refreshes at the second interval defined on the left. This allows you to see the state of the find or to cancel the find if you see information you were searching for.

Locating Documents

The Documents tab allows you to gain access to any documents to which you have references in your mailbox. You are also able to search for documents from this interface and then view, open, save, or view the properties of the document. By default, when you click on the Documents tab, you see documents that contain your name anywhere in the Subject or Author fields. Figure 13.14 shows the Documents tab and a list of documents associated with Eric Raff.

FIGURE 13.14
GroupWise WebAccess provides access to your documents.

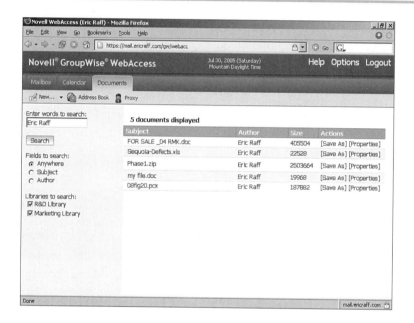

Configuring Mailbox Options

As we discussed in Chapter 11, "Customizing GroupWise," you have many options for customizing your mailbox, such as the signature, default send options, password, and so on. The GroupWise WebAccess client gives you access to the more commonly used options. Click the Options link in the upper right of the main WebAccess screen, and the screen shown in Figure 13.15 is displayed.

FIGURE 13.15
You can configure your mailbox options from the GroupWise WebAccess client using this screen (Send Options shown).

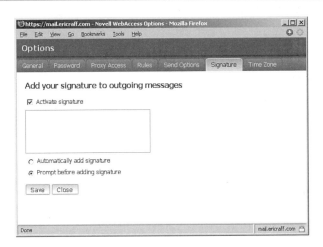

The following tabs are available in the Mailbox Options screen:

- **General**—Used to configure the number of messages displayed in one screen.

- **Password**—Used to change your GroupWise password.

- **Proxy Access**—Used to grant or modify proxy rights to others for accessing your mailbox.

- **Rules**—Used to set up basic rules (Delete, Forward, Move to Folder, Reply, Vacation).

- **Send Options**—Includes default classification, priority, reply, and notification options.

- **Signature**—Used to provide the text to be added at the end of sent messages.

- **Time Zone**—Used to configure your local time zone. This applies only to the GroupWise WebAccess account, not to your master mailbox.

Make your selections and click Save to apply them to your mailbox.

Summary

In this chapter, we discussed how you can access GroupWise whether you are traveling, at an Internet kiosk, or have Internet access using a web browser. This chapter walked you through the process of using GroupWise on a standard web browser. The WebAccess client gives you access to all your GroupWise information from a web browser.

GroupWise Cross-Platform Client

This appendix provides information about the GroupWise cross-platform client. This client is supported on the Linux and Macintosh platforms, allowing access to your GroupWise account from either of these platforms. Because the overall look and feel of the cross-platform client have not been updated from GroupWise version 6.5, this appendix focuses on the new features of the GroupWise 7 cross-platform client and how they work.

It is assumed that the cross-platform client is already installed. Novell provides good documentation on how to install and run the cross-platform clients. Check with your GroupWise administrator for information on where to obtain the cross-platform client for your particular operating system. You can also download the latest cross-platform client from http://download.novell.com. Just search for "Cross-Platform Client."

New Features

Even though the GroupWise 7 cross-platform client does not incorporate the new look and feel of the Windows client, it has received significant enhancements. These enhancements bring it closer to a fully functional mail client with the same basic feature set you are accustomed to in the Windows client. Most of these new features were present in the Windows client, so they are a welcome addition to the cross-platform client.

All-Day Events

New to GroupWise 7 are all-day events or appointments. This feature has also been introduced into the cross-platform client. Figure A.1 illustrates how to create an all-day appointment in the cross-platform client for Linux. Note the All Day Event check box on the right side.

FIGURE A.1
Creating an all-day event in the cross-platform Linux client.

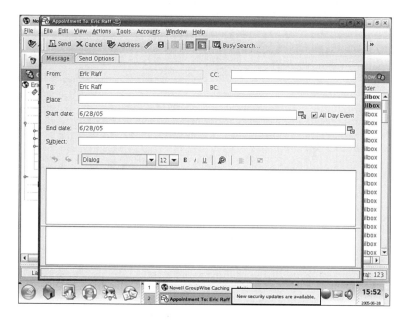

Mailbox Cleanup Options

You can now set your mailbox cleanup options through the cross-platform client. This allows you to use the auto-archive feature or mailbox cleanup settings. You access the mailbox cleanup options by choosing Tools, Options and then selecting the Cleanup tab. Figure A.2 displays the default cleanup options.

Reply Text Formatting

Another new feature to GroupWise 7 that has been exposed in the cross-platform client is the set of reply formatting options. This feature allows you to configure the formatting of text when you reply to a message. You can configure the client so that your text is at the top or bottom of the original message.

There are different formats that you define for text email or HTML-based messages. You configure the reply text formatting option by choosing Tools, Options and then selecting the Default Actions tab. Figure A.3 displays the reply options.

FIGURE A.2
You can now manage your mailbox cleanup options.

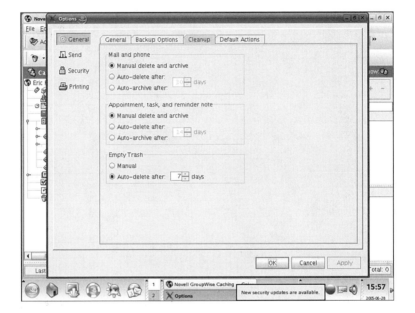

Spell Checking

The GroupWise 7 cross-platform client supports two new spell-checking features.

One is the spell check as-you-type feature. This allows you to visually see misspelled words underlined in red in the message body of a new item you are composing. You can right-click on the misspelled word and select from a list of correct spellings.

The second spell-checking enhancement is the overall spell check option. This allows you to click the Spell Check toolbar button to begin spell checking the Subject and Message body fields. To configure the spell-checking options, choose Tools, Options and then select the General tab, as shown in Figure A.4. These options are at the bottom of the screen.

FIGURE A.3
Defining the reply formatting options.

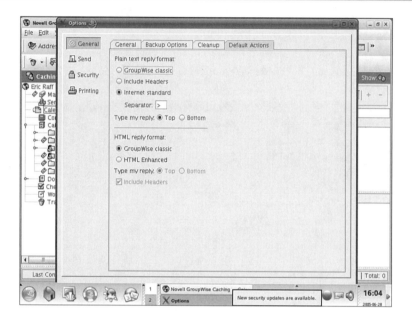

Default Compose and Read Fonts

You can now define the default compose and read fonts that you want to use in the cross-platform client. These settings are defined under the Tools, Options, General tab, as shown in Figure A.4. You can configure the default fonts for composing in plain-text and HTML formats. You can also define the default read font for text-based messages. When you are reading HTML-based messages, the sender of the message defined the font and format.

Show Hidden Files

The Show Hidden Files setting is configured from the Tools, Options, General tab, as shown in Figure A.4. When you check the Show Hidden Files option, you can then see all folders and files that are hidden in Linux. This capability is helpful if you need to attach files that may be hidden because you can see them from the Browse option when attaching files.

FIGURE A.4
Defining the spell-checking options.

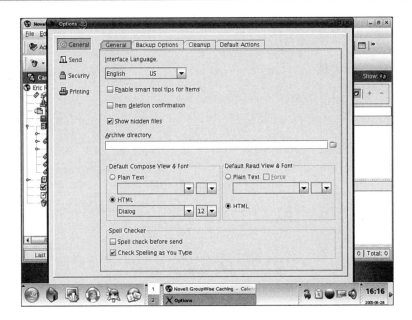

GWCheck Support for the Macintosh

The GWCheck program that is used to repair GroupWise cache mailboxes can now be run on the Macintosh platform. To locate the option to repair your cache mailbox, choose Tools, Repair Mailbox.

This feature is significant. If there are GroupWise database problems and you are in cache mode, you can now repair the databases on the Macintosh platform.

Support for Rules

A welcome addition to the GroupWise 7 cross-platform client is the capability to manage GroupWise rules. You access the rule settings by choosing Tools, Rules. Figure A.5 displays the rules interface. You manage your rules just as you would on the Windows client; the interface is the same. Chapter 8, "Advanced Features," explains how to use the powerful GroupWise rules engine.

FIGURE A.5
The cross-platform rules interface.

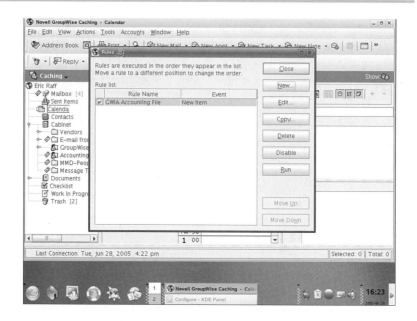

Filter Support

One of the powerful and very useful features of the GroupWise client is the capability to apply filters against your data. The cross-platform client now allows you to use the filter option. You access the filter through the interlocking circles icon to the right of your Toolbar. The only limitation is that you currently cannot save filters to reuse them.

Junk Mail Handling

GroupWise 6.5 introduced the Junk Mail Handling feature. The cross-platform client now allows you to manage the junk mail settings just as you would from a Windows 6.5 or 7 client. Junk mail settings are managed through the Tools, Junk Mail Handling interface. Right-clicking a message that was sent from an Internet user gives you the option to use the junk mail features against the message as well. Figure A.6 displays the basic junk mail interface. For more information about configuring the junk mail settings, see Chapter 8.

FIGURE A.6
The cross-platform junk mail handling interface.

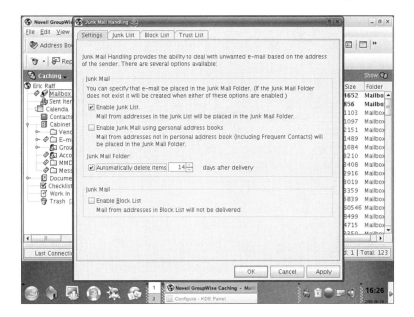

Cache Mode Backup and Restore

The cross-platform client now allows you to automatically back up and restore items from your cache mailbox. This allows you to manage your own backups of your GroupWise data and easily restore mail if it is deleted from your main cache mailbox. To use this feature, you must first define a path to your backup location. This is done through the Tools, Options, Backup Options tab. Figure A.7 displays the backup options screen. After you define the backup path, you can manually back up your mailbox when you desire (by choosing Tools, Backup Mailbox), or you can let GroupWise automatically back it up every few days based on your settings.

After a backup has been run against your cache mailbox, you can access the contents of the backed-up mailbox by choosing File, Open Backup. When you open the backup, you will see *only* the mail that exists in the backup that does *not* exist in your cache mailbox. This makes it simple to find what you need to restore because you do not have to sift through all the mail in the backup, only that mail that is missing from your cache mailbox. So, if you back up your mailbox and then immediately open it, you should not see anything because no mail has been deleted from the cache mailbox yet.

FIGURE A.7
The cross-platform backup options.

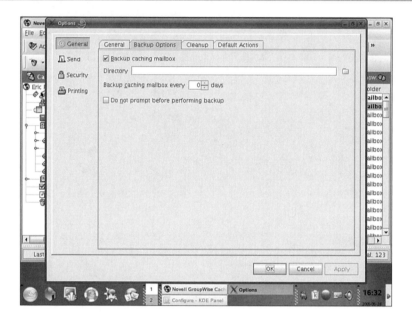

Summary

The GroupWise 7 cross-platform client now has many of the features that were previously standard in the Windows client. This makes the cross-platform client much more functional, so now it is a truly viable solution for the Macintosh and Linux platforms.

GroupWise Startup Options

The GroupWise Startup screen, shown in Figure B.1, is an introductory screen you might see when you run the GroupWise client software. You often will see the Startup screen when you run the GroupWise program for the first time after installation.

FIGURE B.1
The GroupWise Startup screen prompts for critical startup information.

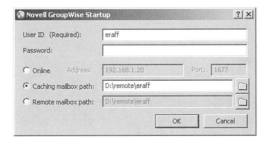

The GroupWise Startup screen will appear if, for some reason, the GroupWise system does not recognize your network login ID or your GroupWise user ID. In this situation, you are prompted to enter the startup information. The GroupWise system requires this information to be able to locate your master mailbox on the network.

If the Startup screen appears, the first item to check is your GroupWise user ID. If you have entered the correct ID and you still receive this prompt, the GroupWise client does not know where to connect. If you are prompted with a password prompt, your GroupWise client knows where to connect and needs you to enter your GroupWise password.

If your user ID is correct and you receive this prompt, you need to provide GroupWise with instructions for connecting to your mailbox.

NOTE

GroupWise will try several methods to identify where to connect to your mailbox. It is usually rare that the GroupWise client will not be able to figure out where to connect to your online mailbox if you have entered the correct user ID for your GroupWise system.

Helping GroupWise Locate Your Mailbox

Depending on your system's configuration, you will need to provide the GroupWise client with one of the following pieces of information:

- TCP/IP address and port
- The path to your caching mailbox
- The path to your remote mailbox

This information is required every time the GroupWise client loads. After you provide this information, your computer will remember these settings, so you are not prompted for them each time you run GroupWise.

Entering Online Information

To access your master mailbox, you need to provide your username and password and a valid DNS name or TCP/IP address and port in the Online Address and Port fields.

The Online Address field requires the DNS name or IP address of the post office agent. This is *not* the IP address of your workstation. The Port field requires an IP port number. Again, you need to ask your system administrator for the information to be entered. You could also ask another GroupWise user to check the Help, About GroupWise screen and tell you the IP address that appears in the dialog box (the default GroupWise port number is 1677, but that can be configured differently by the GroupWise administrator).

TIP

If you check with another GroupWise user, this user does not need to be located in the same GroupWise post office as your mailbox. If you enter another GroupWise post office's IP address and port to connect to, your GroupWise client will be redirected to your post office automatically. Your GroupWise client will then remember the proper location to connect to.

Entering Caching Information

If you are using GroupWise in the cache mode (explained in Chapter 10, "Remote Access"), you will need to enter a local path to your GroupWise cache directory. You might need to open Windows Explorer to discover this path, or you can ask your administrator. A sample path was shown earlier in Figure B.1.

Entering Remote Information

If you are starting GroupWise in the remote mode (explained in Chapter 10), you will need to enter a local path to your GroupWise remote directory. You might need to open Windows Explorer to discover this path, or you can ask your administrator. A sample path was shown earlier in Figure B.1.

Connecting to GroupWise

After you enable GroupWise to locate your messages by following the preceding instructions, you should be able to click OK to log on to your GroupWise system. When you click OK, you will see a message indicating that you are connecting to GroupWise.

If GroupWise still cannot find your mailbox after you enter an IP address and port (this usually occurs as a result of a system failure), it will run in remote or cache mode if either mode has been set up on your computer. You can still use GroupWise offline and send and receive messages when the system comes back online.

Calling Up the Startup Dialog Box

You can instruct GroupWise to display the GroupWise Startup screen every time it launches by simply adding a few characters to the GroupWise startup properties. Startup properties are parameters stored along with the GroupWise icon (depending on the version of Windows you are using) that tell GroupWise what to do when it launches. Often, it is necessary to bring up the Startup screen when multiple users run GroupWise from the same computer.

To bring up the GroupWise Startup screen upon launching, follow these steps:

1. Right-click the GroupWise icon and select Properties from the menu.

2. Click the Shortcut tab.

3. Place the cursor in the Target field and go to the end of the command line.

4. Add a space, followed by **/@u-?**, after the GRPWISE.EXE command. Be sure to include a space between the command line and the / character. Figure B.2 shows the Properties screen with an example of the correct parameter syntax.

5. Click OK. The next time you double-click the GroupWise icon, you will see the GroupWise Startup screen.

FIGURE B.2
Use this syntax to force GroupWise to launch with the Startup screen displayed.

If you want to create multiple GroupWise icons, one for each person who uses the computer, follow the same steps listed previously, but substitute each user's

GroupWise ID in place of the question mark in step 4. This permits several users to run GroupWise from a single machine; however, all users will share the same GroupWise default settings, such as default view.

NOTE

All users who run GroupWise from a shared computer should set passwords on their GroupWise mailboxes. This prevents the users from accessing each other's mailboxes. Passwords are also required for other access modes such as WebAccess and remote modes.

To allow multiple users on the same machine to have different default settings in GroupWise, you must enable multiple user logins for Windows by creating multiple user profiles. Refer to your Windows documentation for instructions.

Other Useful GroupWise Startup Options

In addition to the /@u-? startup option described previously, you can use several other startup options to alter the behavior of GroupWise 7. Table B.1 describes several of these useful GroupWise startup options, and you can find a complete list of startup switches in the GroupWise documentation located on the Novell website at www.novell.com/documentation/lg/gw7/index.html under the heading "Using Startup Options."

TABLE B.1
Useful GroupWise Startup Switches

SYNTAX	FUNCTION
/@u-userID	Allows you to launch GroupWise and access your mail box from another user's computer while the other user is still logged on to the network.
/b1	Launches GroupWise without displaying the GroupWise splash screen (but does not actually speed up the loading of the program).
/c	Causes GroupWise to check for unopened items. If unopened items exist in your mailbox, GroupWise opens as usual. If no unopened items are found, GroupWise does not load.
/cm	Causes GroupWise to check for unopened items. If unopened items exist in your mailbox, you will hear an

TABLE B.1
Useful GroupWise Startup Switches (continued)

SYNTAX	FUNCTION
	audible beep and GroupWise will open minimized. If no unopened items are found, GroupWise will not load.
/iabs	Causes the Address Book application to load. This results in a slightly slower GroupWise launch time but causes the Address Book to open much quicker when you access it for the first time in GroupWise. This also helps with the opening of the first email item because the Address Book is already initialized.
/pc	Allows you to launch GroupWise and point to a specific path for the cache mailbox.
/pr	Allows you to launch GroupWise and point it to a specific path for the remote mailbox.

You can string multiple GroupWise startup switches together on the program line simply by placing a space between the startup switches.

GroupWise Resources

If you have read the entire *Novell GroupWise 7 User's Handbook* and are still uncertain as to how to perform a function in GroupWise, check the index at the back of the book for topics you might have missed. If you still can't find the answer, you should investigate the GroupWise Online Help system. This appendix explains how to use the Online Help resources available for GroupWise.

Using the F1 Key

The F1 (Help) key provides immediate context-sensitive help for most screens in the GroupWise client program. Simply press F1 at any time within the GroupWise client for assistance with your current task.

Using the Help Button

In most GroupWise dialog boxes, a Help button is available for quick assistance with the options in that dialog box. Click this button to view an in-depth explanation of the dialog box or feature you're using. The help information typically explains options and provides examples of how to use the dialog box.

About Toolbar Help

If you allow the mouse pointer to rest for more than a second or two over any Toolbar button, a pop-up window appears, telling you what function that button performs.

Using the Help Menu

The Help menu offers different options depending on the features of GroupWise with which you're working. For example, in the main GroupWise screen, the Help menu topics cover general GroupWise features. In the Address Book, the Help menu topics relate to using the Address Book.

From the main GroupWise screen, the Help, Help Topics option opens the screen shown in Figure C.1.

FIGURE C.1
The GroupWise Help screen provides detailed assistance on GroupWise features.

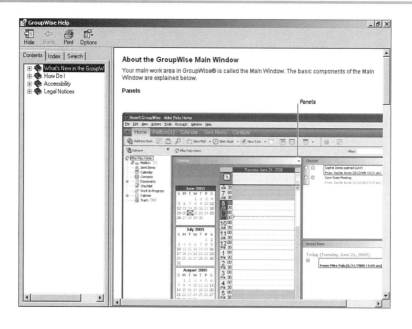

With the Contents tab selected, you can navigate to your desired topic by expanding the headings in the left pane and then highlighting the specific topic you want to view.

With the Index tab selected, you can type the first few letters of the topic you want to view, and the list will automatically scroll to that topic.

With the Search tab selected, you can enter a search string and click the List Topics button to see topics related to your search criteria.

When you have located the topic you want to learn about, double-click that topic or click the Display button.

Viewing the Online GroupWise User's Guide

Click Help, User's Guide to access the GroupWise documentation from the Novell website. You can view the documentation in HTML format, or you can download the PDF file to view with Adobe Acrobat Reader.

You can also access the GroupWise User's Guide by pointing your web browser to the following URL:

http://www.novell.com/documentation/lg/gw7/index.html

Information About GroupWise Cool Solutions

The Cool Solutions option under the Help menu launches your default web browser and takes you to the Novell GroupWise magazine website at www.novell.com/coolsolutions/gwmag/index.html.

GroupWise Cool Solutions is an online GroupWise magazine that is updated frequently with the latest tips and tricks for using GroupWise.

Accessing the Novell GroupWise Product Information Page

You can access general information about the entire GroupWise product, including the GroupWise clients and the GroupWise administration system, by clicking Help, Novell GroupWise Home Page or by pointing your web browser to www.novell.com/products/groupwise.

Tip of the Day

When you click Help, Tip of the Day, you see the screen shown in Figure C.2.

This feature presents a Tip of the Day every time you launch GroupWise if you select the Show Tips at Startup Option at the bottom of the dialog box.

FIGURE C.2
The Tip of the Day feature lets you improve your GroupWise skills one day at a time.

NOTE

If the Tip of the Day add-on has not been installed, you will not see the Tip of the Day option on the Help menu. Check with your system administrator or help desk to see whether the Tip of the Day is enabled for your GroupWise system.

About GroupWise

The Help, About GroupWise screen, shown in Figure C.3, is useful when you are troubleshooting problems with GroupWise.

The Program Release line shows you the exact version and release date of the GroupWise client you are running, as well as the location from which you are running the client (such as your local hard drive or a network location).

The Username line shows your GroupWise user ID and your GroupWise file ID. (The file ID is used to identify which files in the GroupWise post office message repository relate to your GroupWise mailbox. This information is useful for support personnel working on GroupWise system-level problems.)

The Post Office line specifies in which post office your GroupWise mailbox is located. Depending on your GroupWise system's configuration, there may be many post offices within your organization.

The TCP/IP Address and TCP/IP Port lines define where the GroupWise client is connected in online mode. If running in remote or cache mode, the client will report "Path to Post Office" with the path to your cache or remote mailbox.

FIGURE C.3
The About GroupWise screen provides useful system information.

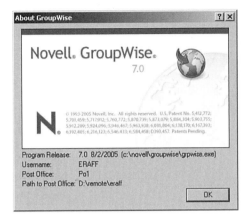

POP Versus IMAP Accounts

This appendix provides additional information about what a POP or IMAP account is and what type of account may meet your needs the best. Chapter 8, "Advanced Features," explains how to enable your GroupWise 7 client to use a POP or IMAP account.

POP3 and IMAP4: What They Are

POP3 and IMAP4 are considered standard mail access methods or protocols. They are used to access messages stored on a mail server. Because they are industry-recognized standards, literally dozens of different "clients" (the GroupWise client being just one of them) support the ability to access your mail on a mail server through one or both of these protocols. POP3 and IMAP4 are never used when you want to send mail; they are strictly used for retrieving mail items stored on a server. Also, when the GroupWise client communicates with a GroupWise post office, it does not use POP or IMAP, but a proprietary encrypted and compressed connection directly to the post office agent. So, with that high-level introduction on what POP3 and IMAP4 are, let's explore which protocol could best meet your needs when accessing your Internet accounts mailbox.

Comparing POP3 to IMAP4

The following sections provide more detailed explanation of how POP3 and IMAP4 behave and what their strengths and weaknesses are.

POP3

The POP3 protocol is simply a standard way of accessing a mail server and downloading your mail from this server. POP3 provides support for getting mail from one folder: the Mailbox. It does not support multiple folders or keep mail organized between multiple folders on the server side. By default, when you set up a POP3 account and download your mail, it is removed from the server. Hence, your mail now exists exclusively on the machine where you are running the POP3 client. Also, by default, the POP3 protocol downloads the entire message regardless of size when you connect. The POP3 protocol does the following:

- Changes made to mail items on the local client (deleting mail) are not replicated back up to the server-side mailbox.

- You can configure the client to leave messages on the server. This capability may be useful if you will be accessing your mailbox from other clients such as a web browser that communicates directly with the Internet server. Figure D.1 displays the Advanced tab where you can configure GroupWise to leave mail on the server.

FIGURE D.1
When configuring a POP account, you can leave the mail on the server.

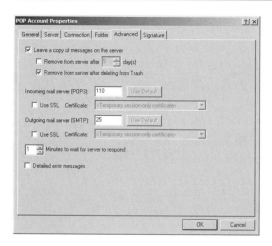

- POP3 does not support server-side folders. This means that the only folder you can download via a POP connection is the Mailbox folder. If you have created additional folders in your Internet account, you will not be able to synchronize them with a POP connection.

IMAP4

The IMAP4 protocol is also a standard way of accessing a mail server and downloading your mail from this server. IMAP is a newer, more robust, and feature-rich protocol. It has support for multiple folders on the server side and, by default, does not remove the mail from the server when a connection is made and mail downloaded. IMAP downloads only the header of the mail message by default. This way, you can see the Subject, From, and Size fields of the message. If the message is large, you will know how large it is before reading it and the rest of the mail message is downloaded. An IMAP4 account does the following:

- Messages stay on the server and are not removed from the server when you synchronize your client.

- When you synchronize, only the headers of the mail messages are downloaded. The header contains the From, To, and Subject fields and the size of the entire message. When you open a message, it is then downloaded to your local computer in its entirety, meaning the message body and any attachments. This allows you to potentially delete mail without having to download the entire message. This capability can be useful if you receive a great deal of junk mail.

- IMAP is designed to keep the local message store in sync with the server side. Hence, if you drag an email item to a different folder from the client, it will be synchronized up to the server and reflect the change there.

- Performance over a dial-up connection is somewhat faster on IMAP compared to a POP connection.

- All folders are synchronized, not just the Mailbox folder. This allows you to organize mail in folders on the server and see the same folder structure from your GroupWise client through the IMAP account.

- Losing your server connection can cause problems. Because the initial sync downloads just the message headers, if you lose the connection when you are browsing through your mail, you will not be able to read new mail. Any old mail that has already been downloaded is accessible, of course.

SYMBOLS

A

J – K – L

M

status

checking (Sent Items folder), 13,
122-124

tracking, 289-290

subject lines, changing, 58, 188

threading, 102

Trash

restoring from, 66

smart purges, 19

types

appointments, 49

discussion notes, 52

mail items, 48

phone messages, 52

reminder notes, 51-52

tasks, 50

unarchiving, 116

undeleting (Trash), 127

unread messages, marking as
(WebAccess Client), 41

viewing (Trash), 18

Microsoft Base Cryptographic Provider
version 1.0, 186

Microsoft Enhanced Cryptographic
Provider version 1.0, 186

MIME Encoding option (Send Options tab),
289

modems, Remote Mode connections, 252,
259-261

Modify Options access right (Proxy), 178

modifying

rules, 171

subject lines (messages), 188

monitoring meeting status, 156

Month & Calendar view (Calendar), 138

Month Display Option option (Calendar
options), 299

Month view (Calendar), 135, 138

Move to Folder action (rules), 174

Move/Link Selections to Folders command
(Edit menu), 101

moving

Calendar items to Checklist, 140

folders in Cabinet listings, 100

messages

to Checklist, 120

into folders, 101

QuickViewer, 28

multi-user calendars, 163-164

Multi-User List dialog, 164

Multi-User view (Calendar), 136-138

multiple calendars, 29, 132

multiple HTML signatures, 33

multiple windows (Mailbox), opening via
Proxy feature, 180

My Certificates dialog options, 298-299

My Subject (messages), changing, 188

N

Name Completion Position (Address
Book), 76

Name Completion Search Order interface
(Address Book), 74-75

Name Format option (Address Book), 74

names

Address Book (WebAccess) searches,
344

auto-name completion, 41, 54, 343

Nav bar, 10

customizing, 27, 307

folders

adding to, 307

navigating, 12

resetting, 307

Q – R

removing
- messages, 125-126
- rules, 171

Rename option (Signature tab options), 286

renaming folders (Cabinet), 100-101

Repair Mailbox command (Tools menu), 216

repairing Mailbox, 216-218

Reply action (rules), 174

Reply button (Toolbar), 62

reply formatting options (GroupWise cross-platform client), 358

Reply Requested option (Send Options tab), 289

Reply to All option (Reply button), 62

Reply to Sender option (Reply button), 62

replying to messages, 62-63
- discussion area messages, 189-190
- inline reply/forward layout, 28

requesting
- items, Remote Mode master system connections, 267-270
- meetings, 49

Require Password to Complete Routed Item option (Security tab options), 291

rescheduling posted appointments (Calendar), 145

Resend command (Actions menu), 127

resending messages, Sent Items folder, 13, 126-127

Reset command (newsgroups), 205

resizing main GroupWise screen, 20

resources
- About GroupWise screen, 374
- GroupWise Cool Solutions Online Magazine, 373
- GroupWise Home Page, 373
- GroupWise User's Guide, 373
- Tip of the Day, 373

restoring
- cache mailboxes, GroupWise cross-platform client, 363
- messages from Trash, 66

retracting
- appointments, 156
- messages, Sent Items folder, 14, 124-126
- notes, 156
- tasks, 156

return notifications (messages), 289-290

rooms, scheduling (sending appointments), 149

rules, 170
- actions
  - Accept, 174
  - assigning, 173-174
  - Delegate, 173
  - Delete/Decline, 174
  - Forward, 173
  - Link to Folder, 174
  - Mark as Private, 174
  - Move to Folder, 174
  - Reply, 174
  - Send Mail, 173
  - Stop Rule Processing, 174
- creating, 170, 174
- function of, 170
- managing, GroupWise cross-platform client, 361
- modifying, 171

Rules tab (WebAccess mailbox options), 355

S

S/MIME Compliance Check option (Security tab options), 293

Save As command (File menu), 61, 117

Save As formats, support for, 35

T

W

X – Y – Z